FINDING JUDAISM
IN THE TORAH

A Search for the Theology
Behind Judaism

Carl J. Palash

Dedication

With many thanks to the current and past members and participating Rabbis of the Congregation Rodeph Sholom Torah Study Group for making our meetings a highlight of the week.

CONTENTS

Foreword

I wrote these papers while participating in the Torah Study Group at New York City's Congregation Rodeph Sholom over the past twenty years. About thirty of us met each Saturday morning for an hour to read and discuss the Torah. Often, only several verses were covered during a session, so it was not unusual for a Book to take a year or more to finish. Every six months, we stopped and held a *siyum*, where people presented papers on their views of what was read. Many of my papers were written for these *siyums.*

We in the Study Group had diverse backgrounds, but in almost all cases had one thing in common – little background in Torah. Most grew up in non-Orthodox families, with little formal training in Judaism. My impression, nevertheless, was that all viewed the meeting as a high point of the week. There was often an air of excitement trying to decipher the meaning of the few verses we read. Not having formal training, we felt as if we were reading the Torah with fresh eyes.

The meaning lifted from the text typically reflected each person's background or interests. An English professor drew parallels with classical literature. A stockbroker, whose passion was a desire for a rapprochement of the various branches of Judaism, liked to look at the text from the perspectives of a Reform, Conservative and Orthodox Jew. One person saw it as an attempt by the ancient priests to press their case, and others applied psychology, business management or other modern disciplines to reach conclusions.

While I am a market economist, I did not try to interpret the Torah in terms of economics or the marketplace. I was interested in getting to the roots of Judaism. Attending Shabbat services on a regular basis when my two boys were in the Rodeph Sholom Day School, I heard the rabbis emphasize a number of ideas. I was never sure whether they represented Judaism, liberal American thought or psychology. I kept hearing the importance of the Torah, although I was sure Reform Judaism did not adhere to all its tenets. I decided to find exactly what was the basis of Judaism by participating in the Torah Study Group.

By applying the analytical approach learned as an economist, I tried to answer the question, "What is the theological point of the passage?" I focused on what it says rather than what I wanted it to say. This is not as easy as it sounds. I have heard some Jews assert rationales for parts of the Torah they find discomforting, even when they are clearly opposed to the written word. For instance, some say Abraham is testing God in the Akedah, despite the text's explicit statement to the contrary. Also, many Reform Jews do not like the emphasis on commandments or punishment approach to persuade people to follow them. My *General Theory* paper (Chapter 7) was met by much discomfort and dismay when presented at a *sium*. But, there is no way to get around the fact that commandments and threat of punishment are integral parts of the Torah. While the Torah clearly can be interpreted in many ways, any conclusion needs to be firmly backed by the text, otherwise one could be confounding the religion with make-believe.

I am familiar with a similar problem in my work as a market economist. I forecasted economic data for traders. For example, if I expected the upcoming jobs report to be strong, they may short bonds ahead of the release. However, once the data printed, I had to forget my forecast and quickly conclude whether the figures were strong or weak. If I downplayed a print that ran counter to my forecast, traders could lose money as the market moved against the implication of my analysis. Similarly, for purposes of Torah analysis, I tried to discern the meaning of the text in its own terms and not what I wanted it to say.

Using a consistent approach, or, perhaps because the Torah is internally consistent in a theological sense, the following papers have coherence despite being written over many years. They construct a Jewish theology, although some of the conclusions are controversial and do not match prevalent ideas in Judaism practiced today. Some Reform rabbis have found my comprehensive approach dubious, because it ignores the historical-analytical conclusion that the Torah comprises material from several writers. They argue that since each of the writers had a different agenda, there cannot be a unifying theme across the Book. My papers argue otherwise, and I wonder whether the Torah's editors made sure it was so. I suspect that emphasizing the multiple sources of the Torah helps justify one's choosing which parts of the Torah to observe. If defunct priests wrote the Kosher laws, for example, why should they be followed?

In total, these papers tackle big issues as well as specific events in the Torah with logic and textual proof. Some of the answers, I believe, resolve issues in a satisfying way for a modern reader. For example, the Torah's acknowledgement of a chaotic part of the universe establishes the validity of free will and argues against predetermination. It offers a reason why bad things can happen independently of God. Other answers resolve questions about events often viewed to be mysterious, such as where Cain found a wife, Jacob's wrestling with an angel, and why God told Isaac not to travel to Egypt to avoid a famine. Finally, some of the analysis may help the interested reader of the Torah feel more comfortable with apparent inconsistencies in the text, such as blaming Pharaoh for keeping the Israelites as slaves even though it is God who hardens his heart.

Not everyone will view the results of the analysis favorably. Traditional Orthodox may reject the notion of chaos in the universe, believing God controls everything. Reform Jews may not like the idea that the Book of Genesis is meant to justify the need for laws, commandments, and threat of punishment. Many people will not like the idea of a separation between God and Jews. However, I hope that even in disagreement readers will find my approach provocative. In particular, I hope my papers help interested Jews find a better understanding and meaning of their religion. While my papers focused on understanding the underpinnings of Judaism, they should be meaningful and insightful for people of other religions, as well. I also hope no one takes offense at my use of masculine words — He and Him — to refer to God. I do so only to make the text flow smoothly.

Quotations from the Torah and the broader Tanakh are taken from the World English Bible. I've altered some to make for a smoother read. The substance of the quotations did not change.

Besides thanking the current and past members and participating Rabbis of the Congregation Rodeph Sholom Torah Study Group for making our meetings so exciting and enlightening, I would like to thank the following individuals for giving me encouragement and advice on pulling this book together: Rabbi Evan Hoffman, Guy Bailey, Barbara Guss, Linda Pollack, Mick Prater, Jane and Larry Swinney, and Monica Swinney. Finally, I thank my wife, Beverly Miller, and my sons, Aaron and Ross, for encouraging me to pursue this journey.

Overview

M y analysis takes the Torah (the Five Books of Moses — Genesis, Exodus, Leviticus, Numbers and Deuteronomy) as the ultimate source of information about God and the basis for Judaism. The papers are not presented in the chronological order they were written. Instead, they follow a progression that I believe builds a theological basis for Judaism.

Bottom Line of the Torah

The Torah indicates what is needed for God to reside in the Israelite community. God's presence is desirable because it will help achieve material or worldly success. This is essentially the covenant -- creating a society compatible for God's presence and receiving His help in exchange.

This bottom line runs counter to a belief, possibly widespread and certainly an historical focus of theology in all the major religions, that religion aims to bring a person up to God. It also runs counter to the Jewish tradition of Tikkun Olam, which posits that people are meant to help God achieve His goals in the world. These ideas turn the Torah on its head.

The requirements for God's presence include a monotheistic belief and fear of God, ritual, ethics, and embodiment of religion-based actions in everyday life. Acknowledgment and fear of God as the Lord ensure that everyone follows one set of laws. Ritual reinforces these two requirements and provides a way of communicating with God. The rules of ethics boil down to having respect for others. Embodiment of religion-based actions in everyday life remind Jews to act like God or to feel as if they are in His presence. They form another set of restrictions, besides rules of ethics, to inspire good behavior by people. From a practical perspective, the requirements create a society marked by respect for others.

The Torah explores different ways to achieve this society over the first four Books. They include the reward approach, a quid pro quo relationship with God, a set of general guidelines, and a detailed code of law. To motivate adherence to commandments, Leviticus and Deuteronomy introduce the concepts of people as God's property and of love between God and the Israelites.

These multiple approaches probably account for the widespread perceptions the Torah is not internally coherent and a reader can conclude anything he wants from the text. These perceptions fail to appreciate that the many ways the Torah posits for following the religion have the same goal -- to prompt people to behave properly.

The covenantal promise of worldly success ironically may explain why the Israelites turn to other gods during the Exodus as well as when they live in the Promised Land. The connection between God and success is difficult to discern. And, without a clear connection, other factors, such as cost considerations, could determine which god to worship. Generally, God's role in the world cannot be proved, but the absence of success is observable and an issue for this covenant. People who adhere to the commandments expect Godly benefits, and the absence of the latter could undermine their beliefs. The prophets (included in the broader collection of the cannon, called the Tanakh) address this problem by emphasizing the longer-term consequences — including those in the after-life — of adhering or not to the covenant. They also argue that God would resurrect the Israelite people after disaster struck, as long as at least a remnant remained true to Him. And, some promise saviors.

Who Is Responsible?

Besides addressing how to make society compatible for God, the Torah struggles with the question of who is responsible for society's destiny – God or people? This question fits nicely with the goal of bringing God down to help. Can people leave everything for God to accomplish if He resides in their midst? The Torah disabuses this idea. Genesis shows God helping the Patriarchs only after they attempt to solve problems themselves. Later, some of the prophets' pronouncements appear to be situation specific, so cannot be applied automatically to similar events in subsequent years. People would need to make their own decisions.

Why Do Bad Things Happen?

A question that kept turning up in the Torah Group, as well as in services, is why bad things happen. Blaming God is perplexing, if one has the idea that He is all-powerful and all knowing. Why does He let a bad thing happen? This line of thought could lead to disillusionment with Judaism.

I found three answers in the Torah. Bad things can represent a test by God of a Jew's commitment to the covenant. The Akedah and the Story of Job put the main character through a terrible experience to test his adherence to God's commandments. Indirectly, God's wrath can entail collateral damage. The Israelites' reaction to God's destruction of Korah's family in Numbers suggests innocent people can be caught up in the punishment. Finally, although controversial, I argue a chaotic element was left over from Creation, allowing random events to occur independently of God.

There is ample evidence in the text that He is not all-knowing. He is not necessarily to blame for unfortunate situations. It could be bad luck. Orthodox rabbis who read the papers found exception to the possibility of randomness. They apparently think God is responsible for everything at all times. Reform rabbis, in contrast, felt comfortable with the idea.

I speculate that God permits chaos for three reasons — to generate demand for Him, to provide an opportunity for people to create, and to serve as a threat for not following the commandments. The most interesting rationale is providing opportunities to create. It is based on the implication of the first Ten Commandments that people are to act like God.

Permitting a random element in the world has other important theological implications. Free choice is not the problem so many theologians have struggled with -- their attempt to reconcile individual responsibility with God's presumed omniscience/omnipotence is not necessary. People do have responsibility, since there is room to make decisions independently of Him. And, history is not predetermined, undermining the approach to history found, for example, in the Book of Daniel.

A random misfortune begs the question why God doesn't come quickly to undo it? Why didn't God quickly prevent the Nazis from exterminating European Jews? I have not been able to find an entirely satisfactory answer from the Torah, although it contains precedents for God's procrastination, some risking the end of the covenantal line. God enables Sarah to have a child only at an old age when it seems she would never produce an heir. He waits for the last minute to save Isaac in the Akedah. And, He takes His time freeing the Israelites from Egyptian slavery.

The absence of God in difficult times can be explained a number of theological ways. The Torah shows God's preference for not becoming involved in everyday problems. Double penalties are attached to those who require God to resolve a problem in both Leviticus and Numbers. There are examples from Genesis through Exodus where people are expected to attempt solving a problem before God intervenes. Should God respond to all problems, people might not have an incentive to do so. A non-predictable response time would force people to act, since they cannot be sure whether God will help in time. The Torah does not support Micah's prescription for someone in dire straits to act humbly and wait for God's salvation.

The Relationship Between God and the Israelites

The relationship between God and the Israelites changes over the course of the Five Books. Exodus establishes a separation between God and the Israelites at Mount Sinai, with a guideline approach introduced to emphasize individual decision-making within a set of rules. The Israelites reject this approach in the Golden Calf episode and desire God to lead. God bends and substitutes a code approach requiring the Israelites to follow laws without question. Numbers concludes with a realization that the guideline approach is, in fact, needed, but softens it by showing God helping in the background. Finally, Deuteronomy implies that Jews can change the commandments to meet new needs.

An exact relationship between God and the Israelites is constructed over the episodes in Exodus covering the crossing of the Sea of Reeds to Mount Sinai. The relationship evolves into one emphasizing separation from God and self-reliance on the part of the Israelites. The Israelites are meant to have the power to make decisions and help direct their own destiny.

The first set of Ten Commandments can be understood in terms of this relationship. The key is the Commandment to honor the Shabbat — Israelites should rest on the Sabbath because God did. Generalizing this rationale implies the Israelites are to act like God. If they are to rest on Shabbat because God did, why shouldn't they also mimic God's other actions? They know Him to be powerful, creative and law-making — qualities required for self-reliance. Anarchy, however, could result if each person acts this way. To prevent this, a supreme Lord God is needed to be the ultimate source of laws and power — thus the first Commandment and a justification for monotheism. The last six Commandments go further to prevent anarchy by establishing boundaries between one Israelite and another. This way of dissecting the Ten Commandments leads to an endogenous theory of ethics. If each person is to act like God, then each should treat another as if he were approaching God – that is, with respect.

Such interpretation of the Ten Commandments sheds light on the obscure reference to the Nephilim in Genesis. There, God apparently tries to make humans like gods by having them procreate with divine beings. The attempt does not work, as it results in much evil. Being god-like is not the answer. The Ten Commandments take a different approach, implying that people should act like God but within a framework of rules.

Unfortunately, the Torah acknowledges that it may be too difficult for people to act with the independence and power to direct their destiny. The Israelites want to rely on God. After the Golden Calf episode, and, more importantly after Moses asks for help, God replaces ethical guidelines with a detailed code of law. The code intrudes in peoples' lives without offering explanation. In effect, He meets the Israelites' desire for dependency by restricting their behavior. Restrictions could make it easier for people to live their lives, curtailing the need to make decisions.

Even the code approach, however, does not persuade the Israelites to adhere to the religion. They turn to other gods during their travels to the Promised Land as well as after they arrive. The prophets complain the Israelites sacrifice to other gods, take credit themselves for prosperity, and neglect the poor. Deuteronomy can be viewed as reforming the religion to address these concerns. It embodies some of the prophets' ideas and introduces the concept of love to portray the relationship between the Israelites and God. In so doing, it posits a psychological reason to follow the laws and commandments.

Adhering to the Laws and Commandments

As long as Jews follow these laws and commandments, God will not abandon them. Jews should not feel they are alone in the world, as God will help them. He will do so, though, when He decides. And, He could act in the background, as suggested by the story of Balaam and Balak in Numbers. God performs miracles, such as parting the Sea of Reeds, but for the most part they are not supernatural. A "fear of God" is needed to discern a miracle from natural events.

A Personal Relationship With God?

The idea of a personal God is not supported by the text in Exodus through Book of Numbers. Instead, Jews are to approach God with awe and respect. The effectiveness of unconditional prayers asking for God's help is dubious. Almost all requests to God require a promise to do something in return.

All this changes when Deuteronomy asserts a love relationship with God. Love presumably means unconditional mutual assistance, although a positive response to prayer does not necessarily follow. Moses' prayer, to be permitted to enter the Promised Land, for example, is rejected by God. A love relationship has mixed implications. The concept helps bind the Israelites to the covenant and the commandments, but weakens the emphasis on self help found in the earlier Books. The latter implication could have dire consequences.

The personal relationships that exist for the Patriarchs in Genesis and for Moses in Exodus are exceptions to the general relationships between the Israelites and God established in the first four Books. Even the Patriarchs, however, need to follow God's commandments. For example, much is often made of Abraham's argument with God about saving Sodom, seemingly implying it is possible to question God's decisions. Importantly, no commandment is involved in the event. God merely informs Abraham of His intentions, thus opening the door for argumentation. In contrast, since God commands Abraham to sacrifice Isaac, it is not surprising he proceeds without question. Abraham understands that questioning God's commandments is not permitted. Similarly, God commands Jonah to go to Nineveh, so Jonah's protest and attempted escape are not acceptable.

God's Wrath

God's wrath or threat of punishment is viewed uncomfortably by many Jews. They prefer a compassionate God, ready to help people solve problems. Their concern is overdone. The episodes where God kills Israelites follow their turning toward other gods or against the God-appointed leadership. It is not a general response to breaking a commandment. That His reaction is more the exception than the rule is underscored by the episodes in Numbers being followed immediately by commandments restricting extreme punishment or innovating in a way that would prevent inadvertent deaths.

Jews do not have to be concerned about feeling the effects of

God's wrath for individual transgressions. God's anger addresses group misconduct. Generally, the message from the Torah is that God wants to minimize His role in Israelite society, leaving enforcement of the commandments to its leadership.

God's Compassion

Jews prefer a compassionate God, and this side of Him clearly comes through. Explicit commandments regarding caring for widows and orphans are examples. The commandment to leave a portion of grain on the field for the poor is another. The latter is a mirror image of the commandment to bring the first fruits of the harvest for sacrifice to God. The symmetry between the two shows that both caring for the poor and ritual are needed to obtain God's benevolence, consistent with the message from the Prophets.

Other Issues

Besides addressing these large issues, the following chapters contain non-traditional explanations for specific events in the Torah, some of which are typically viewed as mysterious. Here are examples:

A General Theory of the Torah (Chapter 7) offers a way of seeing theologically how the Book of Genesis fits with the other four books of the Torah. Genesis is not just a collection of stories to provide background to the Jewish people. The "reward approach" to keeping people on the right track does not work in Genesis, so the threat of punishment in the subsequent Books of the Torah is justified.

How Many Gods Are There? (Chapter 8) argues that Adonai and Elohim may represent two separate entities, with curious implications that resolve a lot of small, apparent inconsistencies in the Books of Genesis, Exodus and Numbers. Being created in God's image may not be what it is cracked up to be.

Analysis of Akedah (Chapter 9) provides a rationale for God's decision to test Abraham. It relates to the potential problem that a person who prospers may take all the credit and move away from God – a concern found elsewhere in the Torah, as well.

An Incorrect Interpretattion of the Torah? (Chatper 10) looks at how the Patriarchs dealt with near-holocaust experiences. It explains the purpose of Jacob's struggle with the Angel. He is to have the self-confidence to solve problems, himself — as did Abraham and Isaac.

Conjectures on the Joseph Story (Chapter 12) shows why Joseph, among the sons of Jacob, was the most apt to prosper and succeed in Egypt. He had his idol-worshipping mother, Rachel, to thank.

Understanding the Haggadah (Chapter 14) argues that interpreting Passover as a celebration of freedom misses the holiday's original aim, which is to reaffirm Jews' obligations to God for freeing them from Egypt. The chapter also links Zipporah's spreading of blood on the legs of Moses' son to the spreading of lamb's blood on the Israelites' doorposts to sprinkling blood around the altar in the Tabernacle. All can be interpreted as binding the Israelites and God together in a sort of marital ceremony.

Purpose of the Plagues (Chapter 13) explains why God hardens Pharaoh's heart and why Pharaoh still has free choice but fails to make the right decision – which is not whether to free the Israelites but whether to acknowledge a fear of God.

What God Wants (Chapter 3) traces the development of God's relationship with the Israelites in the post-Egypt chapters of Exodus. It moves from a quid quo pro to a guideline approach.

Ritual (Chapter 15) analyzes what the detailed instructions for the building of the Mishkan and the problems evident in the Golden Calf episode might mean for current religious practices.

What God Settles For (Chapter 5) shows the religion changing to accommodate people's demands. The biblical text argues against many standard explanations for the Laws. The idea the Laws are meant to separate Jews from other societies, for example, cannot be the reason.

A Living Leviticus (Chapters 16-24) discusses what the sacrificial system means for current prayer practice and provides theological rationales for keeping Kosher, purification rituals and sex-related prohibitions. The rationale for the latter provides a way to make homosexuality biblically acceptable.

Numero Uno in the Book of Numbers (Chapters 25-31) constructs a social hierarchy that fails to satisfy God's requirements. A commitment by all the people to God, not just by their leaders, is needed to obtain God's approval. Non-conformity within society is acceptable.

Deuteronomy: A Reformation of the Religion (Chapters 32-35) shows how Judaism is to be reformed. A rearrangement of two passages in the Book, however, led to a mistaken inclusion of separation of meat and dairy products in the Kosher laws.

Practicing the Religion (Chapters 36-40) begins by offering reasons why the Israelites turned to other gods. They found difficulty seeing the connection between God or his prophets and worldly success. The prophets address this problem by emphasizing longer-run consequences of adhering to God or not. Ezra and Nehemiah try restrictive laws, unsuccessfully.

A Theory of Ethics from Amos (Chapter 41) derives an answer to Cain's question, "Am I my brother's keeper?" The answer is yes, at least to some extent. It also examines the question of whether individuals are responsible for the moral character of their society.

David Unhinged (Chapter 42) argues that the story of David shows how believing one communicates with God can lead to sin and have harmful consequences.

A Job on Job (Chapter 43) highlights the mistake that can be made from applying facile theological rationales to explain events.

Why is Esther in the Bible? (Chapter 47) draws a connection between Purim and Passover.

An Analysis of Song of Songs (Chapter 48) shows how this poetic piece is a critique of Solomon and complaint about the centralization of the religion in Jerusalem.

GOD

T his section examines God's depiction in the Torah. The first chapter shows God is not omniscient. There are many instances when He is not sure what will happen next. Arguably, a level of chaos was left over in the Creation. This is important. Chaos permits people to have the free will to make decisions and events to happen independently of God. The second chapter offers reasons why God permits chaos.

Chapter 1 - *A Theory Of God*

The first step in deriving a theology of Judaism is to form an idea about the nature of God. This chapter, written for a class on logically proving God's existence, argues that the Torah does not depict God as omniscient.

G od typically is conceived as all-powerful and knowing. A rigorous definition of this concept is called an Absolutely Perfect Being (APB). An APB knows everything. At any moment, his knowledge covers all time – past, present and future -- and space. From this definition, the necessity of the existence of an APB can be proven through logic. This definition, however, is not consistent with the Torah's portrayal of God.

Torah's Portrayal of God

The definition of God as an APB does not fit with the characteristics, actions and concept of God in the Torah. The all-knowing aspect of an APB is the problem. God does not know everything in advance. Instead, there are times when He appears uncertain about how events will evolve.

Perhaps a subtle example is God's planting the Trees of Life and Knowledge in the Garden of Eden. He allows Adam and Eve to decide whether to eat them or not. God understands not everything is in His control.

In the story of Noah, man's wickedness is so great God "was sorry that He had made man on the earth, and it grieved him in His heart." These are inappropriate feelings had He known in advance what would happen to His creations.

In the most pre-determined episode in the Torah – Exodus – God demonstrates uncertainty. At the start, God tells Moses to perform two pieces of magic to persuade the Israelites that he, in fact, represents Him. But, God adds a third piece just in case the Israelites are not convinced by the first two. An all-knowing God would not need such a contingency.

In Chapter 13, God chooses the longer route out of Egypt through the wilderness rather than the land of the Philistines because he is not sure of the Israelite reaction to warfare. God says, "Lest perhaps the people change their minds when they see war, and they return to Egypt." God attaches a probability to the possibility the Israelites would not choose the result He desires. He does not demonstrate the complete knowledge of future events required of an APB.

Chaos

God's uncertainty implies a level of chaos in the universe, which allows events to occur independently of Him. Although God imposes order on chaos at the beginning of Genesis, the text does not guarantee all of it is eliminated. Instead, a residual may have been left over from the Creation. God acknowledges this residual by not calling the creation of man good. He is uncertain how mankind will evolve.

The existence of chaos can be found in the story of the Tower of Babel. God feels people are confused in trying to be like gods by reaching for the heavens. They do not know their place in the world order. If He does not intercede, people would take the wrong track. He recognizes a chaotic porton of the world could evolve independently of His desires. So, He introduces different languages to prevent them from attaining their goal.

In Exodus, the Amalek represent chaos. They practice evil and are without constraint. God's admonition to remember to destroy the Amalek shows there always will be an element in the world beyond His control.

Broad Considerations

There are broad, well-known considerations arguing against an all-knowing God. The Akedah does not make sense if there is no free will. God tests Abraham to see if he would follow His commandments. What is the point of the test if Abraham had no free will? Moses' admonition, on behalf of God, for the Israelites to choose life and keep God's commandments also does not make sense if there is no free will. Finally, the entire Torah, with its emphasis on ethics, laws and commandments, belies the idea that there is no free will. Without free will, what is the need for all these rules? The Torah would be a cruel joke.

This is not to say God does not know anything about the future. He clearly knows some future events in the Torah. He tells Abraham and his offspring that their family will develop into a great nation. He also tells Abraham his descendants will spend 400 years in Egypt. He tells Moses what Pharaoh will do. And, at the end of Deuteronomy, God tells Moses that, after his death, the Israelites will go astray and break the covenant. As a result, evils and troubles will befall them because He will "surely hide My face in that day." Future events can be either pre-determined or not.

Conclusion

A strong case can be made from the Torah that events are not all God-determined. In particular, people and random events can influence the path of history.

The existence of chaos has powerful implications, including free will and an explanation why bad things happen to good people independently of God. At the same time, positing such uncertainty does not belie the idea of a powerful God. All it implies is that God is not all knowing.

Chapter 2 - *Why Does God Permit Chaos?*

Why does God allow "bad things" to happen? Why would a benevolent God permit disease, war, etc? Punishment or remnants of primordial chaos could explain this. But, I was interested in whether the guideline approach to the religion, derived in What God Wants (Chapter 3), could offer a reason. I was quite surprised to realize the existence of bad things provides opportunities for people to create, a key implication of the guideline approach. It also encourages a demand for God. Carrying the ideas further led to curious insights about God and the Israelite people. While God permits chaos for people, He does not like it for Himself. As a result, His sanctuary in the world — that is the Israelite community — should be relatively small at any given time.

Several "big picture" conundrums are often heard. Why does God permit inequality, poverty, and war? Why doesn't God quickly try to eliminate them? Why do Jews constitute such a small group if the religion is supposed to be so wonderful? Answers or, at least, conjectures about how to answer them can be constructed on the basis of theology. They follow from an extraordinary insight – God likes chaos except for Himself!

God's desire for people to live in a world of chaos can be derived from three ideas. Chaos promotes a demand for Him – people look for a savior in bad times. People need chaos from which to create, just as God created the world out of chaos. Chaos can be used as a threat to persuade adherence to the commandments.

Chaos Promotes Demand for God

The Torah contains ample evidence that God permits chaos to convince people they need Him. In both the Garden of Eden and Tower of Babel episodes, God comes down hard on people who want to be equal to Him. If they achieve equality, they may decide to be on their own. Concern that people will feel they don't need Him also is addressed in the Akedah and Moses' admonition to the Israelites not to take all the credit themselves when they enter the Promised Land.

After seeing people building a Tower to the sky, God says, "Behold, they are one people, and they have all one language; and this is what they begin to do. Now nothing which they intend to do will be withheld from them." The first part of this statement — "one people ... one language" — seems to suggest God dislikes cooperation in an endeavor. This, however, cannot be the case, since it runs counter to one of the main conclusions of the Torah – there is a partnership between people and God, established as early as the Garden of Eden. The second part of the statement — "nothing will be withheld from them" — is the issue. It indicates concern that people would be as powerful as He. He objects to the absence of an ultimate cap on what can be achieved through cooperation. People would not need Him if they can do everything themselves. God's decision to introduce multiple languages suggests a desire for chaos to sustain people's need of Him.

In the Garden of Eden story, God does not like people attempting to be as powerful as He. The snake is probably truthful when he tells Eve, "God knows that in the day you eat [of the tree of knowledge] your eyes will be opened and you will be like God, knowing good and evil." Eating the apple would be a step toward being like God. This concern prompts God to bar them from the Garden of Eden. He banishes them after saying, "Now that man has become like one of us, knowing good and bad, what if he should stretch out his hand and take also from the tree of life and eat, and live forever!" While there are several ways this thought can be interpreted, one possibility is that were man knowledgeable and immortal he might not need God.

Chaos Enables Creation

God's acceptance of chaos to enable people to create is based on the guideline approach of the first Ten Commandments as derived in *What God Wants* (Chapter 3). While people should not consider themselves God, they should act like Him. Since God created the world out of chaos, people should create out of chaos, too. As a result, there needs to be chaos from which they can create and bring order to the world. Achieving nirvana is never to be. Each generation needs a chaotic world from which to create. As a result, there is never an end to war, disease, and the rest.

This idea would seem to have a better grounding in the theology of the Torah than does Kabbalah, even though both have the same implication that people are to "fix the world," *i.e.,* to create. Kabbalah bases its proclamation on a magical vision of God. God's vessel broke and needs to be repaired.

God's desire for people to create out of chaos begins with Abraham. He sends Abram into a chaotic world when he tells him to leave "your father's house, to the land that I will show you." Breaking away from an established way of life certainly adds chaos to one's life. God recognizes this implication by promising protection, saying, "I will bless those who bless you and I will curse him who curses you." More important than the risk of danger in a chaotic world is the need for Abram to create a new nation in a new land.

Despite God's residing with them, Abraham and his progeny, as well as the Israelites post-Egypt, face difficulties when dealing with the chaotic part of the world. The difficulties occur within their group as well as in their relationships with others. In all these cases, the Israelites need to create by themselves as well as to rely on God to solve their problems.

Chaos as a Threat

The third idea is essentially the traditional view, based on the covenant. If the Israelites do not conform to the commandments, God will disperse them from the Promised Land and inflict other bad consequences. He uses the threat of chaos to persuade the Israelites to act correctly. Although bringing on chaos means destroying His sanctuary within the Israelite society, this sanctuary would be contaminated anyway were the Israelites not to follow the commandments.

The Book of Judges recognizes this traditional theme. God spares some Canaanites from annihilation in the Israelite conquest "that by them I may prove Israel, whether they will keep God's way ... as their fathers did keep it, or not." The Israelites would always be reminded of their need for God's help, which should encourage them to do what's needed -- follow the commandments -- to keep Him in their midst.

This rationale for chaos, however, can run counter to another idea found in the Torah: God does not want to be heavily involved in everyday life; Leviticus specifies a double penalty if God is needed to resolve a dispute. God does not mean to be constantly testing the Jews, with the Akedah and Book of Job containing extraordinary trials. For this reason, the two non-traditional rationales for why God permits chaos — to promote a demand for Him and to allow for people to create — are arguably more in keeping with the broader themes of the Torah than this more traditional explanation.

Why Are Jewish People Few in Number?

The answer resides in a paradox. While God sees value in people living with chaos, He does not like it for Himself. Besides bringing some order in the creation, He attempts to create a sanctuary for Himself in the Israelite society by establishing its laws and commandments. The Israelite society is to be non-chaotic so He can reside in it. To reconcile His need of a non-chaotic sanctuary with His desire for people to be faced with chaos, the Israelite society (Jewish community in more modern times) is to be small. By having only a small sanctuary, there is always much chaos in the rest of the world for people to work with. He minimizes the ordered part of the world, aiming for just enough to satisfy His own requirements. The upshot is that the Jewish people are not numerous.

At first glance, this set of ideas would seem to contradict God's promise to Abram that his progeny will be many. In Genesis, Chapter 13, verse 16, God says, "I will make your offspring as the dust of the earth, so that if a man can number the dust of the earth, then your seed may also be numbered." This promise is driven home in Genesis, Chapter 15, verse 5, when God assures Abram that he should not be concerned about Sarai's barrenness, saying, "Look toward the sky and count the stars, if you are able to count them. So, shall your seed be." Tradition interprets these promises to mean the Israelites are to be numerous. Arguably, they are meant to hold true across generations. So, while Israelites may not be numerous at any point in time, they are when counted over time. This perspective enables the textual promises to be met, even with Jews representing a small group at any moment.

Why do Bad Things Happen?

Finally, "bad things" can happen and persist within this framework by viewing the chaotic nature of the world as a probability distribution. Outliers, such as the Holocaust, can happen despite their low probability of occurrence. The Torah promises, however, that the extreme tail of the distribution — the complete elimination of the Jewish people — will not happen.

Conclusion

Although speculative, these ideas are consistent with the broad theology of the Torah. As in the case of other grand ironies found in the Torah, they argue against conventional religious ideas. In particular, rather than thinking God prefers a world of peace and well-being, one can posit that He allows for a chaotic world to enhance people's demand for Him and to provide an environment within which to create. Prayers for peace may be overly ambitious. Moreover, all the dubious social features found in the Torah, such as slavery, widowhood, poverty, whose presence raises questions about God's intentions or the purpose of the religion, become understood as challenges for people to tackle rather than as acceptable elements of society.

From this perspective, a person's rejection of God in reaction to a bad event is the exact opposite of what is called for. A better theological response would be to increase one's awareness of the need for Him to lower the risk that similarly bad events will happen in the future. The bad event should reinforce the need for God, with the caveat that a person is meant to attempt to solve a problem before God does.

Blaming God for not acting sooner to change a bad event may be more justifiable, since it is questionable how much suffering is necessary to bolster demand for Him or to prompt people to try to solve their problems. Nevertheless, some arguments can be made to explain why God takes His time in coming to the rescue. Time has to be allowed for people to correct the problem themselves. If God acts immediately or after a known, fixed interval, there could be little incentive for people to solve their own problems. Perhaps, uncertainty about God's speed of responsiveness is required to ensure that people do not wait for Him. Without knowing when God will come to help, people must solve problems, themselves.

The Relationship Between God
And The Israelites

The next four chapters focus on the relationship between God and the Israelites as spelled out in the Book of Exodus. Two relationships are established. The first entails the Israelites acting as if they have the power and independence of God, but doing so within guidelines. The second establishes a more dependent relationship.

The Torah Group viewed the episodes following the crossing of the Sea of Reeds as mutually independent, folk-like tales. The episodes involve the well-known stories of God's providing manna to the starving Israelites, Moses' striking a rock to obtain water, and the battle between the Israelites and the Amalek. While apparently distinct events, they can be viewed as a progression of steps defining the relationship between God and the Israelites, moving from one of dependence to one of separation. Starting as a quid pro quo relationship, with God providing help as long as the Israelites obey his commandments, the relationship evolves into one where the Israelites are to make decisions independently of Him but within a set of guidelines based on the commandments.

Chapter 3 - *What God Wants*

This chapter shows how the relationship between the Israelites and God evolves from the time they leave Egypt to when they acquire commandments and laws at Mount Sinai. It moves from dependence to separation. In the end, God is to be acknowledged as the sole ultimate authority. But, the Israelites are to act as if they have the power and independence of God, doing so within ethical and spiritual guidelines.

When the Israelites leave Egypt, their exact relationship with God is not fully defined. Are they to be entirely submissive to His wishes -- substituting God for Pharaoh as slave-master and living only by His dictates? Is the relationship to be a personal one? What exactly does God want of them?

These questions are answered in a sequence of episodes from the crossing of the Sea of Reeds to the revelation at Mount Sinai. Both God and the Israelites change their perceptions of what their relationship should be, starting with one of quid pro quo and ending with one emphasizing reliance on themselves and others rather than God. The evolution is so linear the text could be viewed as didactic rather than historical in nature – it is meant to teach a lesson rather than to portray historical events.

Quid Pro Quo

According to the initial quid pro quo relationship, God will help the Israelites as long as they adhere to Him and follow His commandments. God's first words to the Israelites in the wilderness establish this relationship. He says, "If you will diligently listen to voice of the Lord your God, do that which is right in His eyes, pay attention to His commandments, and keep all His statutes, then I will put none of the diseases on you, which I have put on the Egyptians, for I am the Lord who heals you."

The Israelites in fact had understand this relationship before this episode. In the Song at the Sea, the Israelites praise God because He obliterated their enemy – Pharaoh and his army. They sing, "I will sing to the Lord, for He has triumphed gloriously: the horse and driver He has thrown into the sea." As a result, the Israelites count on God to bring them to their ultimate destination. They end the song with, "You shall bring them [the Israelites] in and plant them in the mountain of your inheritance, the place which You have made for Yourself to dwell in; the sanctuary, Lord, which Your hands have established." As a quid pro quo, they say, "The Lord shall reign for ever and ever." The song suggests the Israelites are willing to acknowledge the supremacy of God because He helped them escape Egypt.

While not obvious, God apparently approves of these thoughts through the voice of Miriam. She is called a prophetess -- one who speaks the word of God. She also is introduced as Aaron's sister, showing a connection to the priesthood. Both put her closer to God than the ordinary Israelite. Miriam's song consists of only two lines, which are similar but not exactly the same as the first two lines of the Song at the Sea. Rather than saying "I will sing to the Lord," she says, "Sing to the Lord," an affirmation of the sentiments just expressed by the Israelites.

Problems With Quid Pro Quo

Problems with a quid pro quo relationship come up quickly. Many Israelites have difficulty distinguishing between God and His agent, Moses, as their savior. Whom are they to credit or blame for good or bad developments -- a person they can see at any time or an invisible god? The Israelites do not recognize God's role in the world but blame Moses for their problems.

They lose their fear of God, which is needed to understand His role in worldly affairs, as discussed in *Purpose of the Plagues* (Chapter 13). Without a fear of God, a quid pro quo relationship may not work since His part of the deal may not be recognized.

The problem of distinguishing between God and Moses surfaces in the wilderness of Sin when the Israelites run out of food. The Israelites vent their anger at Moses and Aaron, telling the two human leaders "you have brought us out into this wilderness, to kill this whole assembly with hunger." But, Moses and Aaron understand the people are mistaken about who took them out of Egypt. The brothers are quick to put the responsibility on God, teaching the Israelites that their welfare is in God's hand as part of the quid pro quo relationship. They say, "At evening, then you shall know the Lord has brought you out from the land of Egypt; and in the morning, then you shall see the glory of the Lord; because He hears your grumblings against the Lord [even though you thought you were complaining against us]. Who are we that you should murmur against us [for we just did God's will]?" The episode suggests that understanding God's role in world events is not an easy accomplishment, raising doubt about the efficacy of a quid quo pro relationship.

Another challenge to the quid quo pro relationship is that even if the Israelites recognize God's role, they could question whether He is upholding His end of the covenant when bad things happen. God's covenant after the crossing of the Sea hints at this problem. While the Israelites emphasized God's power over their enemies, this is not what is actually promised in the covenant. Instead, God promises only not to give them "any of the diseases ... which I have put on the Egyptians." It is a limited promise, consistent with the idea that God cannot be counted on to solve all problems. But, a difference between how the Israelites and how God view the covenant opens the door for questioning His reliability. It could lead to loss of faith in God.

Questioning God's reliability marks this episode. While providing manna, God commands the Israelites not to keep any of it overnight except on the sixth day so that they would not have to gather it on the seventh day, the Sabbath. The Israelites fail to obey this command, keeping extra manna overnight during the workweek. Then, some Israelites go out to gather the manna on the seventh day. God is upset that the quid pro quo relationship does not succeed in prompting the Israelites to follow His commandments. God says in exasperation, "How long will [they] refuse to obey My commandments and teachings?" As in the Book of Genesis, the "reward approach" to persuasion is found wanting (*A General Theory of the Torah*, Chapter 7).

The Israelites, however, are not entirely to blame. Their disobedience may stem from the view that God did not uphold His end of the bargain. When one is led to believe that God will act on your behalf, which the Israelites understood to be the case as expressed in the Song at the Sea, why would God permit any bad thing to happen in the first place? Or, if bad things happen for random reasons, why doesn't God act immediately to correct them? The Israelites encounter problems as soon as they enter the wilderness, despite having God on their side. So, is it surprising that some Israelites do not feel compelled to follow His commandments? They understand that even if they do obey, they could be let down again. Rather than assume God will provide enough manna the next day, they defy God's command and save food overnight or gather manna on the Sabbath.

A feeling of betrayal is a fundamental problem with a quid pro quo relationship. When bad things happen to supposedly undeserving people, feelings of betrayal could lead to disillusionment with God. At Sinai, God says, "If you will obey My voice and keep My covenant, you shall be My own possession from among all the peoples." Some people could blame themselves if their situations don't seem to be commensurate with being God's own possession, but others may blame God for backing out of the deal. Thus, the Torah contains a potentially self-destructive idea. The problem arguably comes to the fore again once the Israelites settle in Canaan, discussed in *Practicing the Religion* (Chapters 36-39).

While the Torah never rids itself of the notion of quid pro quo, it is fascinating that God recognizes its inherent problems and changes this relationship in the remaining episodes in the wilderness. He shows the Israelites that they should be more reliant on themselves and others than on God.

God as Helper

God steps back from directly solving the Israelites' problem at Rephidim, where a lack of water is the issue. He responds to clear evidence of the problems with a quid quo relationship.

Once more, the Israelites are confused about whom is responsible for having brought them out of Egypt, Moses or God. They ask Moses, "Why have you brought us up out of Egypt, to kill us, our children and livestock with thirst?" Moses fears that their confusion could lead to his death. He complains to God, "What shall I do with this people? They are almost ready to stone me." Moses understands the first problem with the quid pro quo relationship – a person (*i.e.*, Moses, himself) can be held responsible for a difficult situation even if he is not responsible -- can have dire consequences.

The Israelites also directly question whether God is upholding his end of the bargain. They say, "Is the Lord present among us or not?" Taking both the problem of incorrect responsibility and perceived unreliability together, God perhaps realizes the Israelites need to put more trust in themselves and their leaders and to reduce their reliance on Him.

As a result, God's instructions for obtaining water emphasize human leadership. Moses is to involve the elders of Israel, thereby giving them part of the credit. God tells Moses to "walk on before the people; take the elders of Israel with you, and take the rod in your hand with which you struck the Nile." In this way, the Israelites can see their leadership involved in solving the drought. To be sure, the Israelites are likely to recognize the rod and understand that God is behind Moses and the elders. God, in this regard, tells Moses that He will "stand before you there on the rock in Horeb," but this seems to be just between the two of them. With the inclusion of the elders and Moses being the one to strike the rock to yield water, the scene is choreographed to demonstrate that people can solve a problem, albeit with God's help.

God as Inspirer

God plays no explicit role in the defeat of Amalek at Rephidim. Joshua and his men prevail during the battle when Moses lifts his hands and are beaten back when Moses drops his hands. People – Aaron (representing the priesthood) and Hur (representing the military) – support Moses' hands, enabling the Israelites to win while giving credit to both sides of society.

The lifting of Moses' hands can be interpreted as inspiring the Israelite warriors to believe God is on their side. Support for this interpretation comes at the end of the episode. Recognizing God's role as one of inspiration, Moses names a newly built altar at the battlefield "Hand upon the throne of the Lord." While the Israelites are to fight their battles themselves, God is there at least for moral support.

The episode, however, leaves open the door for direct help by God, who asserts that He "will utterly blot out the memory of Amalek from under the sky." Emphasis should be placed on the future tense of this statement. It hints at a quid pro quo relationship. Since the Israelites won the battle, themselves, God will destroy their enemy thereafter.

God in the Background

The visit of Moses' father-in-law, Jethro, the priest of Midian, moves the relationship between the Israelites and God further apart. Jethro's recommendation to set up a judicial system demonstrates that Israelites are permitted to implement ideas or practices from outsiders. They are not constrained to live by God's prescriptions alone. To be sure, not every outside idea is acceptable. The Israelites need God's approval to incorporate one. Even Jethro acknowledges the necessity of getting God's consent, as he says, "If you do this thing, and God commands you so, then you will be able to endure." God is seen to be in the background, there to offer guidance as to what is acceptable but not necessarily to find solutions to all of the Israelites' problems.

The episode shows the Israelites are not meant to devote their lives to just submitting to God's commandments. The latter do not cover all elements of society or life. The Israelites are permitted to reach out to other groups to find innovations to improve their society. Isolation from the rest of the world is not required.

Separation at Sinai

Some of these ideas are reiterated at Mount Sinai. God reminds the Israelites that He is responsible for their freedom from Egypt – part of the quid pro quo relationship. He says, "You have seen what I did to the Egyptians, how I bore you on eagles' wings and brought you to Myself." God also aims to prop up the stature of Moses. He says to him, "I come to you in a thick cloud, that the people may hear when I speak with you and may also believe you forever."

However, the most significant message from the encounter is a separation between God and the Israelites. The relationship between God and the Israelites is not to be a personal one. Calling for God does not necessarily bring Him. God, instead, determines when He is with the Israelites. He says, "in every place where *I record* my Name I will come to you and I will bless you." Such separation and one-way relationship fit with the idea that the Israelites are to fend for themselves and not to count on God to be available to help them.

God establishes the separation. After saying to Moses that He will "come down in the sight of all the people, on Mount Sinai," He tells Moses to keep the Israelites away from Him. God says, "You shall set bounds to the people round about, saying 'Be careful that you don't go up onto the mountain or touch its border.'" Even priests cannot approach God. At first, God seems to make them an exception, saying that priests "who come near the Lord must purify themselves, lest the Lord break out against them." After Moses brings up His earlier prohibition, however, God realizes that only Aaron can approach Him. God says, "Go down, and you shall bring Aaron up with you; but don't let the priests and the people break through to come up to the Lord, lest He break forth on them."

The Israelites' reaction confirms that separation from God is the natural response to the situation. After witnessing "the thunders and lightnings, a thick cloud on the mountain, and an exceedingly loud trumpet, all the people who were in the camp trembled." They demand that Moses speak to them rather than God "lest we die," sensing a danger by being near God.

The one exception is when Moses, Aaron, Aaron's sons, and the seventy elders of Israel meet and eat with God. This event has to be viewed as extraordinary, especially since the text acknowledges that God "didn't lay His hand on the leaders of the Israelites." Perhaps, He permits this one personal encounter to cement the commitment of the elders to implement the covenant. That the elders eat with God affirms a partnership between them and Him, consistent with the rules concerning the eating of sacrifices found later in Leviticus (*Implications for Prayer,* Chapter 17).

In sum, the oft-heard notion of a warm, close relationship with God is not well founded in Exodus. The relationship instead is to be one of awe and respect. The awe is apparent in the setting. At Mount Sinai, God "descended on it in fire and the smoke ascended like the smoke of a furnace, and the whole mountain quaked greatly. When the blare of the horn grew louder and louder, Moses spoke, and God answered him by a voice." The respect is seen in God's requirements for the Israelites. He tells Moses to "sanctify them today and tomorrow. Let them wash their clothes...Don't have sexual relations with a woman." The relationship between the Israelites and God is to be a formal one.

Chapter 4 - *The Ten Commandments*
A Non-Traditional
Interpretation

The new relationship between God and the Israelites leads to a non-traditional interpretation of the Ten Commandments. Tradition views the first four Commandments as defining a relationship between Man and God and the last six as independently defining one between Man and Man. In the new interpretation, the last six follow logically from the first four.

Since the Israelites will have some control over their destiny, independently of God, they have to know how to act. The general ideas are found in the Ten Commandments when understood in a non-traditional way. The Israelites are to act like God, while acknowledging Him as the ultimate authority. They are to accomplish both by making decisions themselves, but within the guidelines of His commandments and laws. The notion of everyone acting like God implicitly contains a basis for ethical behavior, but explicit commandments and laws regarding ethics are needed as well.

The Ten Commandments

The Ten Commandments and the subsequent Laws are the framework to guide the Israelites. The Commandments are split between those relating to God (the first four) and those dealing with interpersonal relationships (the last six). Traditionally, the two subsets are viewed to be independent of each other. The new approach, instead, shows they are intertwined. The first four Commandments mean Israelites are to act like God, albeit with the understanding that He is the ultimate authority. Acting like God has powerful and potentially dangerous consequences, since a person might feel permitted to do anything he wants. Anarchy can result. The remaining six commandments prevent this from happening. So, in contrast to the traditional view, there is no dichotomy between the first four and last six Commandments.

The key to the Commandments is found in the rationale for the fourth commandment to work six days and rest on the Sabbath: God created everything in six days and rested on the seventh; therefore, rest on the Sabbath because God rested. It takes just a small step to infer that all actions that imitate God's would be commendable. The only God-like actions with which the Israelites are familiar at this point involve power and decision-making. To imitate God's actions means to exert power — to control one's destiny.

This inference might seem odd, given the widely held views of other attributes of God, such as compassion. However, the desired separation of the Israelites from God underscores the importance of power and decision-making. Since the Israelites are expected to move through history on their own to a large extent, they will need to believe they have the power to make the decisions and take the actions needed to guide their society.

Acting like God encompasses making commandments. This implicit power opens the door for reforming the religion. However, any change presumably would need to be consistent with the intent of the commandments promulgated by God, given the implication of the First Commandment that He is supreme.

Many other parts of the Ten Commandments take on a non-traditional meaning in light of this approach. The first commandment is "I am the Lord your God." The traditional view is that it means to believe in the existence of God. The new view would go as follows. Since all Israelites are expected to act like God, they have to acknowledge one, most powerful authority. Otherwise, the situation could degrade into anarchy with each Israelite regarding himself god-like. The emphasis in this commandment should be on the word Lord, one who rules over all. The rest of the first commandment is "Who brought you out of the land of Egypt, out of the house of bondage." The traditional view says that God has a moral claim on the Israelites. Similar to the traditional view, the new view says that this part of the commandment sets forth immediately the quid pro quo relationship.

The second commandment is "You shall have no other gods before Me." In the traditional view, this commandment states the fundamental dogma of Israel's religion -- there is no other god. In the new view, each Israelite has to know he, himself, is not a god, despite being told (implicitly) to act like Him.

The third commandment prohibits the making of "an idol nor any image of anything that is in the heavens above...You shall not bow down to them nor serve them." According to the traditional view, this commandment forbids worshipping God in the wrong way. The new view might say that constructing and praying to images could make the Israelites dependent on these objects in making decisions. The relationship that evolved in the preceding episodes emphasizes solving problems by oneself.

The fifth commandment is to "honor your father and mother that your days may be long in the land which the Lord your God gives you." In the traditional view, children see parents as a stand-in for God. To honor them will bring happiness and blessing. Alternatively, parents should be honored because they made the decision to enter their child into the covenant. Honoring them helps a person uphold his or her commitment to the covenant, inasmuch as breaking the covenant would dishonor the people who brought him or her into it. And, by living according to the covenant, the Israelites will remain in the Promised Land. Similarly, the third commandment prohibiting the mention of God's name in vain means to prevent the denigration of the covenant, which could happen if God is not treated with respect.

The idea that Israelites are to act like God has within it the basis for ethical behavior. If everyone acts like God, people should approach each other as if they are approaching God, that is with respect.

This implicit basis for ethics may have been too subtle to be effective. It was not understood in the first attempt at having people act like a god — the episode of the Nephilim in Genesis, when divine Beings cohabited with women. This led to

36

problems. "The Lord saw that the wickedness of man was great in the earth, and that every imagination of the thoughts of his heart was only evil continually." In Exodus, when God resurrects the idea of people acting like God, He is explicit that it should be done within the constraints of commandments and laws.

And this is the intent of the last five commandments. They put limits on how far Israelites can incorporate the idea of acting like God in interpersonal relationships. Being told to act like God does not give someone the right to interfere in another's life. Specifically, one is not permitted to murder, commit adultery, steal, bear false witness against neighbors, or covet neighbors' property. The Israelites have to respect the rights and property of others, approaching others in a similar way that they approach God – with respect.

All these latter commandments impose a separation between each and every Israelite, just as there is supposed to be separation between God and the Israelites. As a result, the Israelites are to be a group of separate, but equal people, with each acting like God. This characterization provides, perhaps, a new interpretation of what being a "holy people" means. The Israelites are not meant to be priest-like, but to act like God and to treat others with the respect they would be expected to show God.

The Laws

Although everyone should treat others with respect, the Torah recognizes that not everyone is equal in society. Some are slaves or poor. Women are not viewed to be equal to men. Strangers do not have the same rights as members of the group. The essence of the subsequent Laws is to show how to apply the ethical implications of the Ten Commandments to the treatment of those who are not socially or economically at one's level. In general, the underlying ethics of the Laws can be understood according to the approach Israelites are supposed to take toward other people as well as toward God – they are to approach others with respect.

It is no accident the first Law concerns slaves, who are obviously at the lowest level of the community. Even a slave has certain rights, as the Torah specifies situations where their choices are to be accepted. The same holds true of women, discussed in the law concerning virgins. Similarly, widows and orphans cannot be treated badly even though they are not powerful. Nevertheless, they should not be favored in a dispute just because of their poverty. This law, as well as the prohibition of taking bribes, underscores the evenhandedness implicit in requiring each person to respect another. So important is treating others with respect that the notion transcends the issue of whether two people are enemies. A person cannot appropriate his enemy's animals, even if they are found wandering. Also, a person must come to his enemy's assistance if he is found to be in difficulty, such as with a recalcitrant animal.

The notion of respect also can explain the nature of punishment in the Laws. Some proscribed acts require punishment by death, such as murder and kidnapping. These crimes involve a complete domination of one person over another, with the perpetrator showing no respect at all for the other person. Other crimes, such as striking someone with a stone or fist or damaging another's property, encroach only partly on another person or his property. So, they are assigned a less severe punishment than death. A death sentence in these cases would violate the rights of the perpetrator by more than the crime violated those of the victim. The assignment of punishment to a crime represents a balancing against the lost respect of the victim.

Importantly, punishments are to be performed for the most part by people. Doing so is consistent with the relationship worked out between God and the Israelites for two reasons. Enforcement of the laws is fitting for a people who are to act like God. Also, it is fitting for a relationship meant to minimize dependence on Him.

There are three exceptions where God plays a role in the

adjudication. In the case of misappropriation, where loss of property is alleged by one person against another and God is needed to determine the guilty party, the latter needs to pay the other double. In this case, the guilty party is penalized for requiring God's presence and thereby disturbing the relationship between the Israelites and Him. Other exceptions are the mistreatment of a widow, orphan or poor person. In these cases, the victims may not have the power to defend themselves, which may be why God is required to protect them. Importantly, He will come only if a victim cries out to Him. In a sense, crying out is an action taken in self-defense and consistent with the message found elsewhere in the Torah that God intervenes only after a person acts to solve the problem in question.

Implications for Broad Issues

Why doesn't God just eliminate the inequalities and injustices in society? The answer may be that the Israelites, themselves, need to initiate or implement the changes, as in the case of Jethro. Besides reflecting a separation from God, correcting problems mimic God's creative actions.

Implicit in the Laws is not only the need to respect the rights of others, but also the need to respect the community's institutions. Proposed changes should not aim to overthrow the social or political system. The Law against putting a curse on a "ruler of your people" suggests revolution is not an option, even if the leadership deserves to be removed.

Social structure is a given, even though some of its elements may appear to be contrary to the idea of equality. The acceptance of slavery, the second-class role of women, and the split between the wealthy and poor are examples of a social institution whose possible elimination is not mentioned. Besides social structure, the Laws do not propose changing social realities, such as widowhood or orphans. They are a given.

In total, Judaism, as defined by the Commandments and Laws, represents a conservative rather than radical revolution. It conserves social institutions and accepts social realities. Rather than overturning these institutions, *e.g.*, class structure, or eliminate unfortunate situations, *e.g.*, widowhood, it attempts to instill ethics in dealing with them. This way of looking at the Torah may help to explain why the American Founders relied so heavily on its principles in establishing the U.S. They allowed them to base the new country on law and justice without having to destroy existing institutions such as slavery. Of course, the episode with Jethro demonstrates the Israelites can change their way of doing communal business. The changes presumably need to be consistent with the ethical underpinnings of the Laws, absent direct approval by God.

Finally, dietary laws can be interpreted through the new approach to the Ten Commandments. Since Israelites are supposed to act like God, their diets should be modeled on the sacrifices made to God. Just as only particular parts of animals can be used for sacrifice, Israelites may eat only certain animals or parts of animals. For example, because only unblemished animals can be used for sacrifice, Israelites are not permitted to "eat flesh torn by beasts in the field." Or, as dictated later in Leviticus, Israelites should not eat anything with its blood, in line with the requirement to drain all blood from sacrificial meat. In general, prohibiting certain animals for consumption maps into the restrictions specified by God with respect to sacrifice.

Covenant

Following the Laws, God specifies a covenant with the Israelites. Elements of the new relationship between God and the Israelites mark this covenant, but the quid pro quo notion remains. Consistent with the idea of separation, an angel will lead the Israelites, not God, Himself. However, even with separation, God will come back to help the Israelites. If they obey the angel and follow the Commandments and Laws ("do all that I speak"), God "will be an enemy to your enemies." He will not do everything for the Israelites, though. They must bear the responsibility of destroying any vestiges of pagan religions they come across. Then, God will not only destroy their enemies,

He will bless their "bread and water" (that is, help the Israelites achieve a good standard of living), "take sickness away from your midst," prevent miscarriages and barren women, and specify wide boundaries for the Promised Land." Moreover, God "will fulfill the number of your days." The last benefit could be interpreted to mean the benefits apply to future generations, as well.

The Israelites agree to this covenant, saying, "All the words that the Lord has spoken we will do!" Moses formalizes the vow by throwing bull's blood on the people, similar to Zipporah's idea of connecting with God by being a "bridegroom of blood."

In grand irony, the Torah posits a quid pro quo relationship between God and the Israelites that encompasses commandments requiring the Israelites to make decisions and take actions independently of God. The future is the outcome of both human decision and God's intervention.

Chapter 5 - *What God Settles For*

Having discovered what appeared to be an inspiring message about the essence of Judaism -- calling for independent and decisive actions by Jews within ethical constraints, I came in for a shock with the reading of Chapters 33 and 34 in Exodus. While I could understand the Israelites finding the concept of independence troubling, as seen in the Golden Calf episode, I did not expect Moses to want a more dependent relationship with God, as well. As I read through subsequent chapters, I saw that God bends and reforms the religion to one following a code of rules rather than empowering the Israelites to make decisions within broad guidelines.

U nfortunately, God's desire for the Israelites to act like Himself is difficult to accomplish. The Golden Calf episode shows people wanting to rely on a god to achieve their goals than doing so by themselves. As a result, God gives a second set of commandments meant to be followed without question, providing a code approach to the religion for those who need a strict set of instructions by which to live.

Need for Dependence

God can see the ideals set forth earlier at Mount Sinai are problematical not only from the Golden Calf episode but from the requests made by Moses right after that episode. Moses appears discouraged, spending much time in the Tent of Meeting, away from the people. He seems to need God's support and wants to be certain of receiving divine help. Moses says to God, "Behold, You tell me, 'Bring up this people:' and You haven't let me know whom You will send with me." Moses continues with, "Yet you have said, 'I know you by name, and you have also found favor in My sight.' If I have found favor in Your sight, please show me now Your ways, that I may know You, so that I may find favor in Your sight." Moses does not seem to understand that God's ways have been evident in all His actions thus far. He perhaps is losing faith and needs reinforcement from a restatement of God's attributes.

God bends in response. He says, "My presence will go with you, and I will give you rest." Moses appears somewhat embarrassed by his admitted inadequacy, putting the onus on the need to show other peoples that God is with them. While not denying this reason, God indicates He is willing to take the lead because Moses has "found favor in My sight, and I know you by name." God is willing to compromise as a reward for the extraordinary actions taken by Moses in response to God's demands. This may be the first time the Torah suggests what is required for God to intervene on behalf of an individual. Unfortunately, it appears to require extraordinary behavior.

Moses is still not satisfied. He wants to see God, even though he and the elders already had eaten and drunk in His presence after the earlier covenant. Moses requests, "Oh, let me behold Your Glory." God is willing to compromise again. He says, "I will make all My goodness pass before you." Here, however, the old restrictions remain to some extent. Moses will not be able to see God's face, "for man may not see Me and live." Moses will see only God's back, which in a sense maintains a separation between the two. Also, God's description of Himself uses formal language and said in the third person, again preserving a degree of separation in the encounter. Nevertheless, this segment suggests a basic human need inherent in the Golden Calf episode -- people need to see some physical manifestation of God, perhaps more than once, to be comfortable having a relationship with Him.

The actual nature of God should not have been a surprise to Moses. All the characteristics were evident in God's prior actions or in the Commandments and Laws. First, God is the Lord, which repeats the First Commandment. This characteristic implies the power and almightiness of God. Second, God is "merciful and gracious." These attributes were reflected in the Laws concerning the underprivileged, such as widows. Third, God is "slow to anger, abounding in lovingkindness and truth." God held back His anger, even though exacerbated, when some of the Israelites went out to gather manna on the seventh day.

His kindness and mercifulness also prevented a rupture of the relationship with the Israelites after the Golden Calf episode. Although angered by the sinfulness, God immediately afterward reaffirms His intent on bringing the Israelites to the Promised Land. Fourth, God extends "lovingkindness for thousands [of generations], forgiving iniquity and disobedience and sin; and that will by no means clear the guilty, visiting the iniquity of the fathers on the children, and on the children's children, on the third and on the fourth generation." These characteristics repeat the words of the Second Commandment. To be sure, they reverse the order found in the Second Commandment. Putting the more positive attribute first is understandable given that God is trying to inspire Moses.

Despite not learning anything new, Moses appears satisfied. He bows, asks for forgiveness of the Israelite people, and requests God to "go in the midst of us." Again, this is contrary to the desired separation between God and the Israelites that was derived earlier and shows their desire to have greater dependence on God.

Costs of Dependence

God's response shows there are costs to Moses' request for greater dependence. While God agrees to be more involved, He also makes a new covenant that is narrower than the one made before the Golden Calf episode. It leaves out the earlier promises of blessing the Israelites' "bread and water," "removing sickness," and ensuring procreation. It also does not promise to "fulfill the number of your days," which could be interpreted to mean God's help is not guaranteed to carry over to future generations. And, it does not specify the boundaries of the Promised Land. Having God play an active role in human affairs thus seems to reduce the amount of God's beneficence. Asking more of God's time entails punishment, similar to the double penalties required of offenders whose crime needs to be adjudicated by God.

The subsequent commandments are similarly narrower and

drier than the original set. They deal entirely with the relationship between the Israelites and God, and comprise rules on what to offer Him and which holidays to celebrate. Importantly, they do not offer any rationale, underscoring that the Israelites are now meant to follow the commandments without question — a code approach to the religion.

Strikingly, the commandment about the Sabbath leaves off the rationale that was the basis for understanding the essence of the earlier Ten Commandments – it does not say that the Israelites should rest on the Sabbath because God did so in Creation. Instead, there is no rationale attached at all, consistent with the new code approach. It is as if God has given up expecting the Israelites to act like Him without being overly dependent, but would be satisfied if they just kept to a straight and narrow path in regard to their relationship with Him.

A Reformation of the Religion

The Torah thus downshifts its specification of the religion from one that implicitly requires acting like God to one that is explicitly based on a set of rules. The linear progression from the Sea of Reeds to Mount Sinai -- moving from dependence to separation -- breaks. Not only do the Israelite people express a need for a god and disregard the covenant, Moses, himself, asks to be more dependent on Him. While ordinary people's difficulty in following the first covenant may be understandable, Moses' is not. God responds by redefining what He wants of the Israelites -- in effect, reforming the religion.

Chapter 6 - *What God Wants And Settles For: A Reconciliation*

Imposing a code of laws would seem to be a strange way for God to satisfy the Israelites' desire for more support. While it moves people away from independent decision-making and actions, it lacks a personal touch. It does not eliminate a problem that could make other religions more appealing.

The Torah may be offering two approaches for achieving a God-compatible society – permitting independent actions within ethical guidelines and requiring people to conform to a code of laws. Appreciating this possibility could be the key to uniting the different denominations of Judaism.

There are several possible reasons for the reformation of the religion, moving from the guideline to code approach. Most, however, are not fully defensible or supported by the text. But, one reason — providing different ways to follow the religion — is justifiable and allows for a reconciliation between the guideline and code approaches to Judaism.

Indefensible Reasons for the Reformation

A number of explanations for this shift do not fully explain God's action. These are an act of kindness, an expropriation of the Torah by the priesthood, a desire to separate the Israelites from other societies, a counter example of what would happen to the Israelites if they reject the guideline approach, or a demonstration of the unworkability of the guideline approach.

The reformation shows God's compassion for Moses by helping him in a time of need. He will share the burden of leading the Israelites. God's action, however, entails major shifts in the covenant and laws, implying a longer-term directional change in the religion than would be reasonable if it were a one-time act of kindness.

The Torah was commandeered or expropriated by the priesthood, which was more interested in ruling by decree than in permitting people to act independently within ethical constraints. Stipulating and enforcing laws give power. This reason begs the question why the priesthood allowed the benefits of the covenant to be narrower than the earlier version. Why would the priests have permitted a scaling back of God's promises? If anything, the new covenant should have promised more good prospects for the Israelites than the earlier one.

The commandments and laws are meant to separate the Israelites from other societies. By so doing, they could ensure the survival of the group when they come into contact with others. However, the problems in the Golden Calf episode and Moses' breakdown are internal to the Israelites, not a consequence of external inducements. The intent of the commandments and laws is to ensure proper behavior within the Israelite society regardless of outside influences.

The details of ritual and expanded laws are a counter example to demonstrate what would happen if they reject responsibility to act independently of God. The rituals would be costly, while the laws would intrude into their life styles. Such interpretation has a problem, however. Since the revised approach is the last word on the topic in Exodus, it may be the preferred relationship – taking a hint from the Talmud where the last argument is the right one. If so, it would not be there to convince the Israelites to follow the earlier version of the religion.

Alternatively, the Torah develops the guideline approach to show that it is unworkable and why a code of commandments and laws are needed to attain a monotheistic, ethical society. This development would parallel the construction of the Book of Genesis, which showed why the reward approach does not guarantee good behavior (*A General Theory of the Torah*, Chapter 7). Both explore paths for the religion and find them wanting. The paths – the reward and guideline approaches – lack sufficient restraints. Instead, a more dependent relationship is the only approach that will succeed in ensuring the Israelites are monotheistic and lead an ethical life. The guideline approach returns in subsequent Books of the Torah, however, showing it is still needed.

Problems With a Code-Based Religion

By dropping the idea that Israelites make decisions and act independently of God, the rule-based approach leaves the Israelites and Jews of future generations with potential problems. They will not have learned how to resolve situations or to direct their destiny with little reliance on God. Waiting for God in difficult circumstances can result in disaster, as discussed in *An Incorrect Way of Interpreting the Torah*? (Chapter 10). Moreover, the laws could be viewed as immutable, since God is said to have established them and reasoning behind the laws is not permitted. As a result, Jews could be stuck with commandments that have little meaning after the original purpose no longer is pertinent.

Ironically, the code-based approach could impede ethical development. Society would not be able to change God-given laws if they must be followed without question. In the guideline approach and in the spirit of Jethro, changing the religion's positions on questionable issues would make the Israelite community more ethical.

Also ironically, by not creating a personal relationship with God, the code-based approach could be as unrewarding to some as the guideline approach. Establishing laws does not necessarily reduce the appeal of other religions in which the relationship with a god is personal.

A Reconciliation and Solution

Many of these problems are solved by viewing the two approaches as alternatives rather than substitutes. Jews can choose between them – those who need detailed instructions to live according to the Torah follow the code approach while those who do not need as much supervision follow the guideline approach. The second covenant does not promise God's help in future generations, suggesting the covenant is not binding forever and arguably legitimizing the idea that both approaches are acceptable. A return to the guideline relationship is possible. The Torah may be offering two approaches to God, appealing to a wide range of people.

GENESIS

T he next six chapters offer novel insights into the Book of Genesis. They show how it fits theologically with the rest of the Torah. They also clear up a lot of well-known issues and questions.

A General Theory of the Torah (Chapter 7) explores the shortcomings of the reward approach to the religion. The Book is shown to set the stage for the subsequent commandments and laws, along with the threat of punishment for not following them.

This paper was met by much anguish and denial in the Torah Study Group. The discussion carried through an additional Shabbat meeting, a unique event in the Group. It became clear many Reform Jews do not like the idea that commandments, laws and the threat of punishment are the cornerstones of the religion. They prefer the reward approach, believing that Jews will benefit psychologically by behaving ethically. However, over time, much of the Torah Group came to agree with my analysis – the Book is meant to justify the need for commandments, laws and the threat of punishment to achieve ethical behavior. People eventually realized these latter elements clearly dominate the other Books and this way of looking at Genesis makes logical sense.

How Many Gods Are There? (Chapter 8) unravels problematical features of Genesis by viewing Adonai and Elohim as different entities. This distinction was hard to accept by some, particularly Orthodox Jews, who read the paper.

Why the Akedah? (Chapter 9) finds a motivation for the testing of Abraham and argues the latter's purpose is to show the need to adhere to God's commandments. The chapter also looks at a number of ways this episode has been explained, finding most wanting.

An Incorrect Way of Interpreting the Torah? (Chapter 10) shows how each of the Patriarchs took the initiative to solve a dire problem rather than wait for God's help.

Micah's Mistake (Chapter 11) throws doubt on his well-known prescription for dealing with a bad situation, based on the evidence from Genesis.

Conjectures on the Joseph Story (Chapter 12) answers a number of standard questions regarding this transition to the Book of Exodus.

Chapter 7 - *A General Theory Of The Torah*

The Book of Genesis begins with Creation and ends with Jacob and his family moving to Egypt. In between are the familiar stories of Adam and Eve, Cain and Abel, Noah, and the Jewish Patriarchs – Abraham, Isaac, and Jacob. Most people remember the stories from childhood and, as such, see them as entertaining with a touch of morality. In our Torah group, many people concluded the stories represent tribal underpinnings, told around campfires in the desert. To be sure, they recognized the oddity for a tribe to portray its founding fathers with faults. In the end, there did not seem to be a clear view of the overall purpose of the stories found in Genesis.

What is the theological message of all the stories about the Patriarchs in Genesis? An answer follows from the realization that all the Patriarchs make mistakes despite being prosperous. The reward approach to induce people to behave ethically does not work. Commandments and laws, as well as a threat of punishment, are needed. With this insight, the Book of Genesis becomes an integral part of the Torah. It establishes the need for the commandments, laws and threat of punishment found in the other Four Books.

T he Book of Genesis is often seen as a collection of stories with no strong attachment to the rest of the Torah, outside the establishment of the covenant. In fact, Genesis provides a rationale for the rest of the Torah. As you'll see, my analysis will be from the point of view of an economist. So, in the spirit of John Maynard Keynes, I plan to outline what may be a "general theory" of the Torah. It ties the Book of Genesis together with the other four Books. All can be viewed as approaches by God to get the Israelites to follow His commandments. This is obvious from Exodus to Deuteronomy. The trick is to figure out what Genesis has to do with this goal.

The puzzle begins by realizing that from Abraham to Isaac and then to Jacob, the commandments become less and less a factor in the Patriarchs' relationship with God. With Abraham, God imposes orders and conditions, culminating with the test of the Akedah. With Isaac, God makes only one demand, that he stay in Canaan during the drought. With Jacob, there are no demands. Instead, Jacob imposes a condition on God, saying, "If God will be with me, keep me in this way that I go, and give me bread to eat and clothing to put on, so that I come again to my father's house in peace, [then] the Lord will be my God." God follows through with this condition.

In all three cases, God ensures the Patriarchs are prosperous and promises great things for their future generations. What's going on? What happened to the commandments? Their disappearance is all the more puzzling inasmuch as God comes back with a vengeance when he imposes many commandments on the Israelites at Mount Sinai. So, why does God seemingly drop the commandments as Abraham's line begins to extend? Why does He make them wealthy and promise a favorable future?

I found these questions troubling as we read Isaac and Jacob, knowing the importance of the commandments in the other parts of the Torah. It finally struck me that an answer may be found by looking at the problem from the point of view of an economist – what does it take to persuade people to do something. There are two ways – either through reward or punishment. Economists always talk about incentives and disincentives. Based on this, my idea is that after Abraham and before the enslavement of the Israelites in Egypt, God took the "reward approach," relying on contemporaneous good fortune and the promise of future greatness to persuade Abraham and his progeny to obey the covenant. This did not work. So, what we are reading from Isaac to Joseph is the unfolding of a disaster that culminates in 400 years of slavery.

Did God make a mistake? Did He eventually understand a "reward approach" by itself does not work? As a consequence, did He initiate a "punishment approach" at Mount Sinai? The problem with an affirmative answer to these questions is that God told Abraham what would happen, *i.e.,* that his progeny would spend 400 years in Egypt. He knew from the beginning that the "reward approach" would not prevent the Patriarchs from making mistakes leading to slavery. An alternative explanation, then, is that God wanted to prove to future generations that a pure "reward approach" does not work. Without explicit commandments and the risk of punishment, Isaac, Jacob, and his sons got into trouble. Future Israelites would better understand the need for commandments. This could be the key to how Genesis ties in with the rest of the Torah.

Abraham as Ideal

The problem from God's point of view is to make sure Abraham's line keeps its end of the covenant. While not detailed in the text, the covenant apparently includes commandments, laws and teachings. As God says to Isaac, "Abraham obeyed my voice, and kept My charge, My commandments, My statutes, and My laws."

Abraham is the ideal. Given this, the way to prove a reward approach by itself does not work is to compare the lives of Isaac, Jacob and his sons with that of Abraham. Divergence represents failure of the "reward approach."

Isaac

Life among the Philistines apparently is good for Isaac, just as for Abraham before the Akedah. There is plentiful wells for him to raise sheep. Nothing is obviously wrong with his life until his son, Esau, marries Judith, a Hittite, which "grieves" Isaac and Rebekah. Isaac is at fault for not conveying the need for his son to marry within the family. In contrast, Abraham was adamant that Isaac not marry a Canaanite woman. He has his servant swear that he "will not take a wife for my son of the daughters of the Canaanites, among whom I live. But he shall go to my country, and to my relatives, and take a wife for my son Isaac."

By not preventing Esau from marrying a Hittite, either through admonition as he grew up or by prohibiting it when it was announced, Isaac fails. He seems to understand this at the end. He tells Jacob to marry one of Laban's daughters and not a Canaanite woman. Moreover, Isaac might have been a willing participant in the deceit of the blessing, not wanting to pass the covenant to Esau. Isaac has no hard feeling toward Jacob or about giving him the "blessing of Abraham" *i.e.*, the covenant. Different reactions would be expected if Isaac had been upset about being the victim of deception.

Deceit by itself is not necessarily a fault, since Abraham relied on deceit when he told the Egyptians and Abimelech that Sara was his sister. To be sure, unlike Abraham, Isaac does not ask Rebekah's permission to be called his sister when he tries the same trick. Deceit without approval of participants may be a fault.

Jacob

Jacob and his sons have many faults. First, Jacob's offering his needy brother food on condition of getting the birthright stands in sharp contrast to Abraham's generosity to strangers. Second, Jacob conditions his belief in God on receiving His help on his journey, contrary to Abraham's unconditional adherence to God's commandments. Third, there are suggestions Rachel worshipped idols. She attaches significance to mandrakes and steals her father's house idols. Jacob should have stopped her idolatry when they first met, just as Abraham rejected his father's idol worship (from the midrash). Fourth, Jacob procreates through the maidservants, Zilpah and Bilhah, in contrast to Sarah's rejection of this way of passing on the covenant as shown by her expulsion of Hagar and Ishmael to the desert. Fifth, Jacob's inattention to instructing his children on the covenant is evident. Judah marries a Canaanite woman; Simeon and Levi kill the men of Shechem after Dinah's rape; Reuben has sex with Bilhah, Jacob's concubine; and together his sons sell their brother, Joseph, into slavery. These actions are clearly contrary to the commandments given at Sinai and presumably to Abraham.

Joseph

Finally, Joseph's ability to interpret dreams – a decidedly pagan practice well entrenched in Egyptian culture — is the instrument that enables the family to move to Egypt. Joseph is plausibly open to this pagan practice because of the influence of his idol-worshipping mother, Rachel. Jacob's other sons reject Joseph's dreams. On first blush, they seemingly just dislike the implication of the dreams – they would bow down to him. But, they also could be dismissing this way of divining the future. For the most part, the Torah downplays dreams as precursors of the future. Leviticus explicitly prohibits attempts at divining the future or soothsaying. When dreams play large roles, in Daniel and in Joseph, the protagonists are in the employ of foreigners.

Also worth noting is Joseph's use of the forecast of a famine to appropriate the lands of Egyptian farmers and eventually to enslave them for the Pharaoh. This is not favorably viewed by future Jewish generations, running counter to the spirit if not the law of the Torah. (It also may have precipitated the famine by discouraging farming — an early case of adverse supply-side economics.) However, it is quite appropriate in the context of this chapter. His non-Jewish predilections served not only in enabling Jacob's family to enter Egypt but also in setting a precedent for the enslavement of the Hebrews.

Conclusion

In sum, the faults of Abraham's line increase from generation to generation even though God favors them with economic success. This "reward approach" does not work, and explains why the Israelites are punished by having to endure slavery in Egypt. They have to face the consequences of their forefathers' wrongdoings. The failed approach also explains why they need to be given an explicit set of commandments once their punishment ends. As shown by their ancestors, they could not follow the covenant without them. In this light, Genesis provides the rationale for the large set of commandments and threat of punishment found in the next four Books.

CHAPTER 8 - *How Many Gods Are There?*

Defining Elohim to mean "many gods" – including the gods of other peoples -- and Adonai as "Lord God" not only provides a rational explanation for the first two chapters of Genesis but unravels many apparent puzzles in the rest of the Book, including where Cain found a wife, why Enoch lives only half the number of years as the other descendants of Adam and Eve, and why God tells Isaac not to travel to Egypt to avoid a famine in Canaan. Overall, this chapter offers many curious insights into the particulars of the Book of Genesis. It has little implication for the rest of the Torah, since Adonai completely takes over God's relationship with the Israelites in Exodus. Jews still have an eternal covenant with Elohim, as well as with Adonai, and therefore can be assured that other peoples will never destroy them.

The Torah contains many names of God, including Adonai, Elohim and El Shaddai. Scholars attribute them to different sources. Religious Jews view them as interchangeable. Some analysts view God as having a split personality, with Adonai representing the good side and Elohim the bad. In contrast to these approaches, a case can be made that Adonai and Elohim are distinct entities. Adonai comes across as the supreme leader, while Elohim include all the other gods. Elohim are highlighted when non-Israelites are involved, but there are references suggesting they include Adonai, as well. Adonai may manifest Himself in more than one way, particularly as other gods to non-Israelites. For the most part, when both appear in an episode Elohim echo and imitate Adonai.

Favored Interpretation

Viewing Adonai as the final arbiter and decider of what should be and Elohim as including other gods as well as Adonai sheds new light on Genesis. It changes the interpretation of some events from what is commonly understood and shows how seemingly disparate or even contradictory episodes are mutually consistent.

The Book becomes a much clearer contrast with other ancient religions, such as those of Mesopotamia. The latter posited a multitude of gods who fought among themselves. Genesis offers a different vision. While there are many gods, they are of one voice and subservient to Adonai. Although a singular tense is used with verbs spoken by Elohim, perhaps this is meant to underscore their speaking as one.

Creation

Adonai and Elohim debut in the first two chapters of Genesis, which tell conflicting Creation stories. Chapter 1 spreads the Creation over six days and has God rest on the seventh. Chapter 2 tells of the creation of man and woman in the Garden of Eden. God is called Elohim in Chapter 1 and Adonai in Chapter 2. The common interpretation is that each story stems from a different tradition, so they should be read as separate but equal renditions. In contrast, a theological connection between the two stories can be seen most easily if Elohim and Adonai are considered separate entities. The theological question at issue is whether people should be created god-like.

In Chapter 1, Elohim create man and woman in His "image", in the image of Elohim. This is the only creation not described as "good." The exception typically is taught to mean people choose to be good, as they have free will. Alternatively, the absence of an affirmation could reflect Adonai's unhappiness with it. And, based on the theology in the rest of the Torah, it is easy to see why this might be the case. By creating man and woman in Elohim's image, Elohim put people at almost the same level of God. Their blessing drives home this point. It essentially gives people god-like rule and power over everything on earth. "Elohim blessed them and Elohim said to them, "Be fruitful, multiply, fill the earth, and subdue it. Have dominion over the fish of the sea, over the birds of the sky, and over every living thing that moves on the earth." While this blessing is viewed positively by most people today, being like God, in fact, runs counter to a main theme of the Torah — people are not God.

They should not have unlimited powers.

The theologically more acceptable creation of people is the one formulated by Adonai in Chapter 2. He "formed man from the dust of the ground and breathed into his nostrils the breath of life; and man became a living soul." In Adonai's approach, man is not made "in the image of God" but from the complete opposite – the "dust of the ground." Rather than creating man from the perspective of high example, Adonai creates him from the lowest element of the world.

Although not equal, man and Adonai are to be partners in running the world. Man is put in the Garden of Eden "to dress it and keep it." And, Adonai has man name all the animals — having him act like God. This idea — God is master with people partnering with Him — is an essential part of the relationship between God and Israelites in the rest of the Torah. And, the idea that man should act like God is the essence of the guideline approach found in Exodus. The creation of man and woman in God's image appears to be a problem rather than a glorification of them.

Should Chapter 2 be read to mean Adonai tries a different tack with Adam and Eve since He does not like the creation of man and woman in God's image in Chapter 1? This seems to follow from the Garden of Eden story being told after the seven-day creation story. The text and other considerations, however, argue against this hypothesis. Chapter 2 says Adonai formed Adam when "no plant of the field was yet in the earth, and no herb of the field had yet sprung up for Adonai had not caused it to rain on the earth. There was not a man to till the ground." This description matches the second day, when land and water were separated but there was not yet vegetation, which is created on the third day. It would appear then that Adonai created man before Elohim did. This idea gains support from realizing that having Elohim mimic Adonai is consistent with the pattern found between them in the rest of Genesis. The conclusion from these two observations is not that Adonai does not like aspects of the Elohim-created man and therefore creates Adam and Eve, but that Elohim make a mistake when trying to replicate Adonai's creation of Adam and Eve.

Adonai's attempt to create a subordinate Man does not eliminate the problem that people may try to be like God. Adam and Eve try by eating from the Tree of Knowledge. They know from the serpent that by eating it their "eyes will be opened and [they] will be like God, knowing good and bad." Adonai is concerned that "now that man has become like one of us, knowing good and bad," what if he "also take of the tree of life, and eat and live forever." He is concerned Adam and Eve could become godlike. So, He expels them from the Garden of Eden, to be among the people created by Elohim. Adonai acknowledges the existence of other gods when he says "man has become like one of us...."

From this perspective, men and women in the Elohim line were created in a flawed way. Although not created the same way, Adam and Eve make a decision that transforms them to the same flawed state. Adonai learns early on that something is needed to keep people in their place. Their trying to be in God's image or like Him condemns people to a non-paradisiac existence, similar to the implications of Original Sin!

The upshot of the two creation stories is the establishment of two lines of humankind – the Elohim line and the Adonai line, the latter being the descendants of Adam and Eve. The two sets of people explain why Cain is concerned about being killed by others after being sent into exile by Adonai. Without two lines of men, it is hard to see Cain's concern, since he and Abel are the only children of Adam and Eve at the time. Having two lines also explains how Cain finds a wife. His wife is from the Elohim line.

The distinction between the two lines of people provides novel insights into the history of Adam's descendants in Chapter 5. The odd inclusion of a restatement of how Elohim created and blessed man in verses 1 and 2 now can be seen as an aside to acknowledge the other line of humankind before Adam's line is discussed. The contradistinction of Adam from this line is driven home in verse 3, which says that Adam "became the father of a son in his own likeness, after his image" – not in Elohim's image. This represents almost textual proof that Elohim's creation of man in Elohim's image was a mistake.

This perspective clarifies another odd verse in Chapter 5. Enoch, who "walked with Elohim," is not the ideal person, good enough to be intimate with God. He walks with the wrong god -- with Elohim rather than Adonai. As a result, he lives far fewer years than the other descendents of Adam – 365 as opposed to 782+ years. He is penalized for associating with Elohim rather than Adonai.

The Elohim line of mankind does not extend past the Flood. Chapter 5 ends by saying Noah is a descendent of Adam. He and his family are the only survivors of the Flood. As a result, the rest of history deals solely with the Adonai line. Abraham, for example, is a descendant of Noah's son, Shem.

Elohim, though, do not admit their line is gone after the Flood. They repeat how man was created in Elohims's image in blessing Noah after dry land is reached. Perhaps Elohim's line is not gone after all. Noah or his antecedents may have inter-married with them. Or, perhaps Elohim understand that Adonai's creation of people did not eliminate their desire to be like God. In any case, Elohim's words portend problems ahead.

The Flood

The wickedness of men before the Flood shows that Adonai correctly doubted the wisdom of Elohim's creation. Even Elohim realized the earth was "corrupt." Although the nature of the wickedness is not specified, it appears related to people's behaving as if they are gods. The Flood is preceded by the co-habitation of divine beings – the Nephilim – with women. And, Chapter 6 says the "earth was filled with lawlessness," suggesting anarchy – a result of everyone's thinking of himself as God. Each person operates as if he makes the rules.

Both Adonai and Elohim are involved with the Flood, as it is told twice. Adonai first decides to destroy mankind. Elohim reach the same conclusion and then carry through by instructing Noah on the construction of the Ark and by orchestrating the flood. The dual stories perhaps are meant to preclude the possibility that one God is blamed but not the other. Or, since both the Elohim and Adonai lines (except for Noah) are not behaving correctly, the creators of both lines need to be involved in their destruction.

Noah, however, understands that Adonai is the supreme power. After the Flood, he builds an alter and sacrifices to Adonai but not Elohim. Consistent with the theological message from the Ten Plagues in Exodus, Noah shows a fear of Adonai – he holds Him in awe and respect. Adonai acknowledges Noah's adherence by promising to never destroy the earth or "every living being" because of mankind. He resigns Himself to man's nature, saying "the imagination of man's heart is evil from his youth."

Elohim goes beyond accepting man's evil inclinations by promising his dominance over other living things. Their blessing establishes god-like powers for Adonai's line. They say, "The fear and dread of you will be on every animal of the earth and every bird of the sky." Using the word "fear" suggests that animals should see people as god-like. The only limits on people are not to eat meat with its life-blood in it and not to murder another human being. Essentially, Elohim want to recreate their original conception of men and women. But, this time, they recognize that some restraint is needed, as well.

Tower of Babel

Perhaps because of Elohim's blessing or because of the inclination seen in Adam and Eve, people still want to be god-like after the Flood. Speaking the same language, they decide to work together to build a city and a tower "whose top reaches to the sky." Adonai sees their actions as reflecting the issue He had with Adam and Eve in the Garden of Eden. He says, "Behold, they are one people, and all have one language; and this is what they begin to do. Now nothing will be withheld from them that they intend to do." They will not need God to achieve their goals. Since it is His line, Adonai is the one responsible for correcting the problem. He scatters the people and assigns them a variety of languages.

Abraham

Adonai dominates the story of Abraham, beginning with the command to leave his homeland, but with several exceptions. Elohim, who now should be seen as encompassing all the local gods of the world, make a presence when Abram is ninety-nine. At this time, Adonai has made a covenant with Abraham promising that he would be "exceedingly" numerous. Not to be outdone, Elohim follow with their own covenant and promise of fertility. The language suggests the name Elohim refers to a different god than Adonai. After Adonai makes his covenant, Elohim say, "As for me, behold, this is my covenant with you. You will be the father of a multitude of nations." "As for me" suggests it is their turn to make a covenant now that Adonai has made His. Promising a "multitude of nations" fits with their being gods of other nations.

Curiously, Adonai says, "I am El Shaddai, " the pagan god of fertility according to some scholars, when He makes this covenant. This statement seems to run counter to the idea that Elohim encompasses all the other gods. However, the statement could be read as a metaphor, implying that Adonai has as much power over procreation as El Shaddai. Abram would know the role of this pagan god, so the metaphor would underscore the credibility of the covenant.

The question of credibility arises soon afterwards. Abraham laughs in disbelief when Elohim promises him a son by Sarah, and Sarah laughs when one of the three visitors (representing Adonai) says she will have a son. Adonai is annoyed with her laughter. He says, " Why did Sarah laugh?...Is anything too hard for the Lord? I will return to you ... and Sarah will have a son." He sees that Abraham and Sarah have some doubt about His powers.

Circumcision represents a covenant with Elohim rather than with Adonai. The need for a totemic symbol fits with Elohim's representing gods who require such religious objects. Moreover, Elohim are the ones who insist the covenant be passed down through Isaac rather than Ishmael. Perhaps Elohim are being mischievous, as they break "the rules of primogeniture." Their role in the passing of the covenant may help explain why future generations are not ideal in their adherence to the covenant, as discussed in *A General Theory of the Torah* (Chapter 7). The covenantal line is tainted from being chosen by Elohim.

Elohim dominate again when Abraham and Sarah confront Abimelech, king of Gerer. Elohim speak to Abimelech in a dream, consistent with their being his god. Abraham appears to understand this relationship. He tells Abimilech that he had been afraid because he thought "surely the fear of Elohim is not in this place." And, Abraham prays to Elohim to heal Abimelech, his wife and slave girls, whose wombs were "closed up tight" by Adonai. Abraham seems to know which representation of god applies to people outside of his line and that Elohim have the responsibility for looking after them.

This division of labor is apparent later when Abimelech and Phicol approach Abraham to make a covenant with him. They say Elohim "is with you in all that you do." They seem to think Abraham has a direct connection with their own gods. Abraham may feel uncomfortable with their observation. He invokes the name of Adonai when planting a tamarisk at Beersheba after the purchase of land from Abimelech, almost as a way to wash his hands of such idea and drive home the point that Adonai, not Elohim, is truly his God.

Elohim's responsibilities for outsiders and for having chosen Isaac as the bearer of the covenant are discernible elsewhere. Elohim instruct Abraham to accept Sarah's order that Hagar and her son, Ishmael, leave, removing a threat to Isaac. Then, Elohim look after Hagar and her son in the desert, consistent with Elohim being their god. Adonai comforts and blesses Hagar the first time Sarai orders her to leave, instructing her to return to Abram and Sarai. Adonai perhaps feels responsible for His "ward" Sarai's action in this case.

Another instance demonstrating Elohim's attachment to outsiders is when Abram's name is changed to Abraham. Elohim makes the change, saying, "your name will be Abraham; for the father of a multitude of nations have I made you." Again, Elohim's explanation makes sense — they are the gods of many nations and, as a result, can make nations out of Abraham's offspring. Importantly, their covenant with Abraham would appear to preclude a complete destruction of the Jewish people by non-Jews. It establishes "an everlasting covenant, to be a God to you and to your seed after you." Presumably, if necessary, they would intervene with groups under their purview to prevent a wholesale destruction of the Jews.

The distinction between Elohim and Adonai appears in the Akedah. Elohim put Abraham to the test by ordering him to sacrifice his son, Isaac. But, Adonai's angel stops him from carrying it out. This division can be interpreted to say the test was concocted by the "bad" Elohim and stopped by the "good" Adonai. Adonai, however, appears to have been part of the test from the beginning and to have understood the purpose was to see if Abraham would follow Elohim's commandments. The angel says, "For now I know that you fear God, seeing you have not withheld your son, your only son, from Me."

By specifying "from Me" the angel's explanation suggests that Adonai is one of the Elohim. His inclusion among the Elohim also is indicated in Exodus by the rationale for the sabbath in the first Ten Commandments — that He rested on the seventh day of the Creation.

Nevertheless, the distinction between Adonai and Elohim in the Akedah could reflect other considerations, as well. Perhaps Elohim carry out bad actions in order to keep Adonai "clean." Or, perhaps Elohim command Abraham to sacrifice his son because child sacrifice is part of other religions. Or, perhaps the test is similar to the one imposed on Job. Rather than Satan making a bet with God as in the Job story, here Elohim make a bet with Adonai. In both cases, the bet is whether Adonai's most loyal and devoted follower would remain as such if terrible things happen to him. Adonai is relieved at the end that Abraham remains obedient to commandments even when they come from other gods besides Adonai. Perhaps Adonai wants to ensure the Israelites will honor the covenant made by Elohim to Abraham,

That Abraham obeys the command of Elohim raises the question whether (in retrospect) he violated the Second Commandment not to bow down or serve other gods. He clearly understands Adonai is his God when he plants the tamarisk at Beersheba. He nevertheless seems to recognize the need to deal with other gods, particularly when interacting with other peoples. Perhaps Adonai tightens the restrictions when He issues the Ten Commandments to the Israelites in Exodus.

A sharp distinction between Adonai and Elohim does not occur in the story of Sodom and Gomorrah. Adonai is the one who informs Abraham that He intends to destroy the cities, and it is He who proceeds to do so. The Torah, though, attributes the cities' destruction to Elohim, as well. This case may be easier to explain than the Akedah. In Sodom and Gomorrah, Adonai could be viewed as having the responsibility of "cleaning up" problems with the human line that He had created. Elohim is involved when the cleanup involves people outside of the covenant with Abraham.

Isaac

Elohim appear only once in the Isaac story, when they bless Isaac after Abraham's death. The blessing is made right before Ishmael's line is listed, as if to emphasize that Isaac need not fear his brother. Elohim are not mentioned in the rest of the Isaac story, even though they had chosen Isaac to carry the covenant after Abraham. Perhaps, Isaac holds Elohim responsible for the Akedah and does not want to have anything to do with them. That may be why Adonai tells Isaac not to move to Egypt in the midst of a famine. Adonai's command is typically viewed as inexplicable, but He knows Isaac would have to deal with Elohim there. So, this command may be the second compassionate act of Adonai – the first being His promise to Hagar after she tries to escape from Sarai's displeasure.

Isaac's dislike of Elohim also could explain why he "trembled violently" after learning he had blessed Jacob rather than the first-born Esau. Isaac may have been struck by the realization he had inadvertently repeated Elohim's switch between Ishmael and himself regarding the Covenant — Isaac realizes he did not escape from acting like his enemy. In contrast, psychological reasons are typically used to explain Isaac's response.

Isaac lives a pure life, with few problems, perhaps because of Elohim's absence. Even outsiders know that Isaac has nothing to do with Elohim. Abimelech and Ahuzzath say, "We saw plainly that Adonai was with you."

Jacob

Elohim play a more prominent role than Adonai in the Jacob saga, consistent with the suspect behavior of this Patriarch, as discussed in *A General Theory of the Torah* (Chapter 7).

Jacob's problematic view of Adonai is revealed early on. When Isaac questions his ability to bring back game so quickly, Jacob says, "Because the Lord your God gave me success." Jacob views Adonai as Isaac's God, not his own. Isaac seems to know his son is not closely aligned with Adonai, as his blessing refers to Elohim. Passing along the covenant, Isaac says to Jacob, "May Elohim give you of the dew of heaven ... Let peoples serve you, and nations bow to you..." This reference, however, may be because the blessing involves other nations, which are the purview of Elohim. But, Isaac's understanding of Jacob's relationship with Elohim is seen in his blessing when Jacob is sent to Paddan-aram to take a wife. Isaac says, "May El Shaddai bless you, make you fruitful and multiply you... that you may inherit the land, which Elohim gave to Abraham."

The association of El Shaddai with Elohim is made explicit

later when Elohim appear to Jacob on his return to Canaan. After changing Jacob's name to Israel, Elohim say "I am El Shaddai" and proceeds to command him to "be fruitful and multiply. A nation and a company of nations will be from you, and kings will come out of your loins." El Shaddai seems to be one of the Elohim and steps forward when the blessing involves procreation and nation building.

Adonai first makes a presence in Jacob's earlier dream, promising him a good future. The dream has Jacob being introduced to Adonai, who identifies Himself as the "God of your father Abraham and the God of Isaac." He does not claim to be Jacob's God. The dream also features angels of Elohim going up and down the ladder to the sky. Jacob apparently is familiar with all the gods, Elohim and Adonai. Their multiplicity offers a rationale for why Adonai introduces Himself to Jacob. Without an introduction, Adonai might not have been recognized among the many gods in his dream. Jacob acknowledges the association of the place with more gods than just Adonai. He names it Bethel, which historically was a sanctuary city dedicated to the Canaanite god El.

When Adonai promises a good future for Jacob and his descendants, Jacob, true to form, reacts incorrectly, making Adonai's help on his journey a prerequisite for being his God. More exactly, he makes his adherence to Adonai contingent on Elohim helping him on his journey. It is as if he takes Adonai's promise to mean He will ensure that Elohim will help.

Adonai and Elohim have a complicated relationship with the births of Leah's and Rachel's children and surrogate children. Adonai allows Leah to conceive, after seeing her unloved by Jacob. Leah acknowledges His role by naming her son Reuben, which means "the Lord saw my affliction." Elohim are involved with Rachel and the non-Israelite maids. When Rachel complains to Jacob about her barrenness, his response acknowledges her devotion to Elohim -- "Am I in Elohim's place, who has withheld from you the fruit of the womb?" Appropriately for non-Israelites, it is Elohim who enable Rachel's maid, Bilhah, to conceive and give birth. Rachel says, "Elohim has judged me, and has also heard my voice, and has given me a son." Similarly, Leah understands that Elohim were behind her maid, Zilpah, having a baby. Leah says, "Elohim has given me my wage, because I gave my handmaid to my husband." Finally, it is Elohim who allows Rachel to give birth to Joseph. Rachel first acknowledges Elohim's role, saying "Elohim has taken away my reproach." Then, she appears to understand the desirability of gaining Adonai's favor, as her son's name means "May Adonai add another son to me." Of course, Elohim's association with Joseph's birth bodes well for his later experiences in Egypt.

Elohim appropriately make a presence when pagan rituals or Egyptian-born family members enter into the story. They figure in the conflict between Rachel and Leah over mandrakes, viewed by pagans as a sexual stimulant. Elohim reward Leah with two births after she gave the mandrakes to Rachel. And, when Jacob speaks to Joseph about the latter's sons, he speaks of El Shaddai.

Both Adonai and Elohim tell Jacob it is time to "return to the land of your fathers" or "to the land of your birth" The dual command is understandable for a couple of reasons. Jacob is living in a foreign land, where Elohim has sway. Since Jacob would have to deal with a range of people besides his family in his travels, he will need the help of Elohim as well as Adonai.

While neither Adonai nor Elohim is mentioned when Jacob struggles with a semi-divine person, Jacob understood the person to represent Elohim. In a later chapter, at Bethel, he builds an alter to Elohim, "who appeared to you when you fled from the face of Esau your brother."

Adonai still holds purview of what is happening with Jacob and his family. He comes back to judge Judah's sons, Er and Onan, who are "wicked" and "evil."

Joseph
Adonai shows up one more time in Genesis, when He "was with" Joseph at the start of his road to success in Egypt. Elohim

are then alone in the story, in line with Joseph, his brothers and Jacob all dealing with outsiders. Moreover, Adonai already has pulled back in anticipation of the 400 years of Egyptian slavery that He had predicted to Abraham.

Moses

Elohim dominate the start of Exodus, responding to the Israelites when they cry out for help. It is appropriate for Elohim to have responded, since the Israelites have a covenant with them and the problem is with the people of a foreign land.

Adonai appears when He addresses Moses at the burning bush. After Adonai sees Moses turning aside to look at the bush – an important step by Moses – Elohim call to him. This division makes sense since Moses has been an Egyptian and knows gods as Elohim.

Moses continues to see the distinction between Adonai and Elohim as the episode progresses. Although Adonai speaks to Moses, saying, "I have surely seen the affliction of my people who are in Egypt," Moses asks Elohim, "Who am I that I should go to Pharaoh and that I should bring forth the children of Israel out of Egypt?" In one sense, asking the question of Elohim is understandable as their provenance covers Pharaoh and Egypt. In another sense, Moses is questioning his own qualifications with the gods whom he has known.

Moses shifts to speaking directly to Adonai once Elohim instruct him that from then on Moses should address Adonai. When Adonai says, Adonai "is My name forever," the issue is settled whether future generations of Israelites should worship Adonai or Elohim or both.

Nonetheless, Adonai still recognizes that Elohim deal with others. He later tells Moses that he will be "as Elohim" when speaking to Pharaoh. And, Moses and Jethro, his father-in-law, speak of God as Elohim – again fittingly for a conversation with an outsider.

There is a perplexing scene when Elohim say to Moses, "I am Adonai. I appeared to Abraham, Isaac, and Jacob as El Shaddai, but I was not known to them by my name Adonai." The Patriarchs, of course, did know Adonai. But, they viewed Him separately from Elohim. So, the comment is an accurate description of how the Patriarchs viewed El Shaddai. Perhaps the assertion "I am Adonai" is not meant to be taken literally but as a figurative way of informing Moses that Elohim speak as one with Adonai.

Elohim continue with a long recitation of the covenant they gave to the Patriarchs. The scene may make sense by observing the recitation comes after a terse comment by Adonai that Moses "shall see what I do to Pharaoh." A long, roughly replicative comment by Elohim after a short comment by Adonai mimics the pattern found in Genesis.

Balaam and Balak

Adonai and Elohim reappear in the Book of Number's Balaam/Balak episode. Their interplay is not well specified and requires speculation for a logical interpretation. The Moabite king Balak is concerned the Israelites will overpower him, as they did to the Amorites. He requests the prophet Balaam to put a curse on them. Balaam asks for guidance from Adonai, knowing Him to be God of the Israelites (He later calls Adonai "Lord their God"). Elohim, however, respond, saying "You shall not curse the people, for they are blessed." They perhaps are the conduit between Adonai and a non-Israelite prophet at this point. Balaam appears to understand their role as an intermediary. He attributes the response to Adonai, saying "I can't go beyond the word of Adonai my God, to do less or more."

At this point, there appears to be disagreement between Elohim and Adonai. Elohim come back and allow Balaam to see Balak, but require that he do whatever they command. As soon as Balaam heads out, however, Elohim seem to have a change of heart; "their anger is kindled because he went." Conceivably, Adonai was unhappy with their having allowed Balaam to travel to the king, and His reprimand made them angry. From then on, Adonai figures alone in the episode, as if He could not trust Elohim to act correctly.

Conclusion

This interpretation of Adonai and Elohim as separate entities makes for an atypical read of Genesis. It nevertheless clarifies a number of puzzling aspects of the Book. And, it reconciles some parts, particularly the two creations stories, with the theology in the rest of the Torah. Although acknowledging multiple gods in the Torah might be seen as heretical, it just could be the Torah's way of directly challenging the other religions of the day.

What, however, if the idea of multiple gods is taken at face value? What lessons can be derived for modern Jews? Perhaps most importantly, they should feel that no matter how untoward is the behavior of others it will ultimately fail in the extreme, since Jews have a covenant with Elohim. Indeed, the specifics of the covenant are more forceful in light of this new interpretation of Elohim, as He now is seen to speak for all people. Elohim say, "I will make you exceeding fruitful, and I will make nations of you. Kings will come out of you. ... I will give to you, and to your seed after you the land where you are traveling, all the land of Canaan, for an everlasting possession." Elohim's promise that Jews will be leaders among people is more than mere talk, given that as other peoples' gods they have some control over their actions. And, since they are the gods of all people, they have the right to take the land of Canaan from one group and give it to another.

Jews cannot use the distinction between Adonai and Elohim to justify picking and choosing among laws and commandments. All the requirements specified in Exodus and the other Books come from Adonai. The distinction also does not undercut the notion of monotheism in Judaism. There is still only one Lord God. Adonai is the ultimate god of the Jews. As the last words of the Yom Kippur Service say, "Adonai Hu Elohim." Curiously, Jews pay homage to other gods when they recite the passages of Genesis Chapter 1 in the Kiddush. And, Reform Jews do so again when they read Chapter 1 on the second day of Rosh Hashana.

Chapter 9 - *Why The Akedah?*

The Akedah, or Binding of Isaac, is one of the most troubling episodes in the Torah. God tests Abraham by commanding him to sacrifice his son, Isaac, at Mount Moriah. Of course, God rescinds the harsh commandment at the last minute, providing a ram in Isaac's place. Nevertheless, Jews have found God's role disturbing, perplexed why He would put Abraham through such an ordeal. This chapter offers a motivation for the test that also provides insight into other puzzling aspects of the episode.

T he story of the Akedah is typically regarded to be a stand-alone piece in the Torah. Questions of faith and psychology tend to be the issues. Is Abraham's faith in God being tested? Does he act because he believes God will save the day, having faith that He will not permit such gruesome outcome? How must Abraham feel as he takes Isaac to Mount Moriah?

The typical answers to these questions are not entirely satisfying from a theological perspective. Even the question of faith could be handled in less troubling manner. Theologically compatible answers come from asking what motivated God to test Abraham in the first place. The motivation appears to be concern that a successful person will take all the credit for his good fortune and turn away from God. A person in these circumstances might not feel the need to follow the Commandments. This issue ties the story theologically to the rest of the Torah.

A Motivation

The clue to what motivated God to test Abraham is in the paragraph that precedes the story. There we learn that Abraham settles in peace in Beersheba. Moreover, he prospers, because with wells, his flocks must have grown. The Torah hints at such when it says he "sojourned in the land of Philistines many days." For a nomadic family to have an extended stay in one place means it is quite content with the resources of the area.

So, what problem concerns God? It could be the following. When a group prospers, it may take all the credit and turn away from God. This is a serious issue in the Torah, as it shows up in a number of places. Moses addresses the problem of prosperity before the Israelites enter Canaan, warning that they not attribute their future well-being solely to their own efforts but to give credit to God, as well. Relating the Akedah to Moses' admonition shows the Torah to be symmetrical, with the same problem addressed at the start and end of the story of the Israelites. At the start, God has to see whether Abraham would follow the commandments while living well in Beersheba. At the end, Moses emphasizes that the Israelites should not forget God when times are good.

God may have been uncertain about Abraham because the two had not communicated with each other during the "many days" of Abraham's residence at Beersheba. Perhaps God left Abraham alone to see if he would live correctly without His direct involvement? After this long period of self regulation, God uses the Akedah to determine whether Abraham is still committed to adhering to His commandments. He issues an extreme commandment to see if Abraham would follow it even though it would terminate his family line (and thus the covenant). Abraham, of course, does not waiver.

In this light, it is understandable why God stops communicating with Abraham after the Akedah — another puzzle of the story. Abraham's actions show that he can be trusted to follow God's commandments. God's constant involvement in Abraham's life is not necessary.

Is Faith Being Tested?

Why does God want Abraham to kill his son? This makes the test gruesome. If it were just to see whether Abraham would keep his faith, i.e., believe that God would save him, other calamities could have been inflicted on him. Natural ones, such as an earthquake, would not have put Abraham in such an awkward position. Isaac's life could have been threatened in these circumstances, and God could have saved him at the last moment as Abraham's faith expected would happen.

That this is not how the story was written shows that Abraham's faith is not being tested. What is tested is whether he would follow God's commandments without question. This test requires that Abraham be the executioner. He has to do the unthinkable to show that he puts God's commandments above everything else, including his son's life even though Isaac is the person chosen to carry forward the covenant.

The demonstration of Abraham's commitment to God, as well as God's intervention at the last moment, could be important lessons for Isaac, himself, in light of his future responsibility to uphold the covenant.

There are other reasons why the story is not about faith. If Abraham had faith God would not let him sacrifice Isaac, it would be relatively easy to play the game and take Isaac up the mountain. Abraham would not see it as risking the life of his son, since God would surely not permit such an atrocity. This reasoning implies God lied when he commanded Abraham to sacrifice his son – an idea that Abraham would never have. To be sure, Abraham tells Isaac, ""God will provide himself the lamb for a burnt offering, my son." However, this may have been said just to placate his son. Or, it may have implicitly included Isaac as a potential sacrifice, particularly if Abraham took God at His word.

It is unlikely Abraham knows with any degree of certainty or faith that God would prevent sacrificing Isaac. There is no precedent to believe Abraham ever understood God's intentions. For example, when God tells Abraham that Sarah will give birth, Abraham says, "Oh that Ishmael might live before you!" He had thought — incorrectly — the covenant would be passed down through Ishmael.

Finally, it is unlikely God wants to see if Abraham would act on blind faith, that is, proceed with the sacrifice of Isaac based on the belief that God knows best whatever the outcome. We know from the story of Sodom that God does not demand blind faith. When Abraham argues with God, God is not angry as He would be if He required Abraham to accept His decision on blind faith. On the contrary, He compromises. So, there is no precedent to think God demands blind faith in the Akedah.

Obeying God's Commandments

However, obeying God's commandments is required in the Torah. It does not depend on whether a person has faith or love for God.

From all that precedes the Akedah, Abraham clearly would obey God's commandment to sacrifice his son regardless of what he thought. He always followed God's commands. The only time Abraham questions His intentions is with respect to Sodom. But, God does not command Abraham to do anything in this episode. Instead, God only informs him what He intends to do to the city. Thus, it is wrong to hold up Abraham's acquiescence in the Akedah to his protestation in the case of Sodom.

How could God, who is supposed to be compassionate, just and kind, have concocted such a test? He clearly thinks ensuring the commitment of His chosen leader supersedes these considerations. He puts the future requirements of a Chosen People — to adhere to His commandments — ahead of a difficult chore.

This way of analyzing the Akedah offers insight into why God tries to kill Moses or his son on their way to Egypt. This later episode, often deemed inexplicable or absurd, can be seen as a test of whether Moses will adhere to God. (The similarity to God's test of Abraham is even closer if the afflicted person is seen as Moses' son.) Moses' wife's actions — rubbing blood on his legs and declaring a marital pact with God — affirm such adherence. In this episode, as in the Akedah, God is willing to risk killing His chosen leader's son to be sure the leader will adhere to the covenant before the Israelites move on to the next leg of their journey.

Chapter 10 - *An Incorrect Interpretation Of The Torah?*

The Torah contains evidence of a necessary condition for God to help – people must first attempt to solve problems themselves. Each Patriarch finds himself in a situation with the same potential outcome as the Holocaust – the ending of the Jewish people. Each solves his problem without knowing God would help him. God gives support only afterwards.

W hy do bad things happen to good people? This perennial question was asked in the <u>Jerusalem Report</u>, which talked of how the Holocaust represents a major challenge to Ultra-Orthodox Jews for two reasons. First, they believe their rabbis "speak with divine inspiration and can even see the future." However, most ultra-Orthodox European rabbis told their followers not to emigrate to Palestine or the US as late as 1937. In part, they did not want their followers to mix with Reform Jews or Zionists. It also reflected their view that God would protect and save them. Second, since Ultra-Orthodox Jews believe God controls history, there is the problem of why the great religious communities of Eastern Europe were destroyed, but the 600,000 Jews of Palestine, mostly Zionist and many non-religious, were spared. From the Ultra-Orthodox perspective, why were the bad guys saved and the good guys destroyed?

How could God have let the Holocaust happen to the Orthodox Jews? Weren't they just following the advice of the Prophets? Micah said that in a difficult situation Jews should act ethically and wait until God "pleads my case, and executes judgment for me." The answer may be they misinterpreted the Torah.

To begin, a case can be made from the Torah that God does not fully control history, as discussed in *A Theory of God* (Chapter 1). A remnant of chaos remained after the Creation. As a result, bad things can happen to good people independently of

God, and Micah's prescription of waiting for Him is not necessarily correct. It behooves someone to act to reverse an evil event, since it may have stemmed from the chaotic portion of the universe and not from God. In this light, the Orthodox Jews took the wrong approach of waiting for God rather than trying to solve the problem, themselves.

The correct interpretation of the Torah arguably comes close to the ideas heard often at synagogues – a person has to take an active role in resolving his problems. This can be proved from the Torah by showing that all the Patriarchs take responsibility and action to resolve difficult situations, some of which are potentially as devastating as the Holocaust.

Despite being blessed by God and enjoying economic prosperity, all the Patriarchs face serious difficulties with the people among whom they live. Each finds himself in a situation where he and his line risk annihilation. In this sense, the problems are as significant as the Holocaust. However, unlike the ultra-Orthodox of the Holocaust, the Patriarchs do not rely on God to solve their problems. For the most part, they act to solve them decisively and by themselves. Abraham uses both deceit and force. Isaac moves his family a number of times. Jacob leaves the covenanted land and takes his family to Egypt to avoid famine. For the most part, God appears only after they had solved the problem.

Abraham

Abraham faces many problems and acts forcefully or with ingenuity to resolve them. When he travels to Egypt to avoid famine, he has Sarai pretend to be his sister to avoid being killed. He has to do the same in Gerar, when King Abimelech takes Sarah. In the War of the Five Kings, Abraham frees his nephew Lot from captivity. And, he confronts Abimelech and Phicol over wells.

To be sure, God helps him in difficult situations. In Egypt, God afflicts the Pharaoh and his family with plagues on account of Sarai. Pharaoh understands the connection and sends

Abram and Sarai away. In the other time when Sarah poses as Abraham's sister, God appears to Abimelech in a dream, warning him not to touch Sarah because she is married. God is not mentioned explicitly in Abraham's exploits during the War of the Five Kings, except that afterwards King Melchizedek of Salem attributes Abraham's success to Him. In all these cases, Abraham acts on his own without any knowledge that God would help him.

The most significant problem facing Abraham is Sarah's infertility. Here, Sarah attempts to solve the problem by offering Hagar, her maidservant, as a surrogate mother. Sarah realizes after the birth of Ishmael that this solution is a mistake and demands that Abraham expel Hagar and Ishmael. It is only after this aborted attempt at solving the infertility problem, importantly conceived and implemented without God's help, that God performs a miracle by having Sarah give birth to Isaac.

Isaac

Isaac has troubles, too. First, he, like Abraham, has to pretend that his wife is his sister so Abimelech would not kill him. Then, after he becomes wealthy, the Philistines stop up all his wells and order him to leave their land. This confrontation may not seem as significant as Abraham's saga, as the story is so concise it could seem trivial. However., it may be an extremely important element of Genesis. Water is vital for survival. By denying Isaac and his family wells, the Philistines threaten their very existence. Isaac's continual movements until the Philistines leave his family alone show that he does not wait for God to solve this serious problem. Only after his many moves to find water and resolution of the issue with the Philistines does God intervene, appearing in Isaac's dream and telling him not to be afraid.

Jacob

Jacob is the least commendable of the Patriarchs. He is self-centered and does not prevent his family from sinning. It takes him almost his entire life to be able to resolve a problem without the help of God. He, of course, had a difficult relationship with his uncle Laban. He was tricked into marrying Leah, in servitude for seven years, cheated during this time, and pursued by Laban as he was returning to Isaac. Jacob does not act forcefully to change any of these developments. He stays in servitude until God tells him, "Return to the land of your fathers, and to your relatives, and I will be with you." Then, God provides protection by warning Laban in a dream not to harm Jacob. This would seem to be consistent with the Orthodox Jews' approach of waiting for God to solve a problem. However, as the Jacob story continues, it appears that God does not support this idea.

On his way back to Canaan, Jacob becomes fearful as he approaches Esau in the land of Seir. He takes a couple of steps initially by himself, dividing his group into two camps on either side of the Jordan River. And, he sends a messenger to Esau, hinting at appeasement. But, then his nerve fails, and he prays to God for protection. God does not respond directly. Instead, He sends a man to wrestle with Jacob. This is said to be a mysterious episode, but its purpose becomes clear in the context of this analysis. When Jacob appears to have won, he tells the man, "I won't let you go, unless you bless me." Jacob is still looking for providential help. But, the man replies, "Your name will no longer be called 'Jacob,' but, 'Israel,' for you have fought with God and with men, and have prevailed." God is trying to stiffen Jacob's resolve toward Esau, showing that since he can beat a semi-divine being he can handle Esau. God wants Jacob to tackle the problem himself. The change in Jacob's name to Israel and the wrenching of his hip mean that this should be a permanent change in his nature. Even so, the man blesses Jacob, possibly to indicate that God still supports him. However, Jacob does not rise to the occasion admirably. As his family approaches Esau, he puts his wives and children at the front of the pack, exposing his progeny to risk. The Torah recognizes Jacob's failure to change his nature by continuing to refer to him as "Jacob."

Only late in life does Jacob finally take matters into his own hands, which the Torah underscores by beginning to refer to him as "Israel." He decides to send Benjamin to Egypt, realizing that his family could be destroyed by the famine if he does not defer to the Egyptian ruler's (that is, Joseph's) demand. Then, after learning of Joseph, Jacob decides on his own to travel with his family to Egypt, thereby leaving the covenanted land. After making these difficult decisions, by which he finally takes responsibility for his family's destiny, he learns in a dream that God would be with him on the trip.

The Lesson

It is clear from this analysis that the Patriarchs take actions in difficult situations, with the caveat that this applies to Jacob late in life. While God gives support in most instances, they are not aware that He had or would come to their cause when decisions or actions are needed. These episodes teach that people should not wait for God to solve their problems. They have to make the difficult decisions, themselves. The Orthodox Jews of Eastern Europe assumed wrong. They misread the message of the Torah. By focusing on ritual and study and not fighting to the best of their ability, they did not act to solve their problem as did the Patriarchs. They waited for God to save them.

Chapter 11 - *Micah's Mistake*

Micah, a prophet, lived in the 8th century BCE when Assyria dominated Judah and the surrounding region. Judah was required to pay a heavy tribute to the Assyrian king, Tiglath-pileser.

Micah depicts a society corrupted by the imposition of tribute. Everyone tries to shift the taxation's burden to another, which, in the process, undermines the judicial system and turns family members against each other. This disastrous outcome applies to other societies in similar straits. For example, the post-WWI reparations paid by Germany damaged its social fabric and set the stage for Nazism. Micah is clearly relevant for understanding situations where one country dominates another.

Micah's prescription is to wait for God to come solve the problem. However, it runs counter to Genesis' message that a person must attempt to solve a problem himself before help from God is possible.

M icah addresses the question of what to do in a difficult situation. In his case, Assyria already had destroyed the Northern Kingdom. The Southern Kingdom, Judah, has averted this outcome by paying tribute to Assyria. The difficult situation: Judah cannot end the tribute without being destroyed by Assyria.

What comes through in Micah is the fallout from this tribute. Taxation is heavy; the rich try shifting the tax burden to the poor; people work hard but have nothing to eat; political leaders act without justice; judges, prophets and priests accept bribes; rich men buy favorable verdicts; family members spy and turn on each other. In short, the social fabric is undermined.

Micah blames the Jews' sins for the calamity, and then informs people what to do. A person is to "act justly, to love mercy, and to walk humbly with your God." In other words, even in a difficult situation, a person has to maintain ethical conduct. This admonition would seem to be good advice. But, then Micah goes further, saying a person should wait for God to save him. He must "bear the indignation of God" until God champions his cause and upholds his claim. This will happen because God forgives iniquity and remits transgressions, not maintaining his wrath forever against the remnant of His own people. "He will bring me forth to the light. I will see His righteousness."

Waiting for God, however, is a troubling idea and very possibly a mistaken conclusion from the Torah. It suggests people should not try to solve problems themselves, but have faith and wait for God to save them. The Torah, instead, supports a proactive response to a problem, as discussed in *An Incorrect Way of Interpreting the Torah?* (Chapter 10).

Sole reliance on God to solve a problem may stem from a change in the conception of God made by the Prophets. God became omniscient and omnipotent in their understanding of Him, more powerful than the conception found in the first five Books, discussed in *A Theory of God* (Chapter 1). This revised notion of God does not allow for random developments. God is responsible for all. But, believing in this idea can have dire consequences.

Chapter 12 - *Conjectures On The Joseph Story*

The story of Joseph ends the Book of Genesis. As is well known, Jacob favors Joseph among his twelve sons. Joseph's brothers are resentful and sell him into slavery in Egypt. There, because of his ability to interpret dreams, Joseph rises to be the most powerful official under Pharaoh. He eventually reunites with his father and brothers, thereby setting the stage for the enslavement and subsequent exodus of the Israelites from Egypt. Some have called the episode the best story ever told, as it contains high drama, excitement, intrigue and more.

This chapter explores the reasons for Joseph's ability to assimilate and succeed in Egyptian society. It also answers a traditional question of why Judah's tribe and not Joseph's led the Israelites after their stay in Egypt. Finally, it looks at the story's message on tribal unity.

The Joseph Story tells how Abraham's line leaves the covenanted land to move to Egypt. This may be enough to explain how it fits into the Book of Genesis and Torah. However, other connections provide answers to often-asked questions. Why is Joseph able to enter Egyptian society while his brothers cannot? Why, however, is it Judah's tribe and not Joseph's that leads the Hebrews when they leave Egypt? How does the theme of brotherly disunity fit with the earlier parts of Genesis? And, what is the Story's fundamental message?

Why Joseph Was Successful in Egypt

Joseph's ability to interpret dreams enabled the family to move to Egypt. This skill brought him to Pharaoh's attention and resulted in his appointment as overseer of Egypt. Although not explicit in the text, dream interpretation was a decidedly pagan practice, entrenched in Egyptian culture.

Why did Joseph and not the other brothers develop this practice? Joseph was open to dream interpretation because of his mother, Rachel. The Torah hints that Rachel worshipped idols. She not only took them from her father's house but died for doing so. Earlier, she had let Leah sleep with Jacob in order to get the mandrakes found by her son. Pagans viewed mandrakes as an aphrodisiac. In worshipping idols, Rachel presumably viewed other pagan practices favorably and thus likely predisposed Joseph to them.

Comparing this story with the Exodus story underscores the pagan connection between Rachel and Joseph. For, it stands as a counterpoint to Moses and his mother. Whereas Joseph was an Israelite open to pagan ideas through his mother, Moses was an Egyptian open to Israelite ideas through his mother. The Israelite sojourn in Egypt is framed by two individuals with more in common than might meet the eye.

The sons of Leah, Zilpah and Bilhah reject these pagan practices, denouncing Joseph's dreams. On first blush, they seemingly just dislike the implications of the dreams – that they would bow down to him. But, they also could be dismissing this way of divining the future as foreign. Jacob, being mature, does not complain about the content of the dreams, perhaps realizing they have little intrinsic merit. Instead, Jacob keeps "the matter in mind", possibly concerned that his favorite son is steeped in pagan ideas.

Jacob understands that Joseph strayed from his forefathers' path by the end of the story. But, he loves Joseph so much it does not matter. In blessing his sons, Jacob calls Joseph "a fruitful bough [whose] branches run over the wall." The metaphor of a wall separating Jews from pagan practices is found in "Song of Songs." In Joseph's case, his branches extend over the wall, indicating he became part of the pagan world. Nevertheless, Jacob overlooks Joseph's transgression. He says the "God of your father who will help you" leaving out the names of Abraham and Isaac, presumably recognizing that Abraham and Isaac would not have condoned Joseph's behavior. However, this does not matter since Jacob believes his blessings are more powerful. He says, "the blessings of your father have prevailed above the blessings of the ancient mountains."

As is characteristic of the Book of Genesis, the Torah does not pass judgement on Joseph's ability to interpret dreams. For the most part, the Torah downplays dreams as precursors of the future. And, Leviticus prohibits attempts at divining the future or soothsaying. When dreams play large roles, as in Daniel and Joseph, the protagonists are in the employ of foreigners. Their success results from having mastered this pagan practice.

The Torah says that God was with Joseph in Egypt, indicating approval of what he was doing there. But, this implied approval could be in the context of God's plan to have the Jews spend 400 years in Egypt for failing to live up to the covenant. Nonetheless, the Torah addresses a concern that Joseph would become too much like an Egyptian. This concern is likely the motivation behind the story of Potiphar's wife, who commands Joseph to "lie with me." Joseph first rejects her command to commit adultery as wicked and a sin before God. Then, after she disrobes him, he runs away. With this story, the Torah demonstrates that, despite his predilection for pagan practices, Joseph would not become fully assimilated.

Why Joseph's Tribe Does Not Lead the Israelites

Joseph's absorption of foreign ways helps explain why his tribe does not lead the Hebrews out of Egypt. His descendants were probably more inclined toward Egyptian practices than the other tribes. They were unsuitable to forge a nation different from the surrounding peoples. A tribe whose roots were firmly grounded in the patriarchal heritage was needed to lead the Hebrews back to the Promised Land. An insufficient grounding in Jewish ways, more than the personality differences between Judah and Joseph, may explain why the Joseph tribe took a back seat to Judah's during the Exodus.

Brotherly Disunity

What is the significance of the disunity of Jacob's sons? In general, the Torah places importance on brothers living compatibly with each other. God is beneficent not only to the Patriarchs but also to the children of the Patriarchs who are not on the covenantal line. God tells Abraham that he will make Ishmael a "nation." Esau, too, is successful, as predicted by Isaac's blessing. He meets Jacob accompanied by 400 men. In both cases, the brothers do not become enemies in their adulthood, probably because each is successful and not jealous of the other.

This reward approach may have resulted from God's having learned a lesson from Cain and Abel. God favored Abel, provoking Cain to kill his brother. God wanted to avoid the same result with the Patriarchs' sons and made sure jealousy would not affect them. More generally, God wants to prevent fratricide from destroying the Jewish people.

In this light, the Joseph story is clearly within the scheme of things in the Book of Genesis. Its focus on brotherly disunity and eventual reunion brings home the point that is under the surface in the stories of the earlier generations. That is, there is always the risk that brotherly competition will tear apart the families, but reconciliation is what is to be desired.

The nadir of the Joseph Story is when his brothers throw Joseph into the pit and consider killing him. Similarly, Sarah's command to expel Hagar and Ishmael and the theft of the birthright from Esau are low points of these stories. And, Jacob's theft of Esau's birthright leads to a breakup of the family. But, unlike these earlier stories, the Joseph Story does not rely on God to resolve brotherly disunity, despite Joseph's protestations that God had an ulterior motive for letting it happen. Joseph forgives and bolsters the economic situations of his brothers. He resolves the problem on his own and favorably from God's point of view.

The Fundamental Message of the Story

This solution is probably the fundamental message of the story: the Israelite tribes should, by themselves, act to ensure the unity of the Hebrew nation. A tribe that is harmed by the others should be forgiving and not let the problem destroy the nation.

In the end, however, reconciliation and unity of the Hebrew nation are not sure things. Joseph persists in favoring Rachel's children, giving more clothing (as well as three hundred pieces of silver) to Benjamin than to the other brothers. He does not understand the underlying source of his earlier family problems. This provides another reason why Joseph's tribe is not picked to lead the Hebrews during the Exodus. It may not have fully understood the importance of national unity.

Jacob's blessings to his children are certainly not reconciliatory. They emphasize the differences among the brothers, critical of some and praiseworthy of others. These are not the kind of parting words that would be expected to result in equal, mutually respectful relationships.

After Jacob dies, the brothers fear that Joseph will take revenge on them. They concoct a story about a message left by Jacob that he should forgive them. They view the earlier reconciliation as fragile and solely dependent on Joseph's love and respect for his father. Indeed, they are lucky that Joseph still believes God planned their actions and his subsequent success. As a result, Joseph says he will continue to support them and their children. But, ironically, this ends the story with the same sense of superiority that precipitated the problem in the first place.

Conclusion

This is a strange way to end the story if the message is the desirability of national unity. In an economic sense, the Joseph story ends well, with Jacob's family living on the good grazing land of Goshen. All is not well with the ethical or national character of the people, however, as a sense of inequality remains among them. The subsequent years of slavery and then the commandments and threat of punishment are needed to create a nation based on ethics and marked by tribal unity. As with the Book of Genesis as a whole, the Joseph story shows that God's goals cannot be achieved by the reward approach alone.

EXODUS

T he next three chapters derive curious insights into elements of the Book of Exodus. The first two offer unconventional explanations of the story told at a Passover seder. The third draws comparisons with current religious practices.

Purpose of the Plagues was not primarily to free the Israelites, but to instill a fear of God in Pharaoh and future generations of Jews.

Understanding the Haggadah examines why Moses is not mentioned in the traditional Haggadah.

Ritual relates the instructions for building the Tent of Meeting and behavior of priests to current religious activity.

Chapter 13 - *Purpose Of The Plagues*

The traditional view of the Ten Plagues — they were meant to free the Israelites from Egyptian slavery — has problems. Why did God choose to prolong the enslavement by inflicting ten plagues on the Egyptians, if He is so powerful? How powerful a god is He if He needs ten plagues to convince a mortal to bend to His power? Why not inflict just one, albeit significant? For the same reason, why did He harden the Pharaoh's heart, thereby preventing the Pharaoh from freeing the Israelites? Moreover, by hardening the Pharaoh's heart, didn't He make the Pharaoh the victim rather than the perpetrator of the crime of keeping the Israelites? If God requires people to be ethical, how can He kill the first-born Egyptians?

This chapter provides answers. The Plagues were meant not just to free the Israelites but also to demonstrate how difficult it is to discern God's role in the world. Miracles occur, but one needs a fear of God to perceive them as such. God hardens Pharaoh's heart so he does not yield without acknowledging God's omnipotence. Pharaoh is not a victim since he has free will. However, his choice is not whether to free the Israelites but whether to acknowledge the almightiness of God. He does so only after the killing of the first-born Egyptians, demonstrating that an evil person only understands evil.

The Ten Plagues aim to free the Israelites from Egyptian slavery and demonstrate God's power, according to the traditional view. Several surprising elements, though, raise doubt whether these are the true goals. The first nine Plagues can be explained naturally. Egyptian magicians can duplicate, at least to some extent, the first two Plagues. And, God stiffens Pharaoh's heart to prevent him from permitting the Israelites to leave Egypt. The first two elements throw doubt on God's power. The third element questions whether freeing the Israelites is the main goal.

These problems disappear when the Plagues are read from the point of view of Pharaoh. His perspective is different from that of someone who knows in advance that God is responsible for the Plagues and what the ultimate outcome will be. Pharaoh is never sure what to make of them – are they magic, natural events or the actions of a local god? He does not recognize an omnipotent force behind the Plagues. Before they begin, Pharaoh says, "Who is the Lord, that I should listen to his voice to let Israel go? I don't know the Lord and moreover I will not let Israel go." Keeping his limited understanding in mind, the purpose of the Plagues becomes clear: To demonstrate to Jews of all generations the difficulty of discerning God's role in the world. The episode of the Plagues shows how someone can mistake his own limited understanding for the true factor behind events.

What Does the Pharaoh Know (And Not Know)?

Pharaoh views some of the Plagues as standard magic. He relies on magicians to duplicate them. When his magicians cannot, he seems to acknowledge God's power. However, he considers Him to be a local god with whom he can negotiate. Pharaoh appears to view other Plagues as natural catastrophes, which, while unfortunate, will not recur. In all cases, Pharaoh does not understand what is truly behind the plague.

Moses' earlier response to the burning bush stands in contrast with Pharaoh's reactions to the plagues. The Torah suggests the bush is unusual. In fact, a bush whose leaves look to be burning exists in the Sinai Desert. Moses could have passed it by, considering it just a natural phenomenon. He instead interprets the bush as a "great sight" and takes a step toward it to look more closely. This episode shows Moses to have a different way of seeing the world from that of Pharaoh. Moses considers the possibility of a wondrous world and acknowledges God's responsibility for things he observes. From this perspective, the episode of the burning bush sets up the subsequent plagues as tests of the Pharaoh's ability to see God's role behind events as does Moses.

The Torah says what it takes to understand God's role in events – one has to have a fear of God. Moses tells Pharaoh after the plague of hail, "As soon as I have gone out of the city, I will spread abroad my hands to the Lord. The thunders shall cease, neither shall there be any more hail; that you may know that the earth is the Lord's. <u>But as for you and your servants, I know that you will not yet fear the Lord.</u>" In a biblical context the phrase "fear of God" means acknowledgement of and respect for an all-powerful God who requires moral and ethical behavior. At the start of Exodus, the midwives "feared God" and showed righteous behavior by not following the Pharaoh's orders to kill Hebrew boy babies.

Unlike the midwives, Pharaoh fails on two accounts. He does not recognize the omnipotence of God. Even when acknowledging the Israelite god to have some power, he does not comprehend its full extent -- Pharaoh views God's demands as negotiable. In addition, his prior decision regarding the Israelites – forcing them to gather straw without reducing their other workload -- does not follow the ethical conduct demanded by God. Both shortcomings preclude him from understanding, until the tenth Plague, how an all-powerful God is behind the Plagues. And, the tenth Plague is convincing perhaps because it is in the evil terms Pharaoh understands. Pharaoh could recognize that the slaying of first-born Egyptians was more successful than his father's earlier attempt to kill all the Israelite male babies.

Why Does God Stiffen Pharaoh's Heart?

This line of reasoning can be pushed further to explain why God stiffens Pharaoh's heart. In the Plague of boils, God does not permit Pharaoh to heed the admonitions of his magicians, who understand God's power. Only those who fear God are permitted to discern a miracle when it occurs. In the Plagues of locusts and darkness, God stiffens Pharaoh's heart to stop him from allowing the Israelites to leave on his terms. Here, Pharaoh is not permitted to evade the consequences of under-appreciating God's power — it is not negotiable.

The stiffening of Pharaoh's heart has troubled many. First, it runs counter to the assumed goal of freeing the Israelites. This concern, however, misses the point, which is not to show the most efficient way to free the Israelites but to show what it takes to understand God's role in events. Second, some say Pharaoh does not have free will, since God prevents him from making the decision to let the Israelites leave Egypt. He seems to be the victim, so cannot be viewed as evil. This argument misses another point. Pharaoh does have a choice. It is whether or not to fear God. Ultimately, he does not.

Moses' modest demand underscores that the Plagues are not about an unreasonable request of Pharaoh. Throughout the episode, all Moses demands is for the Israelites to be permitted to leave Egypt for three days to sacrifice to God. He does not ask for their freedom. If he had, Pharaoh's refusals could draw sympathy, as it would be understandably very costly to lose an enslaved people permanently. Instead, the demand for a three-day leave makes the request mundane and secondary. Some might argue that even this demand is onerous because it would threaten Pharaoh's power – the Israelites could demand more if he gave in. However, Pharaoh's own stubborn and ruthless behavior suggests such additional demands would be squashed. The focus of the encounter between Moses and Pharaoh then is not over the control of the Israelites but whether Pharaoh acknowledges the supremacy of God.

These points can be illustrated by looking at each Plague.

The Plagues

In the first Plague, God turns the water of the Nile into blood. However, when the Egyptian magicians turn other water into blood through their spells, "Pharaoh's heart was hardened and he didn't listen to [Moses and Aaron]." The first Plague shows Pharaoh understanding the Plague as ordinary magic. He treats it with disdain.

The magicians are also able to duplicate the second Plague of frogs. Nevertheless, this time Pharaoh becomes somewhat frightened, promising to let the Israelites sacrifice to God if the frogs are removed. But, Pharaoh shifts back to being stubborn when the frogs die, withdrawing his promise. In seeing a "respite," he presumably reconsiders the event as a natural effect of the contaminated Nile.

The third Plague, lice, moves a step further ahead, as the Egyptian magicians are not able to duplicate it. As a result, they understand the power of God, saying to Pharaoh, "This is the finger of God." Pharaoh refuses to acknowledge their insight and just dismisses the problem, his heart stiffening. The different reactions show that nonbelievers can learn to recognize the power of God and see miracles. In this case, the different conclusions reached by the magicians and Pharaoh may reflect, ironically, the narrower focus of the magicians. The magicians acknowledge the power of God on the basis of knowing the limits of their magic. Pharaoh's reaction suggests a broader perspective than that of the magicians. He might have conjectured the dead frogs attracted the lice and concluded the Plague was a natural event.

The fourth Plague, insects, shows the Pharaoh beginning to understand the power of God after seeing only the Israelites spared the onslaught. He gives permission for the Israelites to sacrifice to God within the land, and then bends further to Moses' arguments by saying they can go into the wilderness although not very far. These traveling restrictions, however, mean he believes he has enough power vis-a-vis God to impose limits. He does not fully acknowledge God's omnipotence. To be sure, Pharaoh says, "Pray for me," appearing to acknowledge that God may be behind this Plague. This acknowledgement apparently is not deep or perhaps is said with sarcasm. Once the insects disappear, Pharaoh reverts to his old ways and rescinds his permission.

In the fifth Plague, when Pharaoh learns the Israelites' livestock are not afflicted by pestilence, he nevertheless "was stubborn," refusing to believe that God was responsible for the Plague. Pharaoh seems to view the omission of the Israelites from the plague to be a fluke.

In the sixth Plague, Pharaoh expects his magicians to counter the plague of boils, "but they couldn't stand before Moses because of the boils; for the boils were on the magicians and on all the Egyptians." As Pharaoh still seems to believe the plagues are subject to magic, God, for the first time, stiffens Pharaoh's heart so he wouldn't "listen to them," presumably meaning he would not pay attention to the magicians' admonitions that God is all-powerful. God does not permit Pharaoh to open his mind to the idea of a miracle because Pharaoh does not demonstrate a fear of God. Also, by hardening Pharaoh's heart before he is able to decide on the Israelites' freedom, God implicitly reveals the latter is not His primary concern. If it were, God would have waited to see if Pharaoh decided to let the Israelites leave Egypt.

In the seventh Plague, the only Egyptians to escape the hail are those "who feared the word of the Lord." Pharaoh, himself, appears to give in and acknowledge the omnipotence of God, saying, "I have sinned this time. The Lord is righteous, and I and my people are wicked." However, Moses knows this is not deeply felt. Moses says, "But as for you and your servants, I know that you will not yet fear the Lord God" And, sure enough, the Pharaoh changes his mind when he sees "the rain and the hail and the thunder had ceased." He apparently chalks up the experience to bad weather.

The eighth Plague, locusts, scares Pharaoh, who summons Moses and Aaron "in haste." Pharaoh, however, does not admit to the omnipotence of God. He considers God a local god of the Israelites. He says, "I have sinned against the Lord your God, and against you. Now therefore please forgive my sin again, and pray to the Lord your God, that He may also take away from me this death" God understands this to be a narrow view of His power. He stiffens Pharaoh's heart again so he would ultimately suffer the consequences of choosing not to fear God as omnipotent. With his heart stiffened, Pharaoh reverts to his old ways. He refuses to let the Israelites sacrifice in the Wilderness after the locusts are eliminated.

Pharaoh moves closer to recognizing God as the almighty

during the ninth Plague, darkness. He says, "Go serve the Lord." However, he requires the Israelite flocks and herds to stay behind. By making his consent conditional, the Pharaoh shows he continues to believe himself on equal terms with God and can negotiate with Him. This is unacceptable, and God stiffens his heart.

After the tenth Plague, the slaying of the first-born, Pharaoh finally acknowledges the omnipotence of God. The tenth Plague brings home to Pharaoh just what his father tried to do to the Israelites, but unsuccessfully, when he ordered all Israelite boy babies be thrown into the Nile. By succeeding where Pharaoh's father failed, God finally demonstrates His supremacy to Pharaoh. As a result, Pharaoh tells Moses to take the Israelites out of his country to "serve the Lord." He does not impose conditions, saying they can take their flocks and herds. And, most importantly, he asks Moses to "bless me also." He finally demonstrates a fear of God.

After the Plagues

Jews are troubled by the thought that freedom was obtained through the evil act of slaying the first-born. It may be an evil person only understands evil. While apparent innocents die, it may be that people have to suffer the consequences of their leader's actions. Nonetheless, this outcome is an unacceptable conclusion of the Exodus story. Acknowledging the omnipotence of God only because of an evil act is not tolerable. So, the episode appends Pharaoh's change of heart and his doomed pursuit of the Israelites.

After the Israelites leave Egypt, God tests Pharaoh's new attitude by telling the Israelites to "turn back" in the wilderness and encamp near the sea. Like a fisherman, God uses the Israelites to lure Pharaoh, speculating that Pharaoh will think the Israelites are "entangled in the land" and vulnerable. And again like a fisherman strategizing how to catch a fish, God says He will stiffen Pharaoh's heart if Pharaoh goes for the bait. Sure enough, when Pharaoh learns the Israelites are not returning from the wilderness, he and his courtiers shift back to being against the Israelites. Importantly, Pharaoh changes his view on his own, demonstrating free will. He sees the Exodus as a failure of the Israelites and God to live up to the bargain – they were supposed to have returned after three days. This view of Exodus as a bargaining result once again shows Pharaoh believing he is on equal terms with God. He no longer demonstrates a fear of God. As planned, God stiffens his heart, and the Pharaoh disastrously orders his army after the Israelites.

Conclusion

In sum, throughout the ten Plagues, Pharaoh never displays a fear of God. He does not seem to view the first several Plagues as miraculous. Then, when he finally begins to appreciate the power of God, he views Him as a local god with whom he can negotiate and set conditions. Because of this incomplete appreciation of God's power, God does not let him see the Plagues as miraculous or avoid the consequences of his limited views, purposefully stiffening the Pharaoh's heart. The only Egyptians to view the Plagues as miraculous are the magicians, who understand the power of God in relation to their own limited power, and the courtiers who "feared the Lord's word."

The Israelites learn to fear God only at the end of the episode of the Plagues. In their newfound freedom, but with the Sea of Reeds blocking them, they first lack faith in Him, asking Moses to bring them back to Egypt as the Egyptian army approaches. Moses response is ironic in light of the underlying themes of the episode. He says, "Have no fear! [rather than saying, 'Have no fear other than that of God'] Stand by, and see the salvation of the Lord, which He will work for you today [for which a fear of God is needed]." In fact, the Israelites develop a fear of God once they are safely across the sea. The last verse says, "Israel saw the great work which the Lord did to the Egyptians, and the people feared the Lord; and they believed in the Lord, and in his servant Moses." -- a remarkable closing of the episode of the Plagues in light of this analysis.

Seen this way, God's own interpretation of the Plagues takes on new emphasis. He tells Moses in Chapter 10, "Go in to Pharaoh, for I have hardened his heart, and the heart of his servants, that I may show these my signs in the midst of them, and that *you may tell in the hearing of your son, and of your son's son* what things I have done to Egypt and my signs which I have done among them; *that you may know that I am the Lord.*" The episode of the Plagues is meant not just to create bragging rights about the power of God – the standard emphasis placed on interpreting this passage. The episode is meant to instill a fear of God in Jews of all generations. Then, they can appreciate the possibility there is more than meets the eye in historical events. Unlike the Pharaoh, who saw the world through a limited perspective, they will understand that events may be the work of God, just as in the episode of the Plagues.

Chapter 14 - *Understanding The Haggadah*

The absence of Moses' name from the Haggadah has puzzled many. The Haggadah never seems to tell the entire story even though it is meant to explain the Exodus at a Passover seder.

Nonetheless, there are good reasons for emphasizing God's role. Indeed, the purpose of the seder is not to celebrate the idea of freedom, as is now customary, but to reinforce the need to follow God's commandments.

H aving grown up using the Maxwell House Coffee Haggadah at family seders, I always wondered why this traditional Haggadah centers almost exclusively on God's actions. At the least, one would think Moses should be mentioned. The basis for the near-exclusivity of God in the Haggadah can be found in the Torah. But, the basis for an inclusion of people in the Haggadah is there, as well. Relating the Haggadah to the Torah also brings out the message of the holiday, which is the need for Jews to adhere to the commandments.

Basis for Near-Exclusivity of God in the Haggadah

Focusing exclusively on God's role in extracting the Israelites from Egypt legitimizes God's demand that Jews follow the commandments. We owe Him — the quid pro quo relationship. Deuteronomy's Chapter 6 says, "When your son asks you in time to come, saying, 'What mean the testimonies, statutes, and ordinances, which the Lord our God has commanded you?' then you shall tell your son, 'We were Pharaoh's bondservants in Egypt: and the Lord brought us out of Egypt with a mighty hand....It shall be righteousness to us, if we observe to do all this commandment before the Lord our God, as he has commanded us.'" The significance of Passover is to reaffirm the need to abide by the commandments.

Emphasizing God's power goes to the heart of the covenant between Jews and God. Jews can count on His coming through on the deal. The idea of an all-powerful God who delivered the Israelites from slavery was a wonderful thought for Jewish people who felt politically weak, hopeless, or repressed in the Diaspora. Just as God came to save the Israelites from Egypt, they could hope God would come save them. In this light, it may not be surprising the traditional Haggadah was written between 800 and 1200 CE, when Jews in Europe were expelled from various European countries and generally not treated well.

What About Moses?

Emphasis of God's role centers on His being responsible for the Ten Plagues that convince Pharaoh to free the Israelites. But, should Moses' interaction with the Pharaoh be emphasized as well? The Torah's account suggests not. Moses was not acting as a free agent.

Extracting the Israelites from Egypt did not result from the good bargaining abilities of Moses and Aaron. Their initial encounter with the Pharaoh ends in failure. Moses and Aaron request permission for the Israelites to go into the wilderness for three days to pray to God. Pharaoh responds by increasing the slaves' workload, forcing them to gather straw while making the same number of bricks as before. The Israelites are upset with Moses and Aaron, saying, "May the Lord look at you, and judge, because you have made us a stench to be abhorred in the eyes of Pharaoh and his servants, to put a sword in their hand to kill us."

Moses understands his failure. When God tells him to speak to the Pharaoh again, Moses says, "The children of Israel haven't listened to me. How then shall Pharaoh listen to me?" Consequently, God makes Moses His proxy. God says, "I have made you as God to Pharaoh; and Aaron your brother shall be your prophet. You shall speak all that I command you; and Aaron your brother shall speak to Pharaoh, that he let the children of Israel go out of his land." Moses is no longer acting as a free agent. He is to say only what God tells him and to be a conduit for the supernatural. Moses' actions are really God's.

The supernatural dominates the start of God's showdown

with Pharaoh. He instructs Moses and Aaron to turn their staff into a snake. The ensuing competition with the magicians does not have dialogue, a subtle way to underscore the irrationality of the event. Moses and Aaron clearly act as agents of God, performing deeds beyond their natural abilities. They are not directly responsible for what occurs. This leaves no basis for believing that Moses and Aaron play roles independent of God when they subsequently announce the Ten Plagues.

Do People Deserve Any Credit for the Exodus?

Moses and other Israelites, however, play independent roles before God steps in. They had to do something by themselves before God would help, consistent with the actions of the Patriarchs discussed in *An Incorrect Interpretation of the Torah?* (Chapter 10). They deserve to be highlighted in a broader telling of the story.

Chapter 1 of Exodus shows the Israelites helping themselves. When the Pharaoh commands the midwives to kill newly born boys, they ignore his command and let the Israelite male babies live. God is pleased and rewards the midwives. Pharaoh then repeats his command to kill newly born males, but this time the Israelites, with one exception, make no attempt to thwart it. Consequently, his command is carried out. The exception, of course, is Moses' mother, who sends him floating down the Nile in a wicker basket. She shows that a person's action can make a difference.

Chapter 2 has the Israelites pulling God toward them. Only after they cry out from their bondage does God take notice of them. Their cries are loud and forceful enough that their entreaties "came up to God." The Haggadah includes this part.

Chapter 3 also drives home the need for people to take the first step. While an angel of God is in the blazing bush, Moses has to decide to "turn aside" to look at "this great sight" before God calls to him. As it is said, "When the Lord saw that he had turned aside to look, God called to him out of the midst of the bush: 'Moses, Moses!'" Conceivably, the story might have ended there if Moses had not turned toward the burning bush.

Finally, in Chapter 4, Zipporah's actions to save her son show the need to make a commitment to God. By circumcising her son and spreading the blood over his legs, Zipporah stops God's attempt to kill her firstborn and asserts that God is now "surely a bridegroom of blood to me." With this action, Moses and his family are seen to be fully committed to His goal. Tangentially, this may have set a precedent for the Israelites' spreading lamb's blood over their doorposts on the fateful night. Later, it may have provided a rationale for sprinkling blood around the altar in the Tabernacle. All three actions can be interpreted as binding the Israelites and God together in common goals.

Should God Get The Credit?

There is a problem giving God the credit for extracting the Israelites -- He was responsible for their being in Egypt in the first place. The whole episode was predetermined. God told Abraham the basic outline of what was to happen. And, He implicitly admits his responsibility in Chapter 6 when he tells Moses to say to the Israelites that He will "<u>redeem</u> you with an outstretched arm, and with great judgments." Using the word "redeem" implies that God "deposited" the Israelites there. We could just as well be resentful of God for having put the Israelites in Egypt as be eternally grateful to Him for having taken them out.

God had a reason for putting the Israelites in Egypt, however. The period of enslavement was punishment for the progressively sinful ways of the Patriarchs, as discussed in *A General Theory of the Torah* (Chapter 7). It was meant to prepare the Israelites for understanding the need for commandments. The Israelites (and future Jews) should be grateful at least for God having decided they were ready to follow His commandments.

The Message in the Haggadah

The importance of adhering to God's commandments is the major message in the Haggadah. It finds support in Chapter 13 of Exodus, where the need to follow the commandments is tied to the Passover holiday. Verse 8 states the holiday should involve eating unleavened bread for seven days. Verse 9 says, "It shall be for a sign to you on your hand and for a memorial between your eyes that the law of the Lord may be in your mouth; for with a strong hand the Lord has brought you out of Egypt."

Tradition views this statement as the rationale for wearing Tefilllin. However, since the statement is in the context of describing how to observe the holiday, it could mean eating unleavened bread should remind Jews to think about the commandments ("that the law of the Lord may be in your mouth") as well as about God's power. The verse says in a somewhat convoluted way that the all-powerful God freed the Israelites for them to uphold the Teaching. The need to observe the commandments is stated to be a central theme of the holiday.

This theme is lost among liberal Jews. Instead, the Haggadah has been rewritten to emphasize freedom from slavery, either literally or psychologically. This makes the Exodus story universally appealing. But, it deemphasizes the need to follow God's commandments and thus is problematical from a religious perspective.

The Torah does not denounce slavery as an institution nor argue that people should free themselves from their own narrow constraints. Rather, references to the Israelites' plight as slaves are made to justify commandments to treat others decently. For example, in Exodus 23, the Israelites are commanded not to "oppress an alien, for you know the heart of an alien, seeing you were aliens in the land of Egypt." The Torah's lesson is that freedom from slavery entails responsibility for others. But, this is not the fundamental message of the Exodus.

Conclusion

The Haggadah's emphasis of God's role in the Exodus is defensible, based on the story told in the Torah. But, expanding its focus to include the role of people would be justifiable, as well. Moses and other people had to make decisions and act before God did what was needed to bring the Israelites out of slavery. God, however, is ultimately responsible for the Exodus. The Haggadah's near-exclusivity is consistent with the primary purpose of Passover — to emphasize the obligation of Jews to follow God's commandments. Glorifying freedom is of secondary importance.

Chapter 15 - *Ritual*

The verses describing the building of the Tent of Meeting are some of the most boring of the Torah. Full of detail that seems antiquated and irrelevant, they go on and on without appearing to hold any message. Moreover, the whole discussion is repeated – first by God to Moses and then, in almost identical language, from Moses to the Israelites. Even so, they contain clues regarding the relationship between God and the Israelites and insights, some quite curious, into current religious practice.

M uch of the second half of the Book of Exodus discusses the rituals to be practiced by the newly freed Israelites. Enormous detail is provided for the building of the Tent of Meeting, the priests' garments, and method of sacrifice. For the most part, modern readers view this discussion as tedious and irrelevant. However, by looking past the details and focusing on the theological underpinnings, it is possible to glimpse the founding principles behind these ritualistic practices and the extent to which current practices are consistent with or have diverged from them. For example, a rationale for innovation in the construction of synagogues can be found in the most unlikely of places. In contrast, the current informal approach to and attempts at innovation in services are not well supported.

God's Place

In a general sense, the Israelite community can be viewed as a sanctuary for God. It allows Him to escape from the chaos that exists elsewhere in the world. Even within the Israelite community, He needs His own space — the Tent of Meeting.

Almost all the rituals discussed in this part of Exodus aim to make the Tent of Meeting and priests acceptable to God. Consistent with the notion of separateness found at Mount Sinai, God does not appear to anyone, anyplace. He resides in a specific place, not sullied by the secular. As He says in Chapter 25, "Let them make Me a sanctuary, that I may dwell among them." Using the term "sanctuary" shows He needs a special place, away from the everyday lives of the Israelites. The term contradicts the often-heard view that the word "them" implies God is in everyone's heart.

God's residence must be distinct from Israelite camp life. It is to be constructed with the best materials and based on specifications provided by Him. Even the odors within the Tent are to be different from those of ordinary camp existence; incense for the Tent is not to be made like that which "you make for yourselves." All the attention to detail, however, does not make the Tent holy. Only God's presence sanctifies it. The Tent is where God will "meet with the children of Israel, and the place shall be sanctified by My glory."

Implicit in God's need for a sanctuary is the idea He will descend to the world. Jews are not meant to ascend to the heavens to reach God. Instead, they are to make their society compatible for God's presence. The reason Moses climbs Mount Sinai to meet God must be because God's sanctuary in the Israelite camp, the Tent of Meeting, is not yet built.

Another important implication of the Tent is God's independence of a specific location. Unlike many pagan gods, His purview is not restricted to one place. The Tent is moveable. Instead, God is attached to a people. He introduces Himself to Moses as "the God of your father, the God of Abraham, the God of Isaac and the God of Jacob" at the burning bush. This idea is not understood by pagans after Assyria destroys the Northern Kingdom in Kings 2, Chapter 17. In response to a complaint by the pagan people who replaced the Israelites in Samaria, the king of Assyria sends them a priest to teach them the "law of the god of the land." Theologically, God is not tied to the land of Israel.

The Tent of Meeting

Two aspects of the Tent's specifications may be theologically significant. The text gives much attention to the lengths, widths, and quantities of items used in its construction. These numbers do not appear to have any mathematical relationship with each other, which may be to deny any religious significance to numerical analysis.

The details, however, are apparently not enough information to construct the Tent. Additional specifications by the Israelites are needed to complete it. This need extends the concept of independent decision making into the non-secular realm. In tremendous irony, the most detailed portion of the Torah hints that people play a role in establishing the place where God resides.

Indeed, the first thing God tells Moses about the Tent of Meeting is to involve the participation of the Israelites. Each person, "whose heart makes him willing," shall bring gifts for the construction of the Tent. The voluntary nature implies people need to demonstrate a desire to construct a relationship with God.

Once built, the maintenance of the Tent is the responsibility of all the Israelites. Unlike the initial contributions, payment for its maintenance is mandatory, borne by each Israelite regardless of his/her feelings toward the project (or God). A person is to pay a half shekel when enrolled in a census — a fixed amount per person, thereby requiring each Israelite to bear the same degree of responsibility for enabling God's presence. This "atonement money" shall be assigned "to the service of the Tent of Meeting." The distinction between the voluntary and involuntary nature of the two sources of funds acknowledges a practical problem with fund raising to this day – it is easier to get people to contribute for the construction of a building than for its upkeep.

There is an exception to the role of the Israelites in building the Tent. The Tabernacle, the central place where God is to reside, is to be made exactly according to God's instructions. Each part of the ark and the other elements of the inner sanctuary, including the priests' vestments, are to be "as the Lord commanded Moses." The Israelites may not innovate where the most direct relationship with God is in play.

The Priesthood

Since the Tent is to be holy, only priests are permitted to approach God. They have to wear special clothing and go through elaborate procedures to become ordained. The specifications acknowledge the problem raised at Mount Sinai — that anyone in God's presence will die. Aaron's robe shall have "a golden bell ... so that the sound of it shall be heard when he comes into the holy place before the Lord and when he goes out, that he may not die."

Even with all these preparations, God's sanctuary still will likely be sullied by men's presence. A "sin offering of atonement" is required for the altar once a year "throughout your generations." This offering is the first allusion in the Torah to a holiday that may have developed into Yom Kippur. While the role of the holiday in cleansing the Israelite people of sin is spelled out in Leviticus 16, this first reference shows the holiday mirroring purification of the sanctuary.

Having a priesthood dedicated to performing ritual practices can be put into practical and theological perspectives. From a practical point of view, the priesthood might be considered an efficient way to maintain a relationship with God. In this arrangement, most Israelites devote their time and effort to supporting and increasing their standard of living. They do not take off a large amount of time to make offerings to God, instead leaving the ritual to the priests. In other words, because of priests, Israelites are able to devote their energies to advancing their society, as God intends them to do. Theologically, the priesthood represents a degree of separation between God and the Israelites, consistent with the relationship desired by Him. Israelites are to approach God through the actions of the priests

Two aspects of the priests' ritual activities deserve mention. The sacrificial rituals are highly structured, with the Torah describing exactly how they are to be done. There is little, if any, leeway in how to address God. The formal nature of the rituals is fitting for a god who is to be the Lord. God is to be treated with much respect. Moreover, since sacrificial animals are presumably of some economic value, communicating with God is not to be free and easy.

Golden Calf Episode

The unacceptability of some rituals is addressed in the Golden Calf episode. There, many incorrect decisions are made regarding how Israelites are to show obedience to God. Just as the Book of Genesis demonstrates the need for commandments, as discussed in *A General Theory of the Torah* (Chapter 7), the Golden Calf fiasco shows why all the detailed attention to ritual in the Torah is required. Without it, people will get it wrong.

Looking underneath the details offers clues on what is unacceptable. The episode can be read from the perspective of Aaron and the Israelites or from that of the reader. All that Aaron and the Israelites know are the Commandments given at Mount Sinai. This knowledge should be enough for them to realize what they are doing is wrong. The reader also knows, besides the Commandments, what God stipulated about rituals in his discourse with Moses. The all-encompassing viewpoint of the reader is the more significant perspective for drawing conclusions about today's religious practices.

The Golden Calf episode certainly contradicts some of the Commandments. Several divergences are seen immediately in the Israelites' request of Aaron to "make us gods which shall go before us, for as for this man Moses, who brought us up out of the land of Egypt – we do not know what has become of him." First, the Israelites want to make an image of God, if not a substitute. As they know, this is prohibited. Second, their desire for a god to lead them contradicts the implication of the Ten Commandments that the Israelites are to act like God and direct their own destiny. This problem is less widely appreciated, but important nonetheless. It suggests rituals do not substitute for personal responsibility. Third, the Israelites make the same mistake made after crossing the Sea of Reeds – they do not attribute their deliverance from slavery to God but to Moses.

After the Golden Calf is made, the people say, perhaps mockingly, "These are your gods, Israel, which brought you up out of the land of Egypt." Aaron tries to save the situation by building an alter before it and declaring the next day a "festival of the Lord" – emphasizing God rather than the Golden Calf. It is not enough. The confusion over responsibility for the exodus – Moses, the Golden Calf or God -- demonstrates the absence of a fear of God. A fear of God is needed to perceive His role in world events.

A reader can recognize other mistakes. A couple of problems are seen in Aaron's response to the Israelites. He says, "Take off the golden rings which are in the ears of your wives, of your sons, and of your daughters, and bring them to me." This demand stands in contrast to the voluntary nature of God's instructions to the Israelites for building the Tent of Meeting. Aaron also establishes a holiday, saying, "Tomorrow shall be a festival of the Lord." God, not people, determines the Israelite holidays, as He had specified three such spiritual days to Moses.

The festival conducted by the Israelites diverges from prescribed practices, as well. People, rather than priests, offer the sacrifices, contradicting the need for separation between God and the Israelites. Restrictions are not placed on eating and drinking, as opposed to God's specifications regarding those parts of a sacrificial animal to be eaten. And, dancing is added to the ceremony, although it is not part of any ritual laid out by God. By identifying these activities with this sacrilegious event, the Torah implicitly would seem to condemn them, in particular, and innovation, in general, in ritual.

Conclusion: Ritual versus the Guideline Approach

When all is said and done, rituals are not enough to satisfy God. After giving instructions on ritual, God tells Moses to say to the Israelites that they must keep the Sabbath because ,it is "holy" and "for in six days the Lord made heaven and earth, and on the seventh day He rested and was refreshed." Remarkably, God chooses to emphasize the Commandment and its justification that form the basis for the guideline approach as analyzed in *What God Wants* (Chapter 3). Rituals do not replace the need for Israelites to make decisions and take actions to direct their destiny within the guidelines of the commandments. Even with rituals, Israelites must act like God in their everyday lives. The secondary significance of ritual is perhaps underscored subtly by Moses, not God, blessing the Israelites after they finish the construction of the Tent of Meeting. The omission of God's blessing suggests ritual is not enough to ensure His approval.

A LIVING LEVITICUS

The next nine chapters discern the relevance of what seems to be the Torah's most anachronistic Book. Leviticus deals with rules concerning sacrifices, the priesthood, keeping Kosher, bodily excretions, sexual relationships, and other idiosyncratic aspects of the religion.

The Book, nevertheless, contains many theological concepts relevant today, despite being grounded in the defunct sacrificial system of the ancient Israelites. It suggests how Jews are to approach God in prayer. It also specifies the basis for how Jews are to approach each other – their interactions are to reflect ethics, spiritual purity and recognition they are all God's property. Caring for the poor has to be balanced against ritual. All are needed for God to pay attention to the Jewish community.

The rules can be mapped to theologically significant points made in Genesis and Exodus. For example, daily practices to achieve spiritual purity, such as keeping Kosher or going to the Mikvah, mirror holy aspects of the Tabernacle and Mount Sinai.

Since the purpose of these spiritually-based actions is to create a suitable environment for God, the idea of forming a close relationship with Him through prayer alone is problematic. Incorporating the actions into everyday life would seem necessary, as well. From a practical standpoint, aiming for spiritual purity serves to reinforce the proper social behavior stemming from ethics. In total, seeing past the anachronistic elements of Leviticus offers a better vision and understanding of current Jewish practices.

Chapter 16 - *Is It Relevant?*

Leviticus focuses on the specifics of a God-compatible society. It contains meaningful insights into current religious practices.

At the end of Exodus, the Israelites finalize a covenant with God that entails unquestioning adherence on their part to a set of rules. God, Himself, will lead them through the wilderness. In Leviticus, the Torah delves into the rules and requirements for the Israelite society to be compatible for God. For a modern, and, particularly, Reform Jew, the descriptions of sacrifice and some of the restraints on life style can be repugnant. However, a theologically meaningful way to read Leviticus is possible.

Purpose of Leviticus

To begin, Leviticus can be viewed as answering the question -- what does it take to make a society hospitable for God? From the Torah's perspective, the answer is important because God is seen being in one place at a time. Since the Israelites want God to be with them on their journey, they have to make sure He will want to be within their midst. By not creating a compatible home, He could desert them, with disastrous results. For the most part, a hospitable place for God requires on-going acknowledgement of his power and authority, keeping spiritually pure, and living ethically.

The idea that God exists in only one place at a time, however, has changed over the years. Today, most believe God is everywhere – perhaps a necessary change, given the Diaspora. Establishing a hospitable place for God to reside, in this case, is not relevant, since He is there regardless. The purpose of Leviticus would seem to be pointless. However, the logic of the Torah suggests God's omnipresence does not imply He will necessarily favor the Jews. For example, He is present in Egypt in Exodus but does not favor the Egyptians. The question Leviticus addresses can be framed differently -- what does it take for God to treat the Jewish community specially? Examining Leviticus from this angle begins to make the Book relevant to the modern reader.

Ritual Versus Ethics?

There is one more general issue to be resolved for a Reform Jew — how many of the commandments in Leviticus are relevant? The sacrificial system is anachronistic. And, some of the requirements do not appear to make much sense. Moreover, the guideline approach to establishing an ethical, monotheistic society does not constrain Jews to follow unquestionably a detailed set of rules. And, importantly for the issue at hand, it accepts God's desire for separation and does not require His continuous presence. Thus, all the specifics of Leviticus may not be needed.

The answer is ironic, given the tendency for Reform rabbis to almost apologize for the chapters in Leviticus dealing with sacrifice and plague and to exude relief and exhilaration once the "Holiness Code" is reached in the course of Torah services. Despite these rabbis' view that the Holiness Code is the most compatible part of Leviticus for Reform Jews, all the specifics of the Code are not necessary from the perspective of the guideline approach. Jews who follow this approach may find other means, and possibly better ones, to achieve an ethical society. In contrast, the guideline approach still requires acknowledgement of God as the Lord. And, the exactness of the commandments regarding ritual in Exodus means there is little, if any, leeway in the guideline approach to innovate in the essentials of this sphere.

Leviticus emphasizes the exactness of ritual not only by the attention to detail in the sacrifices but also through the death of Aaron's sons, Nadab and Abihu, for offering alien fire in the Tabernacle. Their failure to follow the rules denigrated God. As Moses says, God's Holiness and authority are demonstrated by the actions of those near to Him. Aaron's silence is typically seen as demonstrating remorse and sadness over the loss of his children. However, it could be interpreted as acknowledgement that he, himself, is as guilty as his sons for knowingly diverging from prescribed ritual. His guilt harkens back to the episode of the Golden Calf.

The repartee between Moses and Aaron whether to eat the guilt offering is a technical debate regarding ritualistic law. It may be the first talmudic-type discussion in the Torah. The technical issue is not whether a priest in mourning should eat of the sacrificial meal, since this is not an issue addressed in the earlier chapters of Leviticus, but whether a guilty priest should be permitted to eat of the sacrifice. By the rules, a priest is not supposed to partake in a sacrificial meal when the guilt offering involves his own actions. Moses' silence indicates acquiescence that Aaron's own sins preclude him from eating of the guilt offering.

Thus, the exactness of ritual is extremely important. And, from the perspective of a modern Reform Jew, all the implications for how to approach God from Leviticus' chapters on sacrifice are relevant. A Reform rabbi would do better focusing on these chapters than on the Holiness Code.

Chapter 17 - *Implications For Prayer*

The sacrificial system, despite being anachronistic, offers insight into the nature and efficacy of prayer. Praying as a way to come closer to God or to make a request of Him should not be viewed as cost free. Asking for help in the sacrificial system is based on quid pro quo, where the petitioner promises to do something in exchange for God's help. In contrast, prayer now is done unconditionally for the most part, asking God for a favor without promising anything in return.

T he sacrificial system in Leviticus raises two issues regarding prayer – coming close to God and asking for His help.

Sacrifices and Prayer – Coming Close to God?

Rabbis like to point out that the Hebrew word for "sacrifice" means "something brought near" with the implication that prayer brings one close to God. This analysis is not necessarily correct, after seeing how sacrifices are specified in Leviticus. Leviticus distinguishes between those sacrifices that bring a person close to God and those that do not.

The burnt and guilt offerings prescribe a distant relationship between a person, priest or community and God. All the sacrifice is consumed in fire or ejected from the community rather than shared in a meal. For a layman, there is an additional separation when priests serve as intermediaries. A layman sacrifices indirectly to God by putting his hands on the animal before giving it to the priests.

Since these offerings mean to acknowledge God's authority or to acknowledge a violation of His commandments, a distance is kept between the one making a sacrifice and God to underscore respect and awe. One approaches God as one would approach a powerful lord – with humble caution. Only in the case of a layman making a guilt sacrifice could the priests partake in the meal. Here, the the priest is being compensated for acting as the conduit to God.

The sacrifices bringing a layman close to God are those of well-being, free-will or vows. The layman rather than a priest waves the sacrifice. And, the layman shares in the sacrificial meal. Partaking in a sacrificial meal would be a quintessential example of getting close to God. Figuratively, one would be sharing a table with Him.

These sacrifices involve a partnership between people and God. In both thanking God or establishing a vow, the layman can be viewed as partly responsible for his good fortune or is responsible for coming through on the vow. Coming close to God by sharing a meal with Him is justifiable in these cases. It represents a partnership between God and a person.

Nevertheless, Leviticus is careful to restrict the time of such a meal. Well-being meals need to be completed on the day the sacrifice is offered. Votive offering meals can be consumed over two days. The different timeframes recognize that needing God's favor is more important ahead of an action (i.e., to give courage to consummate a vow) than after an event. Sharing a meal with God over two days could boost an individual's commitment to pursue his vow, while restricting it to one day to thank God for a good event might restrain the potential for bragging. Leviticus emphasizes the limited time one could feel close to God by stating if one eats the sacrificial food on the third day, the sacrifice is void and the offending party considered guilty of a sin. In sum, while there is an intention of coming close to God in these cases, it is restrictive in nature.

The significance of sharing a sacrificial meal can be taken a step further by viewing the rules as embodying a set of incentives. Since burnt and guilt offerings are either entirely consumed in fire or eaten by priests, there is less incentive to bring them than offerings for well-being or free will. The rules about sharing sacrificial meals thus encourage individual decision-making or actions, consistent with the ideas promulgated at Mount Sinai.

Examples of Coming Close to God

The Torah recognizes at least a psychological need for people to feel close to God. There are instances when trying to come close to God either happens or is envisioned.

At Mount Sinai, Moses, Aaron, Nadab and the elders share a meal with God, presumably to solidify their adherence to Him. "They saw the God of Israel. Under his feet was like a paved work of sapphire stone, like the skies for clearness." This event is somewhat suspect in the context of the Torah, or at least exceptional, since the risk of the elders dying in the presence of God is recognized a few verses earlier. Later in Exodus, Moses asks to see God, and is shown His back. Both events are extraordinary in the Torah.

The Book of Numbers introduces Nazirites — people who believe they can come close to God independently of the sacrificial system. They are Israelites — presumably not priests nor Levites — who dedicate their lives to getting close to God. They face more restrictions in everyday activities than the ordinary Israelite. A Nazirite cannot cut his hair, eat or drink products from grapes, or tend to the dead. But, he can have sexual relations, which raises doubt about the sufficiency of these restrictions for his acceptability to God. An absence of sexual relations is required to be in God's presence, according to Exodus and Leviticus. The role of a Nazirite thus may be more important for the individual involved than for God. Perhaps, that is the main purpose of prayer, as well.

The idea of individuals coming close to God became prevalent in Judaism and other major religions well after the period covered in the Torah. Rising to God became a goal of mystics and theologians in the Middle Ages. And, it is perhaps a major motivator of religious people today. This is not the purpose of the Torah, however, which is grounded in the real world. Attempting to climb to a higher plane of consciousness is a form of escapism, which is probably enticing when times are bad but runs counter to the intent of the Torah. The Torah means to show how to bring God down to help.

Sacrifices and Asking for God's Help

Sacrifices are not made to ask for unconditional help, contrary to what might be considered part and parcel of a close relationship.

The votive sacrifice is not unconditional. It requires a commitment to do something in return for God's help. This quid pro quo underscores the emphasis on individual responsibility and self-help in the Torah. Later biblical writings understand the personal requirement attached to asking for God's help. In the Book of Samuel, for example, Hannah vows to dedicate her son to God if He grants her wish to give birth.

Genesis and Exodus contain precedence for asking God's help unconditionally. However, these examples are not generally applicable.

Abraham's servant asks God to grant him "success this day, and show kindness to my master Abraham" as he goes to find a wife for Isaac. The request appears to be met, since Rebekah enters the narrative right afterwards. God's responsiveness may be illusionary, though, since Abraham had told the servant God would send an angel before him to ensure a proper wife is found. The request may have had more to do with the servant's lack of knowledge about God than about being instrumental in finding Rebekah.

In Chapter 33 of Exodus, Moses asks God to lead the Israelites Himself, rather than to assign the task to an angel. God agrees to do so, but indicates His consent is highly unusual and given only because of the special relationship He has with Moses. God says, "I will do this thing also that you have spoken; for you have found favor in my sight and I know you by name." This example, as well as the times in Book of Numbers when Moses prays to God, doesn't imply God will respond to unconditional requests by those without a special relationship to Him.

What Kind of Acknowledgement From God?

The text does not mention whether Israelites receive explicit acknowledgement or pardon from God each time they sacrifice. The one time God responds is in Chapter 9, when after a series of sin, burnt and well-being offerings, He appears in the form of fire. His responsiveness in this inaugural ritual may be acknowledgement of a partnership with the Israelites rather than a result of specific requests by the Israelites for His help.

Significantly, well-being sacrifices, which reflect the possibility people are partly responsible for their good fortune, are included in this event. God is approached as a partner, rather than the sole provider of success and happiness whose services need to be requested through the priesthood. The idea of partnership with the entire Israelite community is emphasized in Chapter 9 two ways. Aaron, the priest, steps down from the altar after offering the sacrifices. He does not stand between the people and God but with them as God manifests Himself. And, the text says, "the Presence of the Lord appeared to all the people."

Sacrifices and Commitment

The various sacrifices share a common element in the splashing of blood around the altar. Many Jews today find this aspect of sacrifice gruesome. However, it has a basis in earlier parts of the Torah, from Zipporah's spreading of blood on the legs of Moses or his son to the application of ram's blood on the doorposts of Israelites ahead of the Tenth Plague. Zipporah's assertion that the action represents a "bridegroom of blood" between God and them establishes a rationale for the role of blood in sacrifices. Blood is meant to reaffirm a marital agreement with God. The Israelites re-commit at each sacrifice to follow God's commandments.

Implications for Current Practices

What can be inferred about current prayer practice from this analysis? Here are some thoughts.

The Baruchu and Sh'ma prayers have the appropriate majestic tone as we approach God at the start of services. Praising

God maps into the burnt offering. And, acknowledgement of God as Lord certainly is consistent with the relationship between God and Israelites developed at Mount Sinai.

The She'ma and V'ahavta that follow serve as a commitment to follow His commandments. Essentially, they are equivalent to the marital vows implied by spreading blood around the sacrificial alter. The She'ma reminds Jews that God is the ultimate authority. And, the V'ahavta instructs them to keep the commandments in view at all times and "be mindful of them," as well as to teach them to their children. Although missing in Reform services, a prayer regarding guilt or sinfulness perhaps should be included, as in Leviticus Chapter 9.

However, petitionary prayers, such as in the Amidah in the daily service or those made ad hoc, are questionable. Since they are not conditional requests and don't entail costs, they do not match votive sacrifices. And, they run counter to the theme in the Torah that Jews are not meant to disturb God.

Chapter 18 - *Keeping Kosher*

Keeping Kosher is viewed as anachronistic or meaningless by many modern Jews. But, by showing how it maps into rituals, it can be seen as a way to act like God in everyday life. Keeping Kosher restricts one's diet just as God limits the kinds of foods that can be sacrificed. Separation of meat and dairy, however, is mistakenly included in the Kosher laws.

F ollowing the detailed discussion of sacrifice and the episode with Aaron's sons, Leviticus shifts to an area that is neither ritual nor ethics. Beginning with the Kosher laws (requiring Kosher foods) in Chapter 11, it prescribes ways Israelites are to live their lives. This section enters abruptly, with God telling Moses to inform the Israelites what kinds of animals they are forbidden to eat. Since little justification is given, Jews have rationalized these restrictions through health, economic and other practical considerations. None is fully satisfactory. A more satisfying approach looks for theological reasons. Several such reasons can be inferred from statements made in Chapters 10 and 11, with the most persuasive found in Chapter 11.

A Rationale in Chapter 11

The best theological rationale can be inferred from the commandment to "Sanctify yourselves therefore, and be holy; for I am holy." Israelites need to incorporate aspects of ritual into their everyday lives — acting like God as dictated by the guideline approach.

In this light, the need to keep Kosher, take baths in the mikvah, etc., can be understood by seeing how they map into holy items in the Torah – the Tabernacle and Mount Sinai. That the chapter on Yom Kippur, which deals in part with the purification of the priests and Tabernacle, is in this section of Leviticus supports the idea that keeping Kosher and other actions represent a mapping of ritual requirements into everyday activities.

Kosher Laws map the restrictions on what parts of an animal can be sacrificed to God to food consumption. Just as God has a restricted diet, so should the Israelites. While practical explanations can be given why certain animals are restricted, theologically there is none. God determines the distinction between clean and unclean animals in the episode of Noah's Ark. The division is arbitrary from a human perspective.

Rationales in Chapter 10

Other potential rationales for the Kashrut Laws and similar restrictions can be found in Chapter 10. None is persuasive.

One rationale is that Israelites need to distinguish themselves from others because God is in their midst. It follows from Moses' explanation why God killed Aaron's sons in Chapter 10. Moses says, "This is what the Lord spoke of, saying, '"I will show Myself holy to those who come near me, And before all the people I will be glorified." Moses clearly refers to the priesthood with the terms "those who come near to Me." Priests demonstrate the holiness or special nature of God by strictly following the rituals. It could be inferred the Torah implicitly applies this "near-to-me" idea to the Israelites relative to other groups of people. The Israelites' actions need to be holy to demonstrate God's holiness.

How would the holiness of God be judged from the actions of the Israelites? Up to this point, the Israelites know to act ethically, sacrifice properly, honor the Sabbath, and not worship other gods. By following these commandments, the Israelites already show great respect for God. Further restrictions are presumably unnecessary to demonstrate God's holiness. Moses' explanation as a rationale for keeping Kosher and other restrictions is not without question.

Moses says God asserts His authority before all people through those near to Him. It reasonably means others will obey God's commandments if they see priests following rituals precisely. This assertion is fraught with question when applied to the general issue of why additional restrictions on the Israelites are needed. Non-Israelites would seem to appreciate God's power and authority by His actions, not by the Israelites' actions. As Jethro said, "Blessed be the Lord, who has delivered you out of the hand of the Egyptians and Pharaoh; now I know the Lord is greater than all gods." To impress others, God should make sure the Israelites succeed and prosper.

Moses' statement also could be interpreted to mean God's authority is demonstrated by the Israelites' submission to His commandments. In this case, there would be no difference from their earlier obedience to Pharaoh, and others could conclude that God chose the Israelites because they were used to being slaves. Imposing further restrictions on them would certainly not make God's authority tempting to other groups.

Separation of Meat and Dairy — Not Kosher?

Curiously, separation of meat from dairy is not part of the Kosher laws in Leviticus. The requirement is derived from Exodus, Chapter 23, verse 19, "The first of the first fruits of your ground you shall bring into the house of the Lord your God. You shall not boil a kid in its mother's milk." The second part of the verse was interpreted by the rabbis to mean meat and dairy products should not be eaten together. The commandment, however, does not map into the sacrificial system. Instead, it relates to a Canaanite practice of taking a goat and its kid to the fields and then sacrificing the kid in its mother's milk once the crops are planted, according to a scholar who visited the Torah Study Group. The commandment prevents Israelites from practicing a Canaanite ritual.

The commandment is coupled with a positive commandment to bring the initial output of the fields to the priests for sacrifice. The sacrifice is to be done after the crops ripen, as a well-being sacrifice. It is not done before the crops grow, unlike the Canaanites' practice. Sacrificing ahead of the growing season is inappropriate, since the Israelites might conclude responsibility for a successful crop resides with God and not with them. Sacrificing afterwards correctly attributes at least some of the successful planting to God, but does not diminish the Israelites' prior responsibility for the result.

This interpretation of the commandment implies Abraham did not transgress when he boiled meat in milk curds for the three strangers. His action had nothing to do with agricultural efforts and there is no restriction of this food preparation. How separation of meat and dairy became part of the Kosher laws is addressed in the chapter *Flexibility in the Commandments* (Chapter 35).

Chapter 19 - *Remaining Requirements For Holiness*

The remaining requirements are strange. But, they can be interpreted from God's perspective. Overall, incorporating spiritual behavior into everyday life is a way to act God-like.

T he remaining requirements for holiness apply to situations where there is bodily excretion or a growth on clothing or home. They mark a person, piece of clothing or home as unclean. While not stated explicitly, these visible outpourings may be symptoms of unclean elements rather than the unclean elements, themselves. In other words, the outpourings are not unholy, but reflect some internal corruption.

Is God Responsible for Unholiness?

Since sin and guilt offerings are part of the purification rituals in response to these outpourings, a person's guilt would appear to be involved. This is probably not intended, however. Uncleanness never results from a person's action. Instead, God, Himself, appears to introduce it. As God says in Chapter 14, "When you have come into the land of Canaan, which I give to you for a possession, and I put a spreading mildew in a house in the land of your possession, then he who owns the house shall come and tell the priest, saying, 'There seems to me to be some sort of plague in the house.'"

This idea of God's responsibility for an infliction sounds strange, but it mirrors the corruption brought into the Tabernacle by the presence of people. Just as people introduce uncleanness into the Tabernacle, suggested by the need for the annual purification of the altar specified in Exodus Chapter 30, God introduces uncleanness into human lives. By viewing these phenomena as God-induced, one can conclude their appearance is proof of God's presence in society. Ironically, the Torah may be positing that evidence of God is found not necessarily in exalted places but in the lowest elements, as well.

That unclean elements may look like a disease or pestilence

reflects the idea that God typically operates through natural elements, as in the Ten Plagues. This explains why priests have to evaluate whether the symptoms reflect an action by God or are just natural occurrences.

Childbirth and sexual discharges do not require priestly evaluation to determine they are unclean. The problem apparently is not a result of contamination introduced by God. Their uncleanness maps into another holy place in the Torah – God's presence on Mount Sinai. Moses interprets God's command that people "stay pure" to include a prohibition to "go near a woman" for three days ahead of His appearance on Mount Sinai. Sexual activity is associated with spiritual uncleanness. Since Exodus does not explain this association, the uncleanness of sexual activity and childbirth is as arbitrary as the selection of clean animals. The designations are God-determined and beyond human understanding. There is perhaps a sense with sexual activity and childbirth that human creation oversteps the boundary with God. However, this is not stated explicitly in the Torah. In any case, the uncleanness of childbirth and sexual discharges bracket the chapters on impure skin, clothing and houses, suggesting these natural aspects of life are different from the impurities introduced into Israelite society by God.

An Overall Rationale for Incorporating Ritual

For society to be compatible for God, the Israelites need to sanctify themselves, just as do the priests. There is concern they could inadvertently contaminate the Tabernacle. Chapter 15 says, "Thus you shall separate the children of Israel from their uncleanness, so they will not die in their uncleanness when they defile My tabernacle that is in their midst." According to this rationale, the nearness of God requires all Israelites to be pure, even if they are not directly involved in ritual.

The holiness of the Israelites — imparted to them by God's presence — requires that elements of ritual be incorporated into their everyday lives. In general, rituals are two-sided – God demands certain sacrifices and the Israelites supply them.

Since the Israelites are meant to act like God, incorporating ritual into everyday life means they do so from God's perspective. In other words, the aspects of ritual that are embodied in Kosher restrictions and purification represent God's side of the rituals -- the foods that He will accept as sacrifice, the spiritual corruption of the Tabernacle that needs be cleansed once a year, and the restrictions He requires on sexual activities. In line with God's requirements, the Israelites must ensure their food is special, rid themselves of any spiritual corruption introduced by God, and clean themselves after any sexual activity or discharge. They are to act as if they are copying God's requirements — acting as if they are holy.

Chapter 20 - *Is Ritual Necessary?*

In effect, the commandments for keeping kosher and using the mikvah ironically allow for Judaism to be practiced without a temple or priesthood. They also add another layer to rules requiring ethical behavior. Yom Kippur should not be seen as an excuse to behave improperly.

Since the Israelites embody elements of holiness through following the Kosher and spiritual purification commandments, do they need the organized rituals of the Tabernacle? Why can't they perform the religion's rituals outside the structure of the priesthood and Tabernacle? In Chapter 17, Leviticus answers in the negative by prohibiting well-being sacrifices or spilling of animal blood in the fields. Both are restricted to the Tabernacle. The chapter specifically prohibits well-being sacrifices presumably because this type of sacrifice applies to the situation being discussed – the killing of an animal for food. Generalization of the prohibition to the other types of sacrifice would seem justifiable, since they are less likely to be relevant than the well-being sacrifice in practical situations and thus certainly more suitable for being done in the Tabernacle.

Nevertheless, by requiring keeping Kosher and the purification activities, the Torah establishes the means to ensure the ritualistic part of the religion survives the destruction of the Tabernacle or Temple. Since the laws shift the essence of holiness from the Temple-based rituals to everyday life, they preserve this key aspect of the religion independently of a building, structure or priesthood. This does not mean Israelites are holy per se, as is often concluded, but that their actions mimic the holiness requirements of God's dwelling place. In so doing, the Israelites can maintain a connection to God without the need for an institutional framework.

This perspective leads to another great irony. By denying the need for keeping Kosher and purification activities, Reform

Judaism places greater dependency on ritual than does Orthodoxy in establishing a relationship with God.

Implications for Current Practices

Is it justifiable for the spiritually related rules to be dropped or modified by modern Jews? In general, the answer seems to be no. The rules stem from God's side of the rituals – they reflect what He wants. Since people cannot second-guess His reasoning, there is no room to modify the requirements. For example, Kashrut restrictions have no logical basis and have to be followed without question. Trying to justify the dropping of Kashrut because all food in the US is now produced in a healthy manner misses the point. The laws have nothing to do with health.

Is simply saying a prayer before meals an acceptable substitute for keeping Kosher? The answer is no. Prayer maps into the Israelite side of ritual and is inconsistent with the idea that keeeping Kosher maps into God's side. Meal prayers are often equivalent to well-being sacrifices, thanking God for the bountifulness of food or the health of the family. Keeping Kosher does not represent well-being sacrifices, so a prayer at mealtime would not seem to be a good substitute.

It is more difficult to see how the purification of spiritual corruption associated with skin disease and other excretions can be accomplished in the absence of priests. Perhaps all that is needed is for the affected person to stay away from prayer services, since, if there is spiritual corruption, it is offensive to God.

The Practical Reason for Kashrut and Other Restrictions

The lack of practical rationale is one factor making Kosher requirements and the other unusual commandments so perplexing or unacceptable to modern Jews. They see no reason to act in ways separating Jews from gentiles. However, there may be an unstated rationale underlying all the restrictions, a rationale that addresses a concern that has been debated for 2000 years – are ethics enough to guarantee a good society?

Christians have argued in favor of this proposition, implying that keeping Kosher and other restrictions are unnecessary. The Torah's answer is that both ethics and spiritual purity are needed to ensure a good society. Each gets equal weight within the Torah, as both ethics and spiritual purity are implied by the requirement to act like God and both are spelled out.

Although spiritual purity is not well defined, its sense from the Torah is clear -- that which is needed for a person to act like God or to be suitable in God's presence. Keeeping Kosher and the purification rituals remind Jews they need to act in ways that mimic God or would not offend Him. Whereas ethics requires Jews to treat others with respect, spiritual purity requires their actions be compatible with a close relationship with God. With two sets of criteria to satisfy, Jews would be doubly sure to act appropriately in their everyday lives. The Torah builds multiple fences around the Israelites to ensure a good society, just as one is supposed to build fences around the Torah.

Yom Kippur

For most modern Jews, expiation and spiritual cleaning is a once-a-year event – fasting and praying on Yom Kippur. This holiday is specified in Leviticus Chapter 16 and can be mapped into the annual purification of the altar in the Tabernacle, specified in Exodus Chapter 30. Both remove spiritual impurities.

A cynical Jew might think this annual holiday clears all the sins of the prior year, eliminating the need to keep the commandments. This view cannot be summarily dismissed, given the place in Leviticus where the holiday is established. The chapter on Yom Kippur follows the chapters delineating the rules on sustaining a spiritually pure society. Being last raises the question whether there are unspecified impurities not addressed in the earlier chapters or whether the Israelites will fail to follow all the rules regarding spiritual purity — and thus a catch-all final atonement is allowed for each year. In either case, one wonders whether God can abide a society that is only partly spiritually pure?

These questions do not arise if the chapter on Yom Kippur is misplaced, with the last paragraph, specifying it as an "everlasting statute," tacked on subsequently. Since the chapter begins with God speaking to Moses "after the death of the two sons of Aaron, when they drew near before the Lord, and died," the chapter logically belongs after that episode (Chapter 10) and just before the laws on keeping Kosher, etc. Then, the chapter serves to describe a one-time spiritual cleaning of the Israelite society after this horrendous action by Aaron's sons. And, the remaining chapters specify rules that will maintain the cleanness forever. In this order, the chapter would not undermine the necessity of following these rules throughout the year. Yom Kippur still may make sense as a perennial holiday, addressing in prayer inadvertent sins done during the year.

Chapter 21 - *Sexual Relationships*

New rationales are behind sexually related prohibitions. Under-standing the rationales provides a biblically justifiable acceptance of homosexuality.

A fter Leviticus shows the Israelites how to embody spir-itual purity in their lives, it turns to their personal behavior in Chapter 18, addressing for the most part sexual relationships. Sexual relations with family members are pro-hibited. In addition, marriage and sex with a woman to spite her sister, sex with a woman during her period of unclean-ness, homosexuality, sex with animals, and child sacrifice are banned. Except for the last, these restrictions do not fall under the category of spiritual purity or ethics — they cannot be mapped into holy parts of the Torah.

The Torah recognizes it has moved into a new area. It says these prohibitions are meant to prevent the Israelites from copying "the doings of the land of Egypt in which you lived ... and the doings of the land of Canaan where I bring you." The practices offend God, who views them as "abominations." The abominations were done by "men of the land who were before you, and the land is defiled." So, make sure not to practice them so "the land does not vomit you out, as it vomited out the na-tion that was before you." The rationale is new.

How General Are the Prohibitions?

The abhorrence of these activities applies to all people, not just Israelites. Their practice caused non-Israelites, particu-larly Canaanites, to be expelled from their lands. The omission of the commandment to be holy in this chapter indicates the prohibitions are meant for all people, not just Israelites. The punishments spelled out in Chapter 20, however, apply only to Israelites, as indicated by the inclusion of the commandment to be holy.

What's Wrong With These Activities?

To understand God's distaste for these activities requires mapping them against Noahide laws, applicable to all peoples. Some of the proscribed activities violate God's commandment to "be fruitful and multiply." Child sacrifice destroys human creation while homosexuality and bestiality leave out procreation. The inability to procreate during a woman's period of uncleanness is similarly problematic. Perhaps God views these proscribed activities as misuses of humankind's power of creation?

The relevance of this interpretation to the incest prohibitions is not clear, since incest does not stop procreation. Instead, a key to their understanding might be found in the first case of nakedness in the Torah – Adam and Eve after they eat an apple from the Tree of Knowledge. They make loincloths for themselves when their eyes "were opened." A typical interpretation is they learn to be modest about sex. Alternatively, Adam and Eve realize nakedness is not what God wants. A naked person does not have a fear of God, the latter defined as viewing God with awe and respect. The person wrongly puts himself equal to God. Adam responds to God, "I heard Your voice in the garden, and I was afraid, because I was naked; and I hid myself." Thus, intentionally uncovering the nakedness of close family members could imply the denial of a fear of God. A fear of God is required of all people, not just Israelites, as shown in the episode of the Pharaoh and the Plagues.

The various cases of incest prohibited in the chapter generalize the idea of a person exposing his own nakedness. The first prohibition is not to "approach close relatives to uncover their nakedness." They apparently are equivalent to the person, himself, from the Torah's perspective.

This equivalence perhaps explains why the Torah does not prohibit exposing the nakedness of people not closely related. The less related a person, the less meaningful is nakedness in terms of showing disrespect for God. Indeed, the gradations of punishments in Chapter 20 show the severity softening as the relationship moves away from the immediate family. For example, death is the penalty for uncovering the nakedness of one's father's wife, one's daughter-in-law or marrying a woman and her mother. The penalty downshifts to excommunication for marrying one's sister, and downshifts further to childlessness for uncovering the nakedness of one's uncle's wife.

Ironically, Noah's own behavior appears to conflict with the prohibition. After getting drunk on wine from a vineyard he planted subsequent to the Flood, Noah becomes naked in his tent. He may have felt the creation of the vineyard put him on par with God -- he created life after the Flood, as did God at the Beginning. This sense of god-like behavior is a near-parallel to Utnapishtim becoming immortal (god-like) after the flood in the Gilgamesh story. But, unlike Utnapishtim, Noah needs to be drunk to lose his fear of God. His realization of the sin perhaps explains why he lashes out at his son, Ham, who sees Noah naked.

Sex Prohibitions and the Modern Jew

Most modern Jews have little difficulty accepting the prohibitions against sexual relationships with relatives and others viewed as close by the Torah, perhaps because the Torah's proscriptions are so well ingrained. The big controversy centers on homosexuality. Most people take its prohibition at face value and say homosexuality violates the Torah. However, since the motivation appears to be the absence of procreation, homosexuality could be considered acceptable from the Torah's perspective if childbirth is involved. With artificial insemination and surrogate parenting now available, homosexuality can meet this requirement. Indeed, it may not be a large step in reasoning to say child rearing through adoption falls under the wider concept of population growth. Homosexual relationships could be viewed to be compatible with the Torah if these routes are pursued.

Love your neighbor and stranger in your midst is introduced, as is the concept of separateness.

F rom sexual prohibitions, Leviticus jumps into a variety of commandments pertaining to sacrifice, idol worship and ethics in Chapter 19. The chapter begins by repeating some of the commandments found in Exodus, but throws them together without much order. They apparently need to be acknowledged as requirements for society to be compatible for God, but not much has to be said since they were addressed earlier.

Love

The recitation of these commandments, however, suddenly introduces a new concept -- that of love. In verse 18, the Israelites are admonished to "love your neighbor as yourself." And, in verse 34, they are to love a resident stranger as yourself, "for you were sojourners in the land of Egypt."

These admonishments differ from the concept of respect that implicitly forms the basis for interpersonal relations in the guideline approach. According to this approach, if everyone acts like God, each person has to treat another with the respect shown in approaching God. Instead of modeling interpersonal relations on the relationship between the Israelites and God, the notion of love models them on how a person relates to himself. In this way, it downshifts the rationale behind how one treats another -- one's self is not as ideal a model as God. Basing interpersonal relations on one's self view, though, is probably appropriate for a code-based approach to the religion. Since Israelites are not required to act like God, there is little justification to interpret interpersonal relations according to how one typically relates to Him. And, asserting the admonishment without justification is consistent with the code approach.

There are problems, however, with the idea of love. It conceivably covers more than the respect underlying the guideline approach. Loving a neighbor or stranger as one's self would seem to entail an equality the Torah does not insist upon elsewhere. Both Exodus and Numbers accept social and economic inequalities as natural. Another problem is that a person's view of himself could change along with his social or economic position. The commandment to treat another as oneself imparts flexibility in Jewish ethics that may not have been intended. Given the abrupt introduction of the "love" concept, it conceivably was inserted by the writers of Deuteronomy to provide justification for their introduction of the concept of love between the Israelites and God.

Separation

Chapter 19 also pulls together a diverse collection of commandments, the most curious being the prohibition of mating cattle with other kinds of animal, of sowing two different seeds in a field, and not mixing two kinds of material. These prohibitions emphasize God's desire for the Israelites to be separate from other groups, according to the common interpretation. The latter finds support at the end of Chapter 20, when God says, "I, the Lord, am holy, and have set you apart from the peoples, that you should be mine."

This interpretation has problems, however. If separation is the goal, why are strangers permitted in the midst of the Israelite society and to be treated with love? Earlier parts of the Torah do not insist on separation. For example, Verse 8 Chapter 36 of Exodus says the Tabernacle was made of ten strips of cloth "made of fine twined linen" and wool. In Genesis 30-31, Jacob believes God is responsible for giving him the idea of crossbreeding black and white sheep to get streaked ones.

Perhaps a better reason is to underscore the separation of Israelites from the religious practices of others. This idea is supported by the other prohibitions in Chapter 19, aimed against pagan rituals such as turning to ghosts, cutting facial hair, and making gashes or marks on a person's body.

Chapter 23 - *Priestly And Religious Requirements*

Requirements to be a priest raise a curious issue with regard to prayers. The specification of holidays is potentially more significant than one might think. The Torah comes down hard on blasphemy.

L eviticus turns its attention to religious practices at this point, focusing on the requisites of priesthood, holidays and other features of the non-secular side of life.

Priestly Requirements

Chapter 21 lays out rules for priests. A priest is permitted to approach the dead bodies of his immediate family, but not others. Perhaps the former are viewed theologically as equivalent to his own, just as uncovering their nakedness while alive is akin to uncovering his own. So, a priest does not contaminate himself by approaching them.

More troubling to a modern reader is the requirement in Chapter 21 for a priest to be without physical deformity. It fits with the needed perfection of sacrificial food. All people and items involved in approaching God must be without blemish. What does this mean for individual prayer? Are prayers by deformed people not acceptable? Chapter 22 appears to provide an answer by reiterating that ordinary Israelites only need to be spiritually pure to offer sacrifices. They do not need to be physically perfect to participate in the priestly system of sacrifice. Nevertheless, with Jews now directly addressing God, rather than through priests, a question lingers whether they need to be physically perfect for their prayers to reach God.

Holidays

The specification of holidays in Chapter 23 has several important messages for modern Judaism. Restricting holidays to those specified by God presumably is meant to prevent pagan holidays from being introduced into the religion. The seemingly redundant phrase "and you shall proclaim them sacred days" may commit the Israelites to this list of holidays. They are not to regard any other day as sacred. The restriction confirms that Aaron made a mistake in declaring a holiday during the Golden Calf episode.

In modern times, creating holidays, even if not pagan, could shift the focus of the religion away from the Torah's message. The recent holidays commemorating the Holocaust and celebrating the creation of the State of Israel demonstrate the problem. For many Jews, the validity of the religion is based on these two events rather than the commandments and laws. These holidays legitimize this focus, altering the religion.

A holiday schedule gets people to focus on God at regular, important points of time. It is expanded in Chapter 24 to require a perpetual light in the Tent of Meeting – a daily focus – and a sacrifice of bread each Sabbath – a weekly focus. Most holidays are scheduled at harvest time to thank God, not at planting time to ask His help in growing a crop. Jews are at least partly responsible for achieving a goal. Praying at planting time could engender too much reliance on Him. God's possible role in the success of an enterprise should be recognized after the fact.

Blasphemy

Familiarity with God goes only so far, as shown by the story of the half-Israelite blasphemer. His punishment by stoning for pronouncing "the name Lord in blasphemy" emphasizes the seriousness of treating God with insufficient respect, even by a part-Israelite. The death penalty for blasphemy is clearly the strongest punishment for breaking the Third Commandment, which only says God will not forgive this transgression. The Torah recognizes, though, that severe forms of punishment should not be abused. The story is followed by a restatement of an eye-for-eye, tooth-for-tooth retribution approach to murder. Killing should not be arbitrary.

Chapter 24 - **God's Partner And Property**

Jews should view themselves as God's partners and property. Compassion for the poor and a new basis for ethics follow from these relationships.

T he holidays, particularly the offering of a well-being sacrifice at harvest time, acknowledge a partnership between Israelites and God. A successful harvest is partly a result of God's help as well as people's efforts.

The idea of partnership not only justifies offering some of the harvest directly to God, but also indirectly by giving some to the needy. It as if God redirected a portion of his due to the poor. The latter is to be effected by leaving the grain at the edges of the field or that had fallen on the field.

The requirement to leave a portion of the crop for the poor mirrors the requirement to bring the first fruits of the harvest to the priests. Their symmetrical relationship is elegant proof of the Prophets' admonition that ritual without care for the poor is unacceptable to God. Both are sacrifices from the farmer's perspective. And, Leviticus recognizes the close connection between the two. The commandment to leave grain for the poor follows a restatement of rules of sacrifice.

The implications of the partnership between Jews and God are carried further in Chapter 25. Although surrounded by dubious economic concepts – some discouraging lending and risk taking while others leaving out the role of interest rates in valuing property -- God's ownership of the land is stated explicitly. "The land shall not be sold in perpetuity; for the land is Mine: for you are strangers and sojourners with me." As a result, they have to maintain the land's productivity by resting it every seventh and fiftieth year. Generally, they are to "grant a redemption for the land" that they possess. This environmental requirement would seem to apply to all people, who presumably also use God's land.

Israelites as God's Property

Chapter 25 extends the concept of God's ownership to the Israelites, themselves. They are God's property inasmuch as He freed them from Egypt. This justification may explain why the instructions on treating slaves do not apply to non-Israelites – they are not His property since He did not free them from Egypt.

Because the Israelites are God's property, how they treat one another has obligations. They have to treat each other with the care and respect ordinarily expected toward the property of one's host. They cannot cheat their neighbors in the purchase or sale of land. They also are required to redeem the land of their "brother" who is forced to sell land for financial reasons. Moreover, they cannot take advantage of an unfortunate Israelite's situation by exacting undue interest if he asks for a loan or by treating him badly if he is indentured. Generally, they do not have unrestricted control of each other. One Israelite cannot "rule with vigor over" another. In addition, if a non-Israelite obtains an Israelite as a slave, the latter has the right to be redeemed or bought out of his enslavement. If his family cannot manage to do so, he nevertheless becomes free during the jubilee year. Ultimately, the Israelites are God's servants, not anyone else's.

The implications of being God's property serve as a final way to ensure proper behavior among Israelites. Proper behavior should not only entail the ethics required by the Ten Commandments and Laws received at Mount Sinai, not only the spiritual purity of acting like God or believing to be in His presence, but also the obligations from dealing with God's property.

Numero Uno In The Book Of Numbers

The Book of Numbers resumes the story of the Israelite exodus from Egypt. In addition to retelling events, it constructs a hierarchical social structure and then shows how each level makes mistakes. The Book concludes that all Israelites need to adhere to the commandments to create a society compatible for God.

Chapter 25 - *What's Going On?*

The Book of Numbers is odd. After Leviticus specifies the requirements for having God in the Israelites' midst, Numbers might be expected to relate their successes along the path to the Promised Land. Instead, the Book talks of the Israelites' discontent and disobedience of the covenant. It emphasizes their failure to respect the leadership of Moses and of God, Himself. Such behavior is deemed unacceptable, and there is an absence of tolerance for challenging God or His appointed leaders. A wrathful God kills the perpetrators, not meting out the even-handed justice seen in many of the laws. Nevertheless, after the Israelites understand what is required of them, they reach Canaan.

What's going on? The Book of Numbers examines God's attempt to construct a social hierarchy that would ensure the Israelites' adherence to the covenant. Society's leaders essentially would be God's agents. This social structure, however, fails to elicit acceptable behavior by the leaders or the people. At the end, all the Israelites need to commit to following the commandments, independently of the social hierarchy, for God to help them achieve their goals.

The construction and subsequent failure of the hierarchical structure to ensure an acceptable society are similar to the evolution of the "reward" approach in the Book of Genesis. Both Books can be viewed as demonstrating the inadequacy of an approach to obtain correct behavior by the Israelites.

The first ten chapters of Numbers develop an Israelite hierarchy in which all acknowledge God as Number One. In so doing, they surprisingly establish a separation of church and state. In grand irony, Chapters 11 to 21 show social structure, by itself, does not necessarily result in correct behavior. Both the secular and non-secular leadership make mistakes. The Israelites meet success only when they all agree to act in ways consistent with God's commandments and to acknowledge their sins when they do not. Proper action, nonetheless, does not mean all Israelites must conform to society's norms. The last part of the Book discusses the possibility for diversity within the Israelite society.

With responsibility for acting correctly, people can be viewed as being, along with God, the Number One to ensure the success of society. There is truly to be a partnership between God and the Israelites.

Chapter 26 - *Building A Social Hierarchy*

Secular and non-secular social structures are established, presumably to keep the Israelites on a covenantally consistent path.

T he importance of social leadership in ensuring adherence to the covenant was seen earlier in the Golden Calf episode, when the absence of Moses triggers a demand for another god – "When the people saw that Moses delayed coming down from the mountain, the people gathered themselves together to Aaron, and said to him, "Come, make us gods, which shall go before us; for as for this Moses, the man who brought us up out of the land of Egypt, we don't know what has become of him." Perhaps having seen people turn away from Him when there was a breakdown of social hierarchy, God not only specifies the social structure in Numbers but threatens extreme penalties for those who defy it.

The Book begins by indicating the lines of command in the Israelite community. God is supreme, as He dictates how to construct the social leadership. He speaks to Moses, showing Moses to be the main person under Him. And, with Aaron instructed to join Moses in writing down the census, he is authorized to be Moses' right-hand man.

Numbers downplays the priesthood as the ultimate authority in running society. Throughout the early chapters, God's instructs Moses in all but one case. Aaron receives God's words only when a clan of the Levites, who serve the priests, is involved. Even in Chapter 5 where the rules concerning punishment for transgressions are given, God informs Moses, not Aaron, on the role of priests. Priests are to be agents in the punishment process, not accusers. The Book carefully restricts the roles of priests and the Levites in Israelite society.

Secular Side

Beginning with the secular side of society, God names a man from each tribe to assist Moses. Each is to be the head of his tribe. Is God choosing new leaders or is He naming already established chiefs? Do the selections make them the tribal heads —divine determination— or were they the heads beforehand— tradition?

God's specification of the Israelites leaders by name argues for divine determination. A naming would be unnecessary were God choosing the established leadership — everyone should know them. Chapter 1 Verse 17 emphasizes those chosen are "mentioned by name." God says they are the elected "of the congregation, the princes of the tribes of their fathers; the heads of Israel." His selection makes them the tribal leaders. On balance, the entire tribal leadership is chosen by God and not by traditional processes. Later on, the Book hints that having God choose tribal leaders is problematic for getting the Israelites to adhere to the covenant.

Nonetheless, there is a reason, implicit in the text, why God determines the secular leadership of the Israelites at this point. Being God-chosen gives the Israelite secular leaders as much legitimacy as priests. It undercuts any thought of superiority that might be held by the priesthood, which also is chosen by God.

Non-Secular Side

Chapter One ends by turning to the non-secular and specifying the role of the Levites in Israelite society. The Levites are to be "responsible for the Tabernacle," including its dismantling and reassembling during the Israelites' wanderings. They are to "encamp around the Tabernacle" so that "wrath may not strike the Israelite community." God's wrath is warned of, as well, in prohibiting a "stranger" from helping the Levites dismantle or set up the Tabernacle. Any stranger who does so "shall be put to death."

Prohibiting the Israelites from coming close to the Tabernacle can be interpreted a couple of ways theologically. It fits with the desired separation between God and the Israelites. And, it serves to prevent the Israelites from using the objects of the Tabernacle as idols. For example, if they were permitted to approach the Tabernacle, Israelites could borrow objects from the Tabernacle and treat them as house idols. The Torah hints at this concern by requiring an inventory of the Tabernacle's items, presumably to ensure none goes missing. The Merarites, a Levite clan, are to keep a list of the objects they carry.

Chapters Three and Four specify the role of the Levites in more detail, indicating the part of the Tabernacle for which each clan of Levites is responsible and where each clan is to encamp. The chapters go out of their way to protect the Levites from other Israelites, perhaps because the latter might view them as social parasites who do not contribute to the economic welfare of society. The Levites are "given" to Aaron and his sons. And, God consecrates them in place of the first-born, specifying a stipend for them.

On the flip side, the Levites are not to enforce ritual among the Israelites. This prohibition is mentioned specifically regarding priests' actions, when the Torah says that Aaron and his sons – with no mention of the Levites -- are responsible for adhering to their priestly duties. More generally, the Levites are not agents of the priests to ensure adherence to the covenant by other Israelites. In light of their role as such during the Golden Calf episode, they conceivably could be the equivalent of the Inquisition forces in Spain, going after heretics. Instead, the Torah isolates them from the rest of the Israelite society. Enforcement of the covenant does not entail setting one tribe against the others.

God as Supreme

The first part of Numbers ends in Chapters 7 to 10 in ways that emphasize the supremacy of God. Chapter 7 focuses on the secular side, while Chapter 8 centers on the priesthood and Levites. They show both sides to be subservient to God.

Chapter 7 begins with Moses consecrating the Tabernacle. The tribal chiefs then bring offerings to the newly established Tabernacle, thereby acknowledging God as the supreme ruler. The Torah says the chiefs are those individuals who were chosen earlier to do the census, hinting once again that God had picked them for their posts. God tells Moses to accept the offerings and distribute them to the Levites. This instruction from God leaves no suggestion that the secular leadership is subservient to the priesthood, which might have been implied if priests had issued those orders or if the chiefs gave the offerings directly to the priests.

The tribal leaders are equally important. God instructs Moses to give each chief a day to present his offering. Also, they bring the same items despite the various sizes of the tribes. This "regressive" approach to offerings contrasts with the care taken in Leviticus to ensure sacrifices are tied to "ability to pay." The significance may lie in the coming chapter when all the chiefs are held responsible for the decision not to invade Canaan – the decision cannot be laid on one chief for being more powerful than the rest.

Theologically, independent decision-making in the performance of some religious activities – although not recurrent rituals -- seems to be acceptable. The chiefs, not God, appear to specify the amount and composition of the offerings, in contrast to the exactness of what to sacrifice in Leviticus.

Chapter 8 turns to the priesthood and Levites, indicating how little discretion, if any, they have in relations with God. Once again, it begins with Moses in a position above the non-secular side of the Israelite society. God tells him to instruct Aaron about the lighting of the lamps, reiterating in this one small example the message from Exodus and Leviticus that ritual activities must be performed exactly as specified by God. Then, God tells Moses how to consecrate the Levites so they are "Mine," and informs him about their duties. In so doing, God restates His control over this group. God (and Moses) is seen to be supreme on the non-secular as well as secular side of Israelite society.

God reiterates that the Levites are to be consecrated, not the first-born Israelites. This change makes sense in the context of Numbers, as it more completely splits the secular from the non-secular in Israelite society. Now, there would be no question whether the first-born of any tribe should feel a special relationship to God or things holy. That relationship is reserved for the priests and Levites.

Chapters 9 and 10 talk of three ways to remind the Israelites that God is the Lord. Most interestingly, Chapter 9 repeats the commandment to observe Passover, lending credence to the analysis in *Understanding the Haggadah* (Chapter 14) that the holiday's purpose is to reaffirm the obligation of Jews to follow God's commandments. The Israelites' ready acceptance of this obligation is implied by the angst of some men who were unclean "because of the dead body of a man" and complained, "why are we kept back, that we may not offer the offering of the Lord in its appointed season among the children of Israel?" Their complaint suggests all Israelites felt the importance of partaking in this holiday. And, indeed, God provides an alternative time and way in which they can participate.

The chapter also indicates that a cloud above the Tabernacle would be a direct sign of God's presence. Chapter 10, in the same vein, instructs that blasts from two silver trumpets, blown by priests, would be a reminder to God. When at war, short blasts would enable the Israelites to "be remembered before the Lord your God, and you shall be saved from your enemies." All these appeals to the senses demonstrate people's desire for proof of God. This desire returns when the Israelites reach the Promised Land. There, the prophets rely on magic and extraordinary visions to persuade people to adhere to God.

Thus, the first part of Numbers concludes with an affirmation that God is Number One. Nevertheless, the Book fashions the Israelite leadership as the means to encourage adherence to the covenant. It turns out, however, the leadership — both secular and nonsecular — fail in this effort.

The social hierarchy fails to prevent the people or leaders from digressing from the desired path.

W ith the social hierarchy established, the Book of Numbers relates the Israelites' journey to the Promised Land. One would think these travels should be easy and successful, as God is in their midst. Moreover, the Israelites should be expected to fear God and be mindful of His commandments, with the secular and nonsecular leadership keeping them on the right path. However, just the opposite occurs. People are beset by deprivations of food and water. The priesthood and Levites rebel against Moses. And, the secular leaders lack faith in God. All the parts of the social hierarchy, so carefully constructed in the first few chapters of Numbers, fail to measure up.

Improper Behavior: People Complaining

The Israelites soon complain about lack of food. They blame God rather than think of solving the problem, themselves. And, perhaps it is Moses' fault they complain. After his father-in-law refuses to travel with them, Moses emphasizes the power of God when the Israelites break camp, saying, "Rise up, Lord God, and let your enemies be scattered; and let those who hate you flee before you!" and when they stop, saying Return, O Lord, to the ten thousands of the thousands of Israel." It would seem reasonable for the Israelites to expect such a powerful God to provide them with food, and not just any food but meat.

God initially reacts to the Israelites' complaint by starting a fire around the "uttermost part of the camp." This tentative punishment frightens the Israelites, but does not shock them into attempting to solve their own problem. Instead, they "cried to Moses," looking to the top leadership for a solution. Moses assuages God's anger through prayer, and the fire stops. However, prayer provides only a temporary solution. It does not result in better food.

Complaining then spreads throughout the Israelite camp. It begins with the "mixed multitude among them" interpreted by some to be the non-Israelite contingent of the group that left Egypt. It then widens to include the Israelites, who cry, "Who shall give us meat to eat," remembering fondly the fish they had eaten for free in Egypt. The free fish may have been the rations given to them as slaves. They long for their past lives as slaves without responsibility. For them, slavery is preferable to freedom with its concomitant need to take on responsibility. Finally, Moses, himself, complains to God, "Why have you ... laid the burden of all this people on me?" Moses understands that the people act like infants, who cannot care for themselves.

A Solution

The Israelites do not appear to think the lack of food is for them to solve. The Torah shows they cannot conceive of working together to address their problems. "Moses heard the people weeping throughout their families, every man at the door of his tent," after they are disappointed with God's provision of manna, No communal action is forthcoming.

The solution to the problem is in two parts — everyone needs to take responsibility and those creating social discord need to be eliminated.

The Torah recognizes that responsibility for solving society's problems does not reside just at the top, *i.e.*, with God and Moses, but more broadly within society, itself. God responds to Moses' pleas by having seventy of the Israelite elders obtain "the spirit that is on" Moses, in order for them "to share the burden of the people" with him. God says, "Gather to me seventy men of the elders of Israel, whom you know to be the elders of the people and officers over them; and bring them to the tent of meeting that they may stand there with you." By specifying those "whom you know are elders," He, in effect, admits His earlier selection of secular leadership did not work. Leadership has to be rooted in society. Moses goes further, suggesting everyone in society needs to take responsibility. He says, "Would that all the Lord's people were prophets, that the Lord would put His spirit upon them!"

The punishment for blaming God needs to be more than tentative -- the troublemakers must be eliminated. God inflicts a plague on the complaining people, a harsh punishment to indicate the unacceptability of blaming God for one's troubles. It acknowledges that ringleaders of discontent need to be destroyed or they will contaminate the entire society.

Improper Behavior: Rebellion Within the Leadership

In the next episode, Aaron and Miriam fail to understand the social structure. They feel equal to Moses, having heard God's words directly. They say, "Has the Lord indeed spoken only with Moses? Hasn't He spoken also with us?" They believe they can criticize Moses for marrying a Cushite woman. God sets them straight, stating his special relationship with Moses, "I speak mouth to mouth, even manifestly, and not in dark speeches; and the form of the Lord shall he see." And, He punishes Miriam with a case of scales.

Improper Behavior: Decision-Making Contrary to God's Plans

The next episode gets the secular leadership into trouble. God tells Moses to send a chieftain of each tribe "to spy out the land of Canaan, which I give to the children of Israel." Unfortunately, all but two of the scouts return afraid of the Canaanites and recommend against entering the land. This famous story is traditionally interpreted to show a lack of faith in God. Indeed, God complains in frustration, "How long will this people despise Me and how long will they not believe in Me, for all the signs which I have worked among them?"

Nevertheless, there may be another message. Strikingly, the Israelite chieftains make their own decisions regarding how to proceed with the destiny of the group. They feel the Israelites are unequipped to fight the Canaanites. This decision is inconsistent with God's instructions. The message of the episode, then, may be that while the Israelites are to be involved in shaping their future, the chosen path cannot run counter to God's plans (or commandments). While the Israelites may choose from a wide array of possible paths consistent with God's plans, they cannot select a program that does not belong to this array.

The subsequent chapter, Chapter 15, provides support for this interpretation by reiterating how to ensure the Israelites abide by God's wishes. It first discusses rituals related to acknowledging God's supremacy that must be conducted when in Canaan. These include a reiteration of sacrifices and a newly established need to leave the first baked product for God – "Of the first of your dough you shall give to the Lord, an offering throughout your generations." Then, it indicates how to deal with Israelites who break a commandment. Finally, the chapter ends with an instruction for the Israelites to make "fringes in the borders of their garments ... that you may look on it, and remember all the commandments of the Lord and do them." The Israelites are not to forget the commandments and are to take them into account at all times. Decision-making is to be constrained by the requirement that it be consistent with God's commandments.

Improper Behavior: Rebellion by the Levites

The Levites' turn is next, when Korah and the Reubenites -- Datham, Abiram and On -- rebel against Moses and Aaron. They argue that Moses and Aaron have assumed too much authority. All the Israelites should be considered holy because God is in their midst. They say to Moses and Aaron, "You take too much on you, seeing all the congregation are holy, every one of them, and the Lord is among them: why then do you lift yourselves up above the assembly of the Lord?"

Moses understands this complaint as an attack on God, since God, Himself, had established the social hierarchy. Moses' immediate response is to fall "on his face," as if to apologize to God for their misbehavior. He seems to realize the rebels risk bringing God's wrath against the entire Israelite people. Moses' answer to them is to wait for God's response, implicitly saying the rebels' complaint is against God not him. God, of course, rejects Korah's argument. He destroys the rebels and their families, as "the earth opened its mouth and swallowed them up with their households."

Is God's Wrath a Solution?

Some rabbis are disturbed by the killing of the ringleaders' families, whom they feel are innocent. The wider killing may aim to prevent the potential for revenge to persist across generations. This rationale does not hold, however, as Korah's sons survived. Moses, himself, is concerned the rebels' sins could entail destruction of the whole society. He asks God in Chapter 16 verse 22, "shall one man sin and you will be angry with all the congregation?" God's answer is No, as He instructs Moses to tell the Israelites to "get away from the tents of Korah, Dothan, and Abiram."

Nevertheless, His destruction of almost all the rebels' families leads to a general revolt by the people who apparently see the events involving the deaths of innocents. They complain to Moses and Aaron "You have killed the Lord's people." God responds to their blaming secular leadership in a blunt way, telling Moses and Aaron to "get away from among this congregation that I may consume them in a moment." He sends a plague that kills many and stops only when Aaron stands between "the dead and the living and the plague was stayed."

The Israelites' concern for God's indiscriminate wrath again surfaces after God instructs Moses to "put back the rod of Aaron before the Tent, to be kept for a token against the children of rebellion; that you may make an end of their murmurings against Me, that they not die." The people realize they risk death by approaching the Tabernacle; God might be trying to entrap them by placing the "lesson" so close to it. The Israelites say to Moses, "Everyone who comes near, who comes near to the tent of the Lord, dies: shall we perish all of us?" Indeed, they may have cause for concern, as everyone is punished when serpents are let loose on the people after they complain again about inadequate food.

God, however, does not aim to kill everyone for divergence from ritual. God restricts responsibility for proper ritual and relationship with the Tabernacle to the priesthood. He tells Aaron, "You and your sons and your fathers' house with you shall bear the iniquity of the sanctuary; and you and your sons with you shall bear the iniquity of your priesthood." God restricts the death penalty to only those non-Levites who venture into the sanctuary. The punishment is not to be communal.

The episode ends with God restating the relationship between the Levites and priests, presumably so they behave properly and not challenge the social order. He specifies many of the rituals more precisely than in Leviticus. Also, God gives the priests the right to partake in the sacrificial offerings and assigns all of the tithes to the Levites. In a sense, God sweetens the deal for the priests and Levites, co-opting them into the social hierarchy.

Improper Behavior: Not Adequately Acknowledging God

Finally, in Chapter 20, Moses erroneously disregards God's role in obtaining water from a rock. Although Moses takes "the rod from before the Lord, as He commanded him," he does not cite God's role in having the rock yield water. Moses says, "Hear now, you rebels; shall we bring you forth water out of this rock?" There is no mention of God. Moses' neglect of God stands in contrast to the Israelite people's acknowledgement of Him. They call themselves "the assembly of the Lord," unlike their questioning of God's presence under similar circumstances in Exodus Chapter 17.

God notices Moses' omission. He bans him from entering the Promised Land because he did not "sanctify Me in the eyes of the children of Israel." Thus, while there are many interpretations of why God disallows Moses from leading "this congregation into the land which I have given them," the answer from the approach taken here is that Israelite leaders are not permitted to take all the credit themselves. God's role must be acknowledged.

Chapter 28 - *Consequences Of Improper And Proper Behavior*

Improper behavior results in defeats. The answer to how people should act with God in their midst involves not only making decisions on their own, but committing to act in God-approved ways and to acknowledge a mistake and repent when diverging from them. Importantly, God works behind the scenes in the Balaam/Balak episode.

T he consequences of improper behavior are examined in Chapters 20 and 21 of Numbers. Initially, the Israelites' improper behavior results in their defeat by the Edomites. This is followed by the Canaanite king of Arad taking some Israelites captive in battle. These losses perhaps shock the Israelites into understanding what is required for proper behavior. They finally understand they must commit to acting in ways consistent with God's goals and commands. They say, "If You deliver this people into our hand, we will proscribe their towns." God heard, and the Israelites defeat the Canaanite king.

Right afterwards, however, the Israelites revert to their old ways and complain that God and Moses let them down, failing to give them decent food. This time, the Israelites understand their mistake after God sends serpents among them. They say to Moses, "We have sinned, because we have spoken against the Lord and against you; pray to the Lord, that He take away the serpents from us." God responds by specifying a way for anyone bitten by a snake to be healed -- a bitten people is to look at a copper serpent mounted on a standard. It smacks of pagan ritual, but, at least forces the afflicted people to acknowledge God.

Pulling together the key theological points from these events, the answer to how people should act with God in their midst involves not only making decisions on their own, but committing to act in God-approved ways and to acknowledge a mistake and repent when diverging from them.

The importance of acknowledging a mistake and repenting

harkens back to the story of Judah and Tamar in Genesis. Judah's admission to having had relations with Tamar can be seen as a main point of the story. It shows Judah responded correctly to his sin and thus serves to justify his tribe leading the Israelites in the future.

Consequence of Proper Behavior: Guideline Approach Renewed

With the Israelites exhibiting proper behavior, God renews His separation from them, reestablishing the guideline approach. This time, God plays a supportive, behind-the-scene role, perhaps recognizing the failure of the first attempt at the guideline approach in Exodus. The innovation softens the approach. With God behind them, the Israelites are able to win militarily.

The Israelites' greater responsibility is hinted in a short passage regarding water. In verses 16-20 of Chapter 21, God tolerates the Israelites' confusion over assigning credit for finding wells. Although God told Moses to "gather the people together, and I will give them water," the Israelites sing the praises of their "princes" and "nobles of the people" for digging the wells. Despite the obvious error, the Israelites are not punished by God, unlike in the past. Perhaps He wants them to feel confidence in their leaders as they take on more responsibility.

The tide of military fortune changes for the Israelites in Chapter 21 when they defeat the powerful Sihon, king of the Amorites. The Torah refers to the "Book of the Wars of the Lord" and to bards in describing the location and reputation of Sihon, as if confirmation by outside sources would enhance the significance of the Israelite victory. Consistent with the renewed separation relationship, the victory appears to be achieved without the help of God, as He is not mentioned having partaken in the battle. It mimics the Israelite victory against the Amaleks in Exodus 17, where the Israelites own exertions, including Moses' lifting his arms, are responsible for the win.

In Numbers, however, the Torah does not aim to establish a

complete separation between God and the Israelites. Instead, God is there to help, even if His assistance is not readily apparent. In versus 34 of Numbers Chapter 21, God offers Moses support in defeating Og, king of Bashan, telling him, "Do not fear him, for I give him and all his people and his land into your hand. You shall do to him as you did to Sihon king of the Amorites who dwelt in Heshbon."

Balaam and Balak

The supportive role of God is brought home in the subsequent story of Balaam and Balak — an extremely important episode. It illustrates God's role in ensuring the Israelites' success.

The Moabite king, Balak, asks the prophet Balaam to curse the Israelites. God, however, intervenes to thwart Balak. He instructs Balaam to bless the Israelites instead. Thus, God controls the supernatural channels of the enemy. while the Israelites fight militarily. The split represents a division of labor between the Israelites and God in achieving success.

Moreover, God's role may not be obvious. At one point, a donkey, but not Balaam, sees an angel, underscoring that God's presence is not necessarily visible. The story broadens the horizon of possibilities that should be considered in trying to understand world events. God may be operating in the background. It is a more sophisticated depiction of God's power than the supernatural actions associated with the Prophets.

Chapter 29 - *Diversity In The Promised Land*

Non-uniformity of groups is permitted. Not all inter-group mar-riages are bad. Balance of power among the Israelite tribes is im-portant. Disputes about laws and commandments can be resolved through compromise. Diaspora Jews have an obligation to support Israel.

F ollowing the story of Balaam and Balak, the Book of Numbers finishes with a series of apparently discon-nected episodes, including seduction of the Israelites by Moabite women, Israelite women's inheritance rights, a war against the Midianites, the desire of the Reubenites and Gadites to settle outside Canaan, and the need for Levitical and refugee towns. Amidst all this, God chooses Moses' successor.

There is a common element. Each episode deals with a non-conforming group in Israelite society. After emphasizing the importance of social structure and the need for all Israelites to act in God-approved ways, the Book addresses the question of how nonconformists should be treated. The answer likely helps explain why Judaism has survived – diversity is acceptable as long as it does not run counter to God's commands. The Israel-ite society is not to be a stultified, inflexible structure. How-ever, adherence to God is immutable.

Intermarriage

The first episode, in Chapter 25, addresses an unacceptable divergence from the Israelite society – intermarriage with non-Israelites, in this case seduction by the Moabite women. The Torah does not make a blanket condemnation of intermarriage, since Moses, himself, marries a Cushite woman. The problem appears to be when intermarriage results in Israelites giving up their religion. The Moabite seduction leads to a turning away from God, as the women "called the people to the sacrifices of their gods." The Torah unconditionally condemns seduction leading to idolatry. There is a plague. And, God tells Moses to say, "Take all the chiefs of the people, and hang them up to the

CARL J. PALASH

Lord before the sun, that the fierce anger of the Lord may turn away from Israel." After Phinehas kills an Israelite man and his Maobite woman, God stops the plague and confers a "covenant of peace" to Phinehas and his offspring.

This episode troubles many modern Jews. They do not like the harsh punishment for intermarriage. Nor do they like the idea that someone, such as Phinehas, can act so terribly and attribute his action to God's command. The episode, however, does not truly support those dislikes. The Torah confines the role of executioner to a priest, Phinehas, suggesting enforcement of the covenant is not to be done by everyone, not even the Levites – consistent with the earlier themes of the Torah aimed at preventing both resentment against the Levites and internecine fighting. And, Phinehas acts from the knowledge that God told Moses to have the community punish the transgressors.

Phinehas' actions, however, are somewhat suspect. He goes beyond God's command by killing the Moabite woman as well as the Israelite. Also, the slain Israelite is not necessarily a ringleader, although his being the son of a tribal chief enhances the likelihood. Since God condones Phinehas' actions regardless of his failure to adhere strictly to the commandment, these discrepancies may be insignificant. What may be more significant is the implication that society, rather than God, should be responsible for enforcing the covenant.

Distribution of Land — Women's Rights

The desire not to paint God in a frightening way quickly shows up in Chapter 26, which emphasizes God's fairness in distributing land among the tribes. God tells Moses, "To these the land shall be divided for an inheritance according to the number of names. To the more you shall give the more inheritance, and to the fewer you shall give the less inheritance." Similarly, the Levite towns are to be on land appropriated equitably from the other tribes. God says, "Everyone according to his inheritance which he inherits shall give of his cities to the Levites."

163

The apportionment of the land leads to an exception – the inheritance rights of female orphans. In Chapter 27, God allows them to inherit their father's property as long as they do not have brothers. He adjusts the social laws to accommodate a special group.

In Chapter 36, however, God decides against the transfer of property between two tribes through marriage. The distribution of land among the tribes is to be fixed, even if it entails the rather stringent prohibition against inter-tribal marriage for those women who inherit land. God is sensitive to the balance of power within the Israelite society, willing to impose hardships in some cases to prevent an imbalance among the tribes.

An ironic point stands out from both decisions by God. Since individuals raised the question, it suggests God's instructions do not cover all situations. The reader is left with the impression the religion is not fixed but malleable. The religion can evolve as situations arise.

New Leadership

Back in Chapter 27, the Israelite society experiences a wrenching change when God appoints Joshua to be the successor to Moses. New leadership, however, does not alter rituals or vows. Chapters 28 and 29 specify in detail the rituals and sacrifices of each holiday, while Chapter 30 discusses the implications of vows to God, oneself, or to another. They emphasize God's dominance regardless of who leads.

A Census

A census is recorded after the Moabite-connected plague, a reasonable endeavor after a devastating sickness. Perhaps it was done in anticipation of the invasion of Canaan or to set the groundwork for distribution of the land. Interestingly, God tells Moses and Elazar, Aaron's son, to take the census. Including Elazar violates the separation of church and state established earlier. It may be a justifiable exception, however, since a priest would not have a vested interest in the distribution of land based on the census.

Divergent Interpretations of God's Wishes

The question of divergent interpretations of a commandment is addressed in Chapter 31. God commands, "Avenge the children of Israel on the Midianites." There is no specification of how to do it. And, the Israelite soldiers have a different understanding from Moses'. After successfully defeating the Midianites, the Israelite army returns with captive Medianite women and children and booty. Moses feels they should have killed the women, since they, in their earlier seduction, had "caused the children of Israel, through the counsel of Balaam, to commit trespass against the Lord." God stands by the social structure and rules almost entirely in favor of his commander-in-chief, Moses. His ruling, though, contains some recognition for the soldiers' interpretation of the commandment. They are to kill "every woman who has known man by lying with him," permitting those who did not seduce the Israelites to live. The soldiers are to cleanse themselves and share the booty with the entire Israelite community. Thus, when there is disagreement in interpretation of the laws, the final answer can reflect both sides of the dispute.

Obligations in the Diaspora

The next question of diversity is particularly relevant for the Jews in the Diaspora. Can Jews decide to live outside the land of Israel, and, if so, what are their obligations? In Chapter 32, the tribes of Reuben and Gad request permission to settle on the east side of the Jordan, outside of Canaan. After Moses upbraids them, they volunteer to be "ready armed" to help the rest of the Israelites conquer Canaan. Moses accepts their offer, saying it will make them "guiltless towards the Lord and Israel." Jews are permitted to live outside of Israel, but need to support and help the Jews living there.

Even if Jews in the Diaspora do not support Israel, they are not to be ostracized. This appears to be the import of

Moses' instruction that the Reubenites and Gaddites are to receive land in Canaan if they, in fact, "do not pass over with you armed." This magnanimous gesture is in keeping with the Torah's broader message that Jews are not to be in conflict with each other.

The importance of the Promised Land is emphasized in Chapter 33, in which all the travels of the Israelites are enumerated, emphasizing the hardships they went through to get there, and in Chapter 34, in which the boundaries of Canaan are specified. Jews everywhere must understand Israel as an accomplishment that resulted from their own efforts as well as from God. They should feel a commitment to it, stemming from their own hard work and not just received as a gift.

Non-Israelites within Israel

Ideally, only Israelites should inhabit the land. In Chapter 33, God warns the Israelites that unless they "drive out the inhabitants of the land from before you, then shall those who you let remain of them be as pricks in your eyes, and as thorns in your sides, and they shall vex you in the land in which you dwell." Diversity within the Land does not encompass people of different religion.

Levite and Sanctuary Towns

Nevertheless, the Israelite society can accommodate diversity within itself, as implied by the establishment of towns for Levites and for refugees of unintentional killings in Chapter 35. The diversity is in the framework of "separate but equal." And, it need be accomplished in ways that do not result in internecine conflict. Levite towns are consistent with the established split between the secular and non-secular. Refugee towns seem to be aimed to prevent unintentional killings leading to feuds, consistent with the Torah's desire to prevent fratricide. Nonetheless, the Chapter emphasizes that making exceptions for certain groups should not be abused. It spends much time discussing the need to punish those who murder willingly.

They are not to take advantage of the refugee cities.

Conclusion

The Book of Numbers shows that social hierarchy, despite being carefully constructed, does not result in appropriate behavior. All Israelites, not just the chosen leadership, need to act correctly for God to be in their midst. Only when all the Israelites agree to follow God's commandments and acknowledge and repent for a sin does their destiny become marked by success. The whole Israelite society has responsibility to uphold their end of the covenant and to act independently of God to achieve their goals — although there is room for diversity within the society. They cannot rely on their leaders alone to ensure God's help, which could be in the background. People, as well as God, deserve recognition as "Number One."

Chapter 30 - *God's Wrath And Enforcement Of The Covenant*

Undermining the social structure can bring on God's wrath. But, His anger is a last resort.

God's wrath is well known, but His death threats are restricted to those who attempt to undermine the Israelite social structure. The times the death penalty is applied in the Book of Numbers – when a non-Levite touches the Tabernacle and during the rebellions against Moses and Aaron — have one thing in common: a disregard for the established social order. In the non-Levite case, a person intrudes in the non-secular side of society. In the other cases, rebels attempt to overthrow God-chosen leaders. The Torah appears to believe destruction of social structure risks undermining the covenant. So, the threat of an extreme penalty is needed to dissuade the Israelites from breaking the structure.

There is precedence in the Torah for emphasizing social structure as a way to encourage adherence to the covenant. It is similar to the Torah's reliance on a detailed code of law to satisfy the Israelites' need for dependence, as discussed in *What God Settles For* (Chapter 5). Both solutions impose rigidities on the Israelites to prevent them from making wrong decisions. Also, by requiring social obedience, the Torah, in its typical grand irony, eliminates the need for God's enforcement: respect for social structure substitutes for His wrath. It represents one more example of the religion being constructed in ways to minimize God's direct involvement, similar to how the embodiment of the sacrificial system into everyday life through Kashrut and other practices eliminates the need for God's continuous presence to remind people to adhere to the commandments.

Ultimately, the Torah does not intend the religion to be based on a fear of death for errant behavior. The death penalty is not specified as a way to enforce a variety of commandments in

Chapters 5 and 6 of Numbers. People with an eruption or defiled by a corpse are removed from the camp. A person who wrongs another must give restitution. Regarding a marital covenant, an adulterous woman takes a test to determine her guilt. If guilty, she "will be a curse among her people." Although a one-sided resolution, as it applies to only women, at least it permits all parties to live. In the case of a Nazirite's covenant, in which he vows "to set himself apart for the Lord," a set of rituals is prescribed in the event of an inadvertent transgression.

Immediately after the chapters on punishments for covenantal missteps, a positive relationship with God is emphasized. In Chapter 6, God directs Aaron and his sons to bless the Israelites in words that have become classic. God watches over the Israelites, dealing "kindly and graciously" with them and granting them peace. As the blessings follow the discussion of the Nazirite, they also underscore that devoting oneself to God by becoming a Nazirite is not necessary to receive the benefits of God's presence.

Chapter 31 - *Plausibility*

A comparison with the American post-war experience in Iraq shows many similarities with the behavior of the Israelites described in the Book of Numbers.

How Plausible Is This?

The failure of the Israelites to behave properly after being freed from Egypt by God has perplexed Jews throughout the ages. Why didn't the Israelites act appropriately after seeing God's power first hand? The Israelites' actions gain plausibility in light of the 2003 post-war situation in Iraq. Although involving a power far less than God, the situation contains enough similarities to what is described in the Book of Numbers to warrant comparison. By observing how the Iraqis reacted to their deliverance from a dictator in many of the ways described in Numbers, the Israelites' actions can be appreciated as perhaps natural.

The similarities are surprisingly extensive. Despite being freed from a ruthless dictator by the US, the Iraqis complained about mundane problems, such as inadequate electricity and lack of security, just as the Israelites complained about lack of food and an inability to fight their enemies. The US tried to solve the problem by setting up a Governing Council of Iraqi leaders unaffiliated with the Baathist party, in line with God's designating tribal leaders. The Shiite Ayatollah, however, argued that he is at least as powerful as the US-chosen Governing Council, similar to Aaron's and Miriam's assertion that they had as close a connection to God as did Moses. Iraqi clerics, such as Al-Sadr, rebelled, similar to Korah and his allies. And, the secular leader, Challabi, acted against the interests of the US in telling secrets to the Iranians, a parallel to the tribal chiefs not recommending an invasion of Canaan. Thus, the events in the Wilderness may be more realistic than one might think.

And, turning the analogy around, the Book of Numbers offers

a solution to the Iraqi problem. The Iraqis needed to be given the responsibility for determining their own destiny, including reinstating former Baathist officials with experience – just as God reinstated the community elders when Moses needed help. However, the Iraqis could not make decisions that ran counter to the interests of the US, and the ringleaders of discontent needed to be eliminated or co-opted – just as Korah and his group were killed but the benefits accruing to the Levites re-affirmed. Most importantly, all the Iraqis, not just the leaders chosen by the US, needed to sign on to the endeavor of rebuilding Iraq without crossing the US goals.

Deuteronomy: A Reformation

T he first four books of the Torah develop a religion elegant in construction and motivation. The religion, however, didn't work. Proof comes from the Prophets. Israelites often turned to other gods, took credit for their success rather than acknowledge God's role, and ignored the poor. In difficult times, they dropped notions of equity and justice in social relationships. Amos observed their behavior during periods of success and preached that caring for the poor was more important than sacrificing to God. Micah witnessed the domination of the Israelites by the Assyrians and described the breakdown of the Israelite society. He recommended Israelites walk humbly in the footsteps of God and wait for Him to save them from their difficult situation. These ideas may have percolated through Israelite society from the 8th century BCE, when the Prophets wrote, until the 7th century BCE, when they were systematized into the Book of Deuteronomy

Deuteronomy tweaks the religion of the first four Books in several ways to make it work. First, it reestablishes the importance of the quid pro quo relationship between God and the Israelites. The Israelites' commitment to the commandments is based on indebtedness to God for freeing them from Egypt. Second, the Book rewrites history in ways to enhance or whitewash God's role. God is shown to be directly responsible for Israelite successes and not to be involved when the people make wrong decisions, a different depiction from how the events are described in the earlier Books. Third, Deuteronomy changes the relationship between the Israelites and God from one of separation to one of love – a more familial connection lacking earlier in the Torah but with the undesirable implication of encouraging people to rely heavily on Him. Fourth, the Book insists Israelites not turn to other gods or forget God's role in their success. Fifth, it forcefully blames the problems faced by the Israelites on their failure to follow the commandments.

All these ideas, or at least elements of them, can be found in the first four Books. Deuteronomy changes their emphasis. In so doing, the Book has within it clues on how to alter the religion. Reflecting the grand irony found elsewhere in the Torah, the Book with the reputation for the strictest statement of Judaism shows how the religion can reform itself: a reformation needs to use the elements found within the Torah, but can select those that best allow the religion to be effective. New laws are permitted, contrary to the assertion of otherwise in Deuteronomy, although they need to be consistent with the basic ideas of the religion. There is a hint that some laws can be dropped, as well.

Chapter 32 - *Quid Pro Quo*

Deuteronomy brings back the quid pro quo rationale for adhering to the covenant.

T he first three chapters of Deuteronomy emphasize the indebtedness of the Israelites to God. He directs their travels through the wilderness and is behind their major decisions and victories.

God tells Moses the Israelites have wandered in the wilderness for sufficient time, saying, "You have compassed this mountain long enough: turn northward."
God informs the Israelites when they will prevail against another group. He instructs them to bypass Seir and Moab and not to fight the Ammonites. Instead, they should begin their conquest by attacking Sihon the Amorite. He says, "I have given into your hand Sihon the Amorite, king of Heshbon, and his land; begin to possess it, and contend with him in battle. This day will I begin to put the dread of you and the fear of you on the peoples who are under the whole sky, who shall hear the report of you, and shall tremble, and be in anguish because of you." A succession of victories follows, as God delivers enemies into the Israelites' hands.

After a brief history of their victories, the Israelites are exhorted in Chapter 4 to follow the commandments and laws. They are so ideal their observance will show "your wisdom and understanding in the sight of the peoples." Just in case this motivation does not suffice, the Israelites are told to remember God's power, emphasizing the benefit from keeping Him on their side. They should not forget "the things which your eyes saw, and ... make them known to your children and your children's children." The Passover exhortation to Jews throughout the ages to think of themselves as being in Egypt and at Mount Sinai stems from this directive of Moses. Its purpose is to make modern Jews feel in awe of and beholden to God and thus feel compelled to follow His commandments.

By following the commandments, the Israelites would ensure their stay in the Promised Land. Moses says, "Observe His laws and commandments...that it may be well with you, and that you may increase mightily, as the Lord, the God of your fathers, has promised to you, in a land flowing with milk and honey. " However, if the Israelites "forget the Lord your God, and walk after other gods, and serve them, and worship them, you shall surely perish." The reason to follow the commandments is clearly pitched in quid pro quo terms and grounded in worldly success.

The significance of the quid pro quo approach is underscored in the restatement of the Ten Commandments in Chapter 5. Quite extraordinary in light of the analysis of the first two statements of the Ten Commandments in Exodus, Deuteronomy changes the motivation for honoring the Sabbath in the Fourth Commandment. In Exodus, this commandment was first justified by God having rested on the seventh day, implying the Israelites should act like God. This was the key to the guideline approach. Then, in the first reformation of the religion, when Moses asks for God's help after the Golden Calf episode, the commandment leaves off any rationale, consistent with the shift to an unquestionable code of laws. Finally, Deuteronomy uses this commandment to state the quid pro quo rationale of the second reformation of the religion. After saying that no Israelite should do any work on the Sabbath, it says, "You shall remember that you were a servant in the land of Egypt, and the Lord your God brought you out of there by a mighty hand and by an outstretched arm: therefore the Lord your God commanded you to keep the Sabbath day." As in the other rationales for this Commandment, this one forms the basis for the approach to the religion at this point in the Torah – in this case, quid pro quo.

The reversion to the quid pro quo approach -- the most elementary approach taken when the Israelites first left Egypt -- shows how Deuteronomy borrowed and reshaped elements of the earlier Books of the Torah. Neither the guideline approach nor the code-of-law approach sustained the Israelites' commitment to God. So, Deuteronomy revives the basic approach found in the earlier Books.

Chapter 33 - *White Wash*

History is rewritten to put God and Moses in a more positive light.

W ith a quid pro quo approach as the new basis of the relationship between the Israelites and God, Deuteronomy rewrites history to enhance His role.

Deuteronomy gives explicit credit to God for the Israelites' victories. For example, in Chapter 2 there is little question of God having played a direct role in the conquest of Sihon, king of the Amorites. In contrast, Numbers (Chapter 21) makes no direct mention of Him in this conquest. This Book casts God's partnership with the Israelites as more of a "behind-the-scenes" role, described in the story of Balak and Balaam.

Deuteronomy covers up God's role in the problems faced by the Israelites. It removes any connection of God with the disastrous decision by the scouts regarding the conquest of Canaan, which had led to God's condemning the Israelites to 38 years of additional wandering in the wilderness. Chapter 1 verse 22 attributes the decision to send scouts into Canaan to the Israelites, themselves. Moses says, "You came near to me, everyone of you, and said, 'Let us send men before us, that they may search the land for us and bring us word again of the way by which we must go up, and the cities to which we shall come.'" Numbers (Chapter 13) has God telling Moses to "send you men that they may spy out the land of Canaan...."

Deuteronomy even works to whitewash Moses. In Chapter 1, Moses blames the Israelites rather than his own incorrect behavior for being precluded from entering the Promised Land. Moses says, "The Lord was angry with me because of you, saying, 'You also shall not go in there.'" In Numbers (Chapter 20), Moses' failure to acknowledge God when obtaining water from the rock was the cause of God's anger. God said, "Because you didn't believe in me, to sanctify me in the eyes of the children of Israel, therefore you shall not bring this assembly into the land which I have given them." Moses' punishment in Numbers had nothing to do with the Israelites' actions.

Attempts to whitewash Aaron, the priesthood and the Levites are mixed. Chapter 9 cannot avoid acknowledging God's anger toward Aaron in the Golden Calf episode. It drops, however, the role of the Levite Korah in its mention of the rebellion against Moses and Aaron, blaming only the Reubenites, Dothan and Abiram.

Deuteronomy, in sum, appears to shift blame for the unfavorable parts of the Israelite's history away from God and its leadership and directly onto the people.

Chapter 34 - *A Love Relationship*

Deuteronomy introduces love of God and God's love of the Israelites to motivate adherence to the covenant. The need to follow the commandments remains.

Besides attributing worldly success to God, Deuteronomy introduces and emphasizes the need to love Him. Perhaps this new concept aims to inspire Israelites to follow the commandments for more than just material gain. Love personalizes the religion in a way not done in the earlier Books. Its absence could have been a factor contributing to the failure of the early Israelites to adhere to the religion.

The first reference to a personal relationship with God occurs in Chapter 4. After warning that the Israelites would be scattered if they did not follow the commandments, Moses says that even when scattered, "you shall seek the Lord your God, and you shall find him when you search after him with all your heart and soul...and you shall return to the Lord your God and listen to his voice." This admonishment addresses a situation of exile, unlike the circumstances in the first four Books of the Torah. The religion changes to be effective in this new environment. Individual devotion and fealty to God will bring Him close, contrary to the earlier need for a priesthood to approach God.

The concept of love initially appears to be one-sided. In the "V'ahavta" in Chapter 6, the Israelites are told to "love the Lord your God with all your heart, all your soul, and all your might." There is no statement of reciprocal love from God. Instead, there is further insistence to teach the commandments to their children. This unilateral relationship changes in Chapter 7 when Moses says, "the Lord didn't set his love on you nor choose you because you were more in number than any people; for you were the fewest of all peoples: but because the Lord loves you." The benefit of God's love is stated in the next verse, which describes God as "faithful...who keeps covenant and lovingkindness with them who love him and keep his commandments to a thousand generations." A two-way love relationship is established.

Deuteronomy's love requirement is an addition to the prior Books' demand to follow the commandments. Love does not substitute for them. Each statement of the love relationship insists that Israelites also obey the commandments. In Chapter 11, for example, the Israelites are told to "love the Lord your God and keep his charge, statutes, ordinances and commandments always." In general, the exhortation to love God never stands alone, but is always attached to the need to follow the commandments.

Deuteronomy perhaps bases this new approach to God from the commandment in Leviticus 19 to love thy neighbor or stranger as oneself. In a sense, God is the penultimate stranger. Applying the Leviticus 19 doctrine to a relationship with God, however, turns the guideline approach on its head. In the latter approach, interpersonal relationships are modeled after the respect one shows God. The love approach, in contrast, models a relationship to God on how one treats another person. Although changing the relationship with God may be needed to ensure the Israelites adhere to the religion, it comes with problems.

God loses His exalted nature to some extent if He is treated like another person. The most striking example is in verses 14 and 15 of Chapter 23, where one is instructed to cover up your excrement ... "since the Lord your God walks in the midst of your camp ... and that He may not see an unclean thing and turn away from you." The connection of a truly mundane act with God undercuts His majesty, to say the least. Deuteronomy tries to preserve a sense of distance between the Israelites and God, charging in Chapter 10 to "fear the Lord your God" as well as to love Him. The introduction of love into the relationship, nevertheless, brings God down a notch, as people now can relate to Him on a personal rather than subservient level.

Having a personal relationship with God contradicts some

of the important points in Exodus and Leviticus. The image of God moving around the camp belies His need for a sanctuary within the Israelite society. And, if love of God means coming close to Him, it would run counter to the threat of death for those who do so in Exodus and Leviticus. Deuteronomy recognizes this threat. In Chapter 5, the Israelites say at Mount Sinai, "For who is there of all flesh that has heard the voice of the living God speaking out of the midst of the fire, as we have, and lived?" The problem can be resolved by interpreting love of God as a psychological state that encourages people to be devoted exclusively to Him and, by implication, to be more devoted to following His commandments. From this perspective, the idea of love does not entail coming near to God in a real sense. This interpretation, however, is not commonly held, as many Jews feel their love of God and prayer in fact bring them close to Him.

By undermining the idea of separation between God and the Israelites, the notion of love changes the basis on which ethics is derived in Exodus. There, one treats others with respect, just as one treats God. In Deuteronomy, love of one's neighbor as oneself becomes the basis for ethics. This love-based ethics is more informal than the earlier, respect-based one. Loving another as one's self means there is no clear-cut or fixed boundary between people, in contrast to when respect is the foundation of interpersonal relations. How far one goes in loving another is not clear. With the limit in a love relationship being parity, it would imply uniformity and downplay individualism – which is not part of the religion in the first four Books. And, the relationship to God, as to people, presumably could change according to a person's self-view.

A love relationship can overly emphasize reliance on God for solving one's problems. Shouldn't God prevent a bad event from happening to those who love Him? As discussed in *An Incorrect Intepretation of the Torah*? (Chapter 10), this line of thought could lead to disaster, arguing against solving one's own problems. Deuteronomy's Chapter 11 says if the Israelites "listen diligently to my commandments which I command you this day, to love the Lord your God, and to serve him with all your heart and with all your soul...I will give the rain of your land in its season,...grass in your fields for your cattle, and you shall eat and be full." Loving God brings forth material gains. There is no sense the Israelites need to act themselves to achieve success.

In total, the concept of a love relationship with God may be necessary for people to adhere faithfully to the religion. Love helps cement a commitment to God and the commandments. This concept, though, changes some of the implications of the theology developed in the earlier Books. It also has potentially dangerous implications for how the Israelites respond to difficult situations. Rather than trying to solve a problem by themselves, people could wait for God to clear it up. Sometimes, the solution to one problem creates others.

Potential Sins: Turning to Other Gods and Taking Credit Oneself

The love approach most likely attempts to prevent two potential sins from occurring, both of which are emphasized in Deuteronomy. One is the possibility the Israelites will follow the gods of conquered peoples. The other is their taking all the credit for the conquest of Canaan, forgetting the role of God.

Repeated admonishments in Deuteronomy suggest these transgressions were major problems in the early days of Israel. To prevent turning to other gods, the Israelites in Chapter 7 are told to "consume all the peoples who the Lord your God shall deliver to you; your eye shall not pity them: neither shall you serve their gods; for that will be a snare to you." Regarding the problem of taking personal credit, the Israelites are warned in Chapter 8 that "when you have eaten and are full, and have built goodly houses and lived therein, when your herds and your flocks multiply, your silver and your gold is multiplied, and all that you have is multiplied; then your heart be lifted up, and you forget the Lord your God who brought you forth out of the land of Egypt.... Remember that it is the Lord your God who gives you the power to get wealth." There is clearly a veiled threat the Israelites could lose their wealth if they take all the credit themselves.

Giving God credit for success recurs in Chapter 26. The Israelites are instructed to bring the first fruit of the harvest to the temple for God. They should acknowledge God's contribution to the harvest, particularly since He gave them the land.

Chapter 26 drives home the need for God by recounting how obligated the Israelites should be for God having brought them out of Egypt, emphasizing again the quid pro quo approach. This recounting, subsequently made part of the Haggadah, also may be there to balance the commandment at the end of Chapter 25 not to forget to "blot out the memory of Amalek from under the sky." This famous commandment shifts the burden of defense to the Israelites from God. They cannot count on another set of Ten Plagues to convince the Amalek to have a fear of God, but must destroy them, themselves. This shift of responsibility could engender doubts about whether God is needed. So, Chapter 26 has to repeat God's role in Exodus to remind the Israelites (and future Jews) not to abandon Him, as He helped them in the past and could still do so.

Both transgressions – turning to other gods and taking all the credit for oneself -- represent the same problem. A person who takes all the credit for a success implies, in sense, that he is at least as powerful as God. Putting oneself at or above God's level is equivalent to idolizing oneself. Such implication is unacceptable.

From this perspective, the She'ma prayer, found in Deuteronomy Chapter 6, can be viewed as an assertion not only that there is only one God but you are not Him. The prayer harkens back to the interpretation of the First Commandment in the context of the guideline approach — even though an Israelite is to act like God, he is not Him. There is only one ruler. Following the She'ma, verses 10-12 remind the Israelites that God is responsible for their good fortune, driving home this interpretation of the She'ma not to take all credit for oneself. Verse 14 expands the thought by commanding not to follow other gods.

Worldly rewards will continue to accrue to the Israelites if they adhere to acknowledging God as number one. Loving God is meant to persuade them to do so.

Chapter 35 - *Flexibility*

Deuteronomy shows laws can be changed, although they need to be consistent with the broad themes of the earlier Books. A re-ordering of two commandments results in a mistaken inclusion of separating meat from dairy in the Kashrut laws.

Despite it's insistence on following the commandments and laws, Deuteronomy shows their flexibility. Just before Moses recites the laws in Chapter 6, he tells the Israelites, "Observe [the laws and commandments] willingly and faithfully, that it may be well with you." The laws and commandments set forth, however, contain differences, additions and omissions compared to those found in the first four Books. These changes provide hints on how the religion can be reformed.

Moses' famous charge in Chapter 4 not to change the commandments ("You shall not add to the word which I command you, neither shall you diminish from it, that you may keep the commandments of the Lord your God which I command you.") can take on new meaning. Rather than implying a rigid set of laws, the charge can mean the commandments are broad enough to permit choice of emphasis. Jews should not look outside of the commandments to make the religion meaningful.

New Laws and Omitting Others

Deuteronomy shows that laws can be created to meet new situations. Chapter 20 establishes new laws, for example, regarding the military. They are not based on any specific commandment in the first four Books, but conform to their general ideas. They include exclusion from military duty for those who have built a new house, planted but not harvested a vineyard, is engaged to marry, or is fearful of battle. The new laws reflect a respect for personal needs above those of society. They are consistent with the allowance for diversity among Israelite groups found at the end of Numbers. New laws also restrict how an Israelite army is to treat a conquered town near or far from their homeland. They refine the prohibitions against being influenced by other peoples' religions in Leviticus and Numbers.

Deuteronomy omits some commandments in the earlier Books. For example, the commandment for priests to check mold in one's house is not mentioned, although the need for them to examine skin growth is. Most interestingly, the admonition to love one's neighbor as oneself is left out. The omission of a commandment does not necessarily imply it should not be obeyed, but it does raise the question. The omissions open the possibility of dropping commandments if circumstances warrant.

Some Deuteronomic innovations imply commandments can be suspended, according to tradition. In Chapter 20, the Israelites are permitted to cut down non-fruit bearing trees to "build bulwarks against the city that makes war with you, until it fall." The rabbis understood the last phrase ("until it fall") to mean war can be fought on the Sabbath — suspending the commandment to honor the Sabbath until a war is won. The permissibility to violate a commandment would seem to generalize to any situation deemed critically important.

Deuteronomy, in effect, brings back the guideline approach to make the religion flexible in the face of changing circumstances. The Israelites can introduce new laws so long as they are broadly consistent with the commandments established at Mount Sinai.

Centralization of the Religion?
Deuteronomy repeatedly commands the Israelites to sacrifice at a centralized location, chosen by God. But, it suggests a more varied approach is acceptable under some circumstances. That is because this command may depend on the Israelites being settled as a group in one place. Moses states in Chapter 12, "you shall not do all the things we do here this day, every man doing whatever is right in his own eyes for you haven't yet come to the rest and to the inheritance, which the Lord your

God gives you.. When you go over the Jordan...you shall bring all that I command you: your burnt offerings, and your sacrifices...to the place which the Lord your God shall choose."

Apparently, before settling in Canaan, the Israelites' religious practices were not the same for everyone. The variability was tolerated because the Israelites had not yet reached the Promised Land. How a Jew practices rituals appears tied to the situation. A centralized temple works when all Jews live in Israel, but a decentralized, more varied approach to God is permissible when Jews are scattered around the world.

Separation of Church and State -- A Change

The Book of Numbers establishes a clear separation of the secular and non-secular parts of Israelite society. Deuteronomy drops it. Chapter 17 requires an Israelite king to study the Torah in order to "fear the Lord his God, to keep all the words of this law and these statutes, to do them." The secular leadership is to be constrained by the Torah. In addition, priests join secular magistrates in resolving disputes in Chapter 19. Numbers, in contrast, took care to prevent the priesthood or Levites from judging other Israelites.

Deuteronomy implicitly argues against a complete separation of church and state. Clearly, the changed realities in Israelite society over the years led to this re-assessment and realignment of powers. The priesthood apparently gained power over the secular leadership. The relationship between the religion and government can evolve.

Separating Meat from Dairy – A Mistake?

When repeating the laws and commandments of the prior Books, Deuteronomy may have been less careful than it should have been. Chapter 14 verse 21 repeats the law against boiling a kid in its mother's milk, but its location in the text is not right. It comes before the requirement to set aside a tenth of one's yield for God. In the earlier Books, the prohibition comes after the command to bring the first fruits of the crop to the Temple.

From this reversal of order, Deuteronomy places the prohibition right after the listing of the Kosher food restrictions and, as a result, appears to make it part of them.

This prohibition, though, is not part of the Kashrut restrictions. In Leviticus, the Kosher laws are derived from the food restrictions of the sacrificial system. The laws are meant to bring the holiness of the sacrificial system into a person's life. Boiling a kid does not map into these food restrictions, which is why it is stated separately from Kosher Laws in Leviticus. The prohibition against boiling a kid in its mother's milk aims to prevent the Israelites from practicing a Canaanite ritual, as discussed in *Keeping Kosher* (Chapter 18). In Exodus, the prohibition also is mentioned, but not Kosher laws. Since Exodus at that point is focused on how to acknowledge God through holidays and sacrifices and avoid mentioning the name of other gods, the prohibition there represents further proof that it relates to a Canaanite ritual and not Kosher laws. Deuteronomy ties the prohibition to Kosher laws incorrectly.

Deuteronomy changes the earlier couplet of commandments by replacing "first fruits" of the harvest with a tenth of the yield. Although the two are different measures, they represent the same idea -- one has to share his output with God. The substitution may be an example of Deuteronomy's attempt to make the earlier religion practical – in this case, by specifying the amount of output that constitutes "first fruits." Although a tenth of the yield would seem to be a burdensome "tax," the new law cushions the commandment by allowing the donor to eat the food (in God's presence). Only in the third year is the tithe to be given to Levites, the stranger, the fatherless and widows, showing the need for social responsibility.

Flexibility in Blessings and Curses

As a final way to persuade the Israelites to adhere to the religion, Deuteronomy ends with a dramatic recitation of blessings and especially curses that would ensue depending on whether the Israelites follow the commandments. Given the power of the language, this reward/punishment approach to the religion is what people remember most about the Book. Similar blessings and curses are found in the other Books, nonetheless.

Consistent with the Book's aim to put the onus on the Israelites and not God for the catastrophic turns in their history, this final denouement attributes bad events, such as exiles, on the failure of the Israelites to live up to the commandments. God does not prevent bad things from happening because the Israelites do not deserve His help. God, indeed, predicts the Israelites will "go astray" after Moses' death and will suffer "many evils and troubles" since He will keep His "countenance hidden on that day." In light of our knowledge of history, this prediction stands as a dramatic demonstration of God's prescience. However, the pronouncement also strikes one as a little too accurate.

All is not lost, though. There is flexibility in the forecast. Moses tells the Israelites if they eventually "return to the Lord your God, and obey his voice according to all that I command you this day, you and your children,... then the Lord your God will bring you back and do you good." Once again, it is up to the Israelites to stick with God and live according to the laws to obtain God's help.

Implicit in Moses' promise of salvation is the idea that God does not need a sanctuary to "be there" to help the Israelites. The promise in effect resolves the problem, discussed in *Ritual* (Chapter 15), whether the need of a sanctuary to have God in "one's midst" undermines the religion for a dispersed group of Israelites. Deuteronomy may, indeed, be saving the religion by allowing for flexibility in where God resides.

Conclusion

Most remarkably, Deuteronomy demonstrates how Judaism can be reformed. Besides introducing new concepts regarding the relationship between the Israelites and God, the Book invents laws to meet new circumstances and seems to hint that some can be dropped. New laws, though, have a basis in the laws found in the prior four Books. Generally, Deuteronomy relies on all the approaches found in the previous four Books – the quid pro quo, reward, guideline, and code approaches -- to persuade Israelites to live properly.

Practicing The Religion

The remaining chapters examine portions of the Tanakh that focus on the practice of the religion in the Promised Land.

Why Did the Israelites Turn Away From Adonai (Chapter 36) and *Prophets and Men of God* (Chapter 37) discuss practical reasons why the Israelites did not adhere to the religion. They also examine the "profession" of prophecy.

A Longer-Run Covenant (Chapter 38) shows how the prophets tried to solve the covenantal problem.

Compassion Versus Ritual (Chapter 39) examines the prophets' complaint.

Did Ezra and Nehemiah Have the Answer? (Chapter 40) shows that going beyond the letter of the law does not work.

A Theory of Ethics by Amos (Chapter 41), examines the basis of social responsibility and more espoused by this prophet. A similar examination of the Jonah story is done in *Is the Book of Jonah Kosher?* (Chapter 44).

David Unhinged (Chapter 42) and *A Job on Job* (Chapter 43) demonstrate the pitfalls of believing one talks with God and of applying theology to explain events.

A History Lesson in the Book of Daniel (Chapter 45) argues this Book takes too narrow a view of history, attributing all to God.

Here Comes the Judge (Chapter 46) and *Why is Esther in the Bible?* (Chapter 47) offer reasons for their theological importance.

Making Sense of the Song of Song (Chapter 48) outlines a logical way to read this difficult Book.

Chapter 36 - *Why Did Israelites Turn Away From Adonai?*

Difficulty in discerning both Adonai's role in events and the prophets' credibility may have undermined the Israelites' adherence to the covenant. They may have turned to "less costly" gods when the benefits of staying with Adonai were not readily apparent.

T he relationship between Adonai and the Israelites changes after the Israelites reach the Promised Land. It shifts to more direct interaction from having moved toward separation and minimal involvement while they wandered in the desert. At first, Adonai speaks directly to Joshua and, on occasion, to subsequent secular leaders. But, for the most part, He speaks through prophets and "men of God."

God's active participation, however, doesn't prevent the Israelites from turning to other gods, particularly in the north after the post-Solomon breakaway. Why this was so is a major theological question. Why are other religions more attractive than Judaism? The answer arguably involves the difficulty of discerning the true god or His representatives (the prophets) and the cost of worship.

The initial rejection of a Jerusalem-centered religion by the Northern Kingdom was politically motivated—King Jeroboam feared his subjects would reattach themselves to Judah if they brought sacrifices to the Temple.

Nevertheless, there could have been theologically significant reasons for people to turn to gods other than Adonai. People may have had difficulty discerning Him, given the covenantal promise of worldly success. There does not appear to have been much, if any, difference between the economic conditions of the northern and southern kingdoms. The text provides no evidence the economic situation worsened when people turned to other gods.

Uncertainty about the credibility of prophets and men of God also may have undermined people's connection to

Adonai. Prophets were relied upon to forecast the outcome of an event or to intervene with a god. There were many prophets, each group tied to a particular god. It was likely difficult to decide who among them was right. A prophet's credibility depended on the success of his forecasts and whether he had the power to heal. Samuel's perfect forecasting record demonstrated his being a true prophet. But, for the most part, prophets' forecasts likely had mixed records, making it difficult to determine who had access to God. Even a true prophet may have been unconvincing, since the timing of a dire forecast was not certain and the outcome could be well in the future. The proliferation of prophets, along with their having disciples, suggests a lucrative occupation, nonetheless. Indeed, the text shows competition among them, even within the group professing to represent Adonai.

The absence of quick, direct responses by Adonai to covenantal misdeeds may have weakened people's adherence to the religion. The connection between sin and punishment was not obvious from people's perspectives. "Bad" kings, such as Ahab, reigned for many years. In Ahab's case, Adonai postponed punishment to his "son's days." And, the text says Adonai gave the Northern Kingdom many chances to reform their ways before giving up on them and letting Assyria destroy it. Moreover, bad kings in Judah, such as Rehoboam, Abijam, Menasseh and Amon, survived. Manasseh was blamed for the Babylonian expulsion, which occurred years after his reign. What makes matters worse, Adonai's decision could be discretionary and thus unreliable. For example, He exonerated Abijam for "David's sake," preserving Jerusalem and allowing his son to secede him.

Without a noticeable benefit from maintaining allegiance to Adonai nor certainty of punishment, people may have turned to gods that entail lower costs. This is conjecture, however, since the relative costs of sacrifice among religions are not mentioned in the text. For the Northern Kingdom, to be sure, transportation costs clearly were lower getting to local shrines than traveling to the Temple in Jerusalem. The text hints of the costliness of sacrifice. It mentions the valuable items held in the Temple, indicating sacrifices resulted in wealth accumulation by the priesthood.

Why Stick With Adonai?

Although there may not have been discernible economic benefit from Adonai, the text makes explicit Adonai's powers. It attributes military successes and defeats to Adonai, emphasizes the magic practiced by prophets, and mentions supernatural events. This approach, while seemingly unsophisticated, argues that, at a minimum, Adonai may be acting in the background to influence worldly activities. It posits belief in Adonai's extraordinary powers as a reason to adhere to the religion.

The Israelites may have been impressed by magic because of having lived among the Egyptians for so many years and then among the Canaanites in the Promised Land. Their neighbors' religions may have influenced their view of a god. Magic was the provenance of the priests in these foreign religions — explicitly indicated in Exodus — and the Israelites may have had to see Adonai's magical abilities to be convinced that Moses represented Him or, in the Promised Land, that Adonai was there.

Reliance on magic to convince the Israelites of Adonai's powers has precedence in Exodus. When Moses expresses doubt the Israelites would believe and listen to him, Adonai makes his rod become a snake when thrown on the ground and his hand become covered with scales when put on his bosom. Adonai says if the rod trick doesn't convince them, the scales trick would. Moreover, if neither convinces them, Moses should take water from the Nile and it will turn into blood.

Emphasis on Adonai's powers also is seen in a "rewriting" of the creation story by King Hezekiah. He prayed to Adonai, saying "You alone are God of all kingdoms of the earth. You made the heavens and earth...." While being "God of all kingdoms" can be viewed as consistent with the idea of being Lord

God, the attribution of heavens/earth creation to Adonai alone ignores the interpretation of Genesis Chapter 1 that the creation was the result of a concerted effort by all gods.

Some analysts view the prophets' conception of a universal god as a shift in the religion from an earlier version that portrayed Adonai as a local god for the Israelites. However, the prophets' view has precedence in the First Five Books. Acknowledging God as "God of all kingdoms of the earth" is consistent with the depiction in Genesis that He is the Lord among Elohim and in Exodus that He is the dominant god in Egypt. The prophets may have emphasized this idea to provide hope to the Israelites in dire times.

Some prophets extended the covenant to the after-life, making unprovable assertions of resurrection of the dead and immortality to convince Israelites to adhere to Adonai. These assertions were not included in Deuteronomy, however, even though the latter embodied many of the prophets' ideas. The Deuteronomic writers may not have viewed them as central to the prophets' message. Also, promises of resurrection and immortality run counter to a major theme of the first four Books of Moses — people would be like divine beings, contrary to Adonai's expressed concern about eating from the Tree of Life in the Garden of Eden.

Conclusion

The behavior of the Israelites in the Promised Land has to be viewed as strange. After inhabiting the land promised to them by Adonai, they had trouble discerning Adonai's role or the consequences of diverging from His commandments. There was no obvious economic benefit by adhering to Adonai. And, consequences of not doing so were not immediate, obfuscating cause and effect. Kings and commoners turned to prophets to learn of Adonai's or some other god's plans — to obtain forecasts of future events. But, there were many professed prophets, which might have raised doubts about their validity. In this competitive and uncertain environment, Israelites turned to other gods, worship of whom may have been less costly than that of Adonai.

The theological problem demonstrated by this history may lie with the nature of the covenant. The latter promised worldly success in return for following Adonai's commandments. Without experiencing this benefit, people might lose faith in Adonai. Understanding the covenant to mean Adonai might be there to help, but with no guarantee, apparently was not enough to get people to follow the religion.

Chapter 37 - *Prophets And Men Of God*

Prophets played practical as well as supernatural roles in Israelite society. Their reliance on magic shows people's need to see explicit proof of God's actions to be firmly committed to the covenant. The prophets' profession appears to have been lucrative and, as a result, had many practicing members.

M uch of Adonai's communication to the Israelites was conducted through angels, prophets and men of God. They conveyed His commands regarding leadership decisions, battle plans and situations involving individuals. Taken as a true depiction, these detailed commands show God again changing his relationship to accommodate the needs of the Israelites, from separation and working in the background to close, direct involvement. Taken as a literary device, it underscores the need for an explicit representation of God's actions to persuade people of His role in the world.

Without judging which interpretation is right, the role of prophets and men of God persisted in Judaism at least to Jesus. The persistence of prophets suggests people need explicit evidence of God, even if it requires a "fear of God" to be understood as such. To be sure, others may be comfortable believing God possibly acts in the background. Perhaps, the Torah allows for a variety of ways to envision God's involvement, some explicit and others abstract. The flexibility would mimic the choice between the guideline and code approaches to following the commandments, established in Exodus. It would permit the religion to accommodate a wide range of needs.

Magic and supernatural events are emphasized in the episodes involving prophets. In particular, the idea of resurrection is introduced with Elijah, when he adjures Adonai to bring back to life a woman's son who had stopped breathing. Resurrection continues with Elijah's successor, Elisha. He brings back to life a child of a wealthy family whom he had predicted would be born. Even after Elisha died, a dead man whose body makes contact with his bones comes back to life. Conceivably, all these cases can be explained rationally. But, they show the "value-added" of prophets, bringing the supernatural to bear in resolving a problem. These magical events can be taken several ways. Taken literally — even if the true explanation is more mundane — they underscore people's need to "see" extraordinary proof of Adonai's role in human events. They also can reflect frustration that more realistic evidence did not persuade people to adhere to Adonai. Or, they could be viewed as satirical, making fun of using such unworldly actions.

The existence of prophets attests to the inadequacy of the priesthood as established in Leviticus and Numbers. Priests may not have been easily accessible to those with problems, particularly after the centralization of the religion in Jerusalem. If they were accessible, they likely served as intermediaries in the sacrificial system — in a sense acting as tax collectors. Moreover, at least some priests were corrupt, interested only in taking sacrificial meals for themselves. In contrast, many of the "holy" individuals practiced their profession outside Jerusalem and dealt with ordinary people. In some respects, they acted as a social safety net, providing food during a famine and medical care.

The prophets' advisory role in government shows the separation of church and state, established in Numbers, did not work well. Their conveyance of God's messages to the king can be viewed literally. Or, the prophets can be viewed as intelligent, astute individuals who might have thought their ideas were inspired by God. In almost all cases, ordinary people and kings turned to prophets for forecasts.

Prophets, backed by their disciples, might be viewed as equivalent to the "think tanks" of today, hired by the government to analyze policy options. The prophets' analytical approach was based on the "model" that Adonai controlled events and, as a result, the Israelites had to follow His commandments to succeed in their endeavors.

The proliferation of prophets stands as evidence of the economic well-being in the Promised Land. An agricultural surplus allowed these "service-producing people" to focus on their supposed communication with God. Some may have partaken in the sacrificial meals shared by the priests. Others received contributions from individuals or compensation from the king. Whatever way they supported themselves appears to have been more than satisfactory, inasmuch as they had families as well as disciples.

These and other points can be seen in the following highlights.

Joshua

Adonai speaks directly to Joshua after he takes command of the Israelites. Acquiring this great responsibility, he needs close coaching to lead the Israelites into the Promised Land. The most interesting theological event is Adonai's command that Israelite men born after the exodus from Egypt be circumcised. Adonai's reasoning suggests the circumcision would enhance the Israelites' perception of themselves as a separate, free people. He says, "Today, I have rolled the reproach of Egypt from off of you."

Curiously, the original command to circumcise was made by Elohim, not Adonai. It formalized a covenant in which these other gods implicitly promised not to destroy the Israelites, being an "everlasting covenant." Perhaps Adonai wanted the latest generation of Israelites to reaffirm this covenant before entering Canaan where Elohim reigned. Or, He may have wanted them to be recognizable by Elohim. These explanations are not stated in the text. But, these ways of understanding the purpose of the second circumcision make it consistent with the novel approach taken in interpreting Genesis.

Judges

The theological elements of Judges arguably fit the satirical character of the Book, as discussed in *Here Comes the Judge* (Chapter 46). They exaggerate the problems faced by the religion and the responses to them. Nevertheless, the Book argues for the need of contemporaneous direct proof of God to convince people to adhere to the covenant. Direct proof does not sustain adherence beyond a generation.

The satire begins with the generation of Israelites after Joshua. These people turn to other gods, since they "didn't know the Lord, nor yet the work which He had worked for Israel." The oral or written history of the Exodus apparently was insufficient to persuade Israelites to stay true to Adonai. The satire is in the dubious forgetfulness or theological weakness of the people.

The Israelites can't see the relationship between good events and adhering to Adonai. They do not turn back to Him when He allows enemies to defeat them in battle. They live in peace only under leaders chosen by Adonai or an angel. But, after each of these regimes, the weak-spirited Israelites turn to other gods. People may not have seen the connection between their peaceful existence and attachment to Adonai. Or, cost concerns may have been responsible for the shift.

Even a chosen leader sometimes needs proof of Adonai's supernatural abilities to be fully persuaded of His intent to help beat other nations in battle. Such is the case with Gideon, who demands not only to see Adonai cause dew to fall on a piece of wool overnight but has the chutzpah to ask Him to perform a variation of the trick the next night (another instance of satire?).

Magic is evident again when an angel rises in the flame from a burnt offering to Adonai by Samson's parents. This episode shows, as well, that "men of God" existed then. That is what Samson's parents call the angel who tell them of their impending child.

Elohim make a presence when a ruthless leader, Abimelech, takes command of a group of Israelites without being chosen by Adonai. This group had turned to worshipping other gods, so it would seem to be under the purview of Elohim. Abimelech persuades the people to appoint him their king. Elohim, however, do not support Abimelech, consistent with the theme from Genesis that they act in concert with Adonai. Elohim instigate discord between the people and Abimelech that eventually leads to his death.

Samuel

Samuel grows up attached to Adonai, raised by Eli the priest. Eli may not have been entirely devoted to Adonai, however. He threatens that Elohim will harm Samuel if he does not reveal his dream. And, the dream consists of Adonai predicting the destruction of Eli's family because "his sons brought a curse on themselves and he didn't restrain them."

The Samuel story shows the need to convince people that a person is a true prophet. It suggests there were many so-called prophets practicing at the time, requiring discernment on the part of the people to know whom to believe. A prophet's forecasting record was the standard. Adonai "was with him, and did not let any of his words fall to the ground. All Israel from Dan even to Beersheba knew that Samuel was established to be a prophet of Adonai." This standard of proof is still valid in evaluating models and forecasters today.

Even though Samuel satisfies the test, his sons' bad behavior undermines his credibility. It presages the message from the David story regarding the dubious consequences of believing one hears Adonai, as discussed in *David Unhinged* (Chapter 42). Samuel is raised knowing his mother had pledged him to serve the Lord. He must have been open to the idea of directly communicating with Adonai. And, according to the text, this is what happened. "Adonai revealed Himself to Samuel at Shiloh by the word of the Lord." But, similarly to David, his progeny goes off track. Samuel, in old age, had made his sons judges over Israel. They "didn't walk in His ways, but turned aside after monetary gain, took bribes, and perverted justice." This leads people to demand he appoint a king, overriding his objections. They perhaps understand that Samuel aimed at protecting his sons' positions. He lost his credibility.

Minor Prophets

The history of the split countries, Israel and Judah, after Solomon, is a progression of Adonai-determined events prophesied by a number of minor prophets. This approach to history is similar to the one found in the Book of Daniel (*A History Lesson in the Book of Daniel* Chapter 45).

Most disturbing to Adonai appears to be the worship of other gods by the Israelite kings and their subjects. Practical considerations are responsible. King Jeroboam thinks "Will the kingdom return to the house of David? If this people go up to offer sacrifices in the house of Adonai at Jerusalem, then will the heart of this people turn again to Rehoboam king of Judah; and they will kill me."

The king appears to understand Adonai is the true god, however. The king sends his wife to an Adonai-prophet in Shiloh to obtain a forecast regarding his sick son. Non-Adonai prophets seem to have sensed their second-tier position. The interjection of how a false prophet tricks a true prophet to disobey Adonai demonstrates their resorting to desperate, competitive actions to discredit Adonai-prophets. Nonetheless, the king and his descendants do not give up the false religion, suggesting Judah is viewed as a more immediate concern than the longer-term threats from Adonai's prophets.

Elijah

Elijah's episodes underscore how difficult it is to discern true prophets. In his introductory episode, even actions that appear to be magical are not entirely convincing. Adonai does not allow a jar of flour or jug of oil to run out for a woman who is kind to Elijah. She apparently is not fully convinced he is a messenger of Adonai, though. Only a successful response by Elijah to a personal request for help, when her son is sick, persuades her Elijah is "a man of God and that the word of Adonai is in [his] mouth."

Part of the problem may be there were many prophets in

the Northern Kingdom claiming to communicate with one or other god. Besides Adonai-affiliated prophets, there were 450 attached to Baal and 400 to Asherah. Elijah says he hid 100 Adonai-prophets to protect them from Ahab's wife Jezebel, who had ordered them killed. And, Ahab asks about 400 Adonai-prophets whether he should battle the king of Aram. There is competition even among them. Micaiah is the only one of many Adonai-prophets who advises against the battle. But, Zedekiah, another Adonai-prophet, protests, saying "Which way went the Spirit of Adonai from me to speak to you?" How is anyone to know whom to believe? Micaiah retorts that the outcome of the battle will show who speaks the truth — unhelpful to those making decisions ahead of the event.

People also could view some prophets as biased and not to be trusted. Ahab views Elijah as a personal enemy. He complains that Micaiah "does not prophesy good concerning me, but evil." Ahab perhaps views Adonai-prophets as agents of Judah.

Even Elijah has doubts about being Adonai's prophet. Fleeing from Jezebel's assassins, he cries to Adonai, "Enough! O Adonai, take away my life, for I am not better than my fathers." An angel and then Adonai, Himself, reassure him of his mission and instruct him how to proceed.

Elisha

The striking feature of Elisha's activities as a prophet is the frequency at which he uses magic to help individuals. He helps the widow of one of his disciples fend off creditors by providing her with unlimited oil to sell. And, he uses magic to obtain food during a famine. His efforts suggest men of God provided a social safety net supplied by neither royalty or priesthood.

The recitation of his good works is marred by a story of God's retribution for a group of boys having made fun of Elisha's baldness — having bears kill them after he curses them. It puts neither Elisha nor God in a good light. In a sense, however, there is precedence for God's action in Exodus and Numbers.

God's wrath is shown against people who rebel against Him or his leaders (Moses). Having God set the bears on the boys is consistent with this precedence if Elisha is viewed as his appointed leader. But, the mundane nature of the offense suggests the episode is more akin to satire, as it applies a significant motivation of God's wrath in the Five Books to a silly prank by boys. Alternatively, the role of God in the boys' deaths may have been just a way of explaining an event in terms of the prophets' model, although it is better viewed as random.

Isaiah and Huldah

The prophet Isaiah and the prophetess Huldah forecast and communicate with Adonai for good kings — Hezekiah and Josiah, respectively — who "did that which was right in the eyes of Adonai." The episodes are notable in their depiction of communication between people and Adonai. Hezekiah's prayer is heard directly by Adonai. But, Adonai answers through prophets, as it is Isaiah who brings Adonai's response to him.

Josiah does not pray to Adonai after he becomes concerned He would punish him for the sins of his forefathers. This concern is sparked after reading a "book of the law" that had been found in the House of the Lord by Hilkiah, the high priest. Instead of asking Hilkiah to speak to Adonai, the king sends him and some government officials to Huldah to "inquire of the Lord" on his behalf. People understood that communication with Adonai did not occur through priests or by themselves, but through prophets.

Chapter 38 - *A Longer-Run Covenant*

Prophets pushed ideas of God's help in the long run to convince the Israelites to adhere to the covenant. Their approach is consistent with typical features of current-day forecasting.

T he prophets addressed the difficulty of discerning the near-term benefits of the covenant two ways. They emphasized the longer-run consequences of adhering or not to it, occurring in the real world and the after-life. In addition, the prophets asserted that God will return after a disaster if the Israelites stick with their end of the deal — resurrecting them from a seemingly hopeless situation. These longer-run arguments may have been more appealing to the logically-minded than the magic and miracles highlighted in Kings 2. Nonetheless, the prophets personified putative saviors and painted unrealistic views of the future, showing that explicit examples of God's powers may be needed to persuade at least some people to follow the religion.

Precedence in the Torah

The prophets' two approaches, to an extent, have precedence in Torah. Regarding the longer run, God foretells that Abraham's progeny will be as numerous as the stars and that the Israelites would spend 400 years in Egyptian slavery. Both forecasts relate to the real world. Statements of after-life reward and punishment cannot be found in the Five Books of Moses.

God's steadfastness is clearly seen in Exodus when He returns to free the Israelites after 400 years of slavery. It is important because it counters the risk people would give up on the covenant if their situation appears hopeless. Applying the idea of resurrection to the Israelite people as a whole, which some scholars say is the correct interpretation of the prophets' visions, implies an eventual recovery if they get into serious trouble. And, clearly, the history of the Jews supports the idea. Besides the Exodus, they bounced back from two expulsions from the Promised Land and expulsions, Inquisition and Holocaust in Europe.

The prophets' long-run approaches have a common element with the "behind-the-scene" depiction of God's help in the Balaam/Balak episode. There is no hard evidence of God's role. A fear of God and an assumption that He is acting or will act are required. Where the prophets' approaches differ from Balaam/Balak is their futuristic aspect. There is no immediately observable proof of God's actions in their pronouncements, unlike the possibility inherent in the Balaam/Balak message.

Credibility of the Prophets

The long-run approaches not only necessitated people's belief in God but also their belief in the credibility of the prophets, themselves. The latter would seem to be a given, since Biblical prophets are generally viewed as legitimately conveying God's messages. But, this view may not have been prevalent when they preached. There were many prophets, and it may have been difficult to discern their reliability. As a result, the prophets' tirades could have reflected frustration in trying to convince Israelites to follow the commandments and laws. The prophets were correct about the Assyrian and Babylonian conquests of the Northern Kingdom and Judea. While proof of their predictive success was too late for contemporaries, it may have enhanced their credibility for future generations.

The prophets' tirades are consistent with a couple of generic features of forecasting. Long-term projections often are made to have shock value without risk of being proved wrong soon. Also, the repetitive nature of the pronouncements across prophets is consistent with a tendency for forecasters to stay close to consensus. From a forecaster's perspective, staying close to consensus is a safe foray into the future since he could not fail relative to his colleagues or competitors. A prophet probably was aware of what the others said and did not want to diverge much from the general view. Of course, the general view might have been correct.

Examples of Extraordinary Visions and Personification of Saviors

Some of the prophets bolstered the longer-run benefits of adhering to God by describing extraordinary visions and saviors.

Ezekiel paints pictures of unrealistic beings in the heavens. He includes the promise of a "remnant" of the people surviving and returning to God.

Isaiah (Chapter 11) predicts a new leader "shall grow out of the stump of Jesse" who will derive wisdom and understanding from Adonai. He will not "judge by what he sees or hears." In other words, the new leader will have a fear of God and understand His role behind worldly events. He will not let a current disaster disabuse him of these beliefs. The leader will achieve idealistic goals of justice, "killing the wicked," because "the earth shall be full of the knowledge of Adonai." In addition, exiled Israelites will return to the land (i.e., be resurrected) and defeat their enemies. Isaiah emphasizes the powers of God by describing an extraordinary future where animals of prey live peacefully with their victims.

Other prophets also predict the arrival of a savior. Daniel dreams of "the great prince Michael," whose appearance will coincide with the recovery of those Israelites "written in the book." In addition, "many of those who sleep in the dust of the earth shall awake, some to everlasting life, and some to shame and everlasting contempt." Isaiah (Chapter 9) says a "child is born to us, a son is given; and the government shall be on his shoulder."

Substituting a person for God as the savior or conjuring up extraordinary visions may be rooted in Moses' complaint after the Golden Calf episode that he has never seen God. People may need a visualization to get the point of the argument.

Promoting God

Rather than describing unrealistic angels or person to enhance the idea of God's greatness, Isaiah begins (Chapter 2) by stating His eventual supremacy in the world, another long-run promise that provides a rationale for remaining committed to the covenant in bad times. It foretells a time ("in the latter days") when all people will acknowledge God's supremacy and the wisdom of His "ways." Since God will judge and arbitrate among the nations, they shall never "learn war any more."

This depiction might be viewed as partly fulfilled. Widespread acknowledgement of God's supremacy has happened, if it includes all the religions stemming from Judaism. But, the ultimate result of ending war remains an unrealistic promise. It also fails to recognize why God permits chaos (*Why Does God Permit Chaos?*, Chapter 2).

Resurrection

Isaiah (Chapter 4) uses metaphor to demonstrate the possibility of the Israelites' resurrection after a disaster. The metaphor says "seven women shall take hold of one man in that day, saying, 'We will eat our own bread, and wear our own clothing: only let us be called by your name.'" The "one man" is God, the clue being the word "one." Their own food and clothing means the women will practice their own religion and not turn to others. And, asking to be called by his name implies they want to be linked to Him. The remainder of the paragraph has God acquiescing, bestowing "beauty and glory to the survivors of Israel." God shows His steadfastness, resurrecting the Israelites. But, they have to commit to Him and His commandments.

Conclusion

The prophets' emphasis on the long-run benefits of adhering to God may have helped Judaism survive major catastrophes, as the latter could have undermined Israelites' belief in Him. Predicting God's help in the future was perhaps more convincing than magic or miracles to convince people to adhere to the commandments. A future hope is not subject to immediate failure, in contrast to this being a risk with magic and miracles. Nevertheless, the prophets' reliance on extraordinary visions and saviors shows people still may need a physical manifest-ation to be persuaded by the promise of future help.

Chapter 39 - *Compassion Versus Ritual*

The prophets emphasized the need for compassion rather than ritual to gain God's favor. In a sense, they "tweaked" their model describing the relationship between Israelites and God.

T he prophets are aghast not only at the Israelites' turning to other gods, but at their lack of compassion for the poor. They criticize the emphasis on ritual, including excessive animal sacrifices and wealth accumulation at the Temple. They argue that caring for those in need is more important.

Neglect of the poor may very well have resulted from the dire threats made by Assyria during the times of the prophets. Self-preservation became the norm and the social structure weakened, as Micah describes. Perhaps, the balance between ritual and compassion in the practice of Judaism depends on the political/social/economic conditions at the time — rightly or wrongly.

The first chapter of Isaiah lays out the issue directly. "'What are the multitude of your sacrifices to me?" says the Lord. "I have had enough of the burnt offerings...When you make many prayers, I will not hear...Learn to do well. Seek justice, Relieve the oppressed, Judge the fatherless, Plead for the widow." The Israelites are over-emphasizing ritual and ignoring the commandments regarding social welfare.

Conceivably, Isaiah realizes the ritualistic sacrifices did not prevent the Assyrians from invading Judah. They did not bring God down to help fight the invaders. He concludes that failure to care for others — another mainstay of the religion — is at fault. From a modern perspective, Isaiah sees that his model — God will protect the Israelites if they adhere to Him — is not working and needs to be tweaked. He consequently shifts the model's emphasis from ritual to compassion, hoping that a more balanced ordering of the commandments would elicit the desired response by God.

The prophets are correctly upset that Israelites neglect the poor. The Torah states the duality of ritual and caring by framing the harvest between bringing the first fruits to the Temple (ritual) and leaving fallen grain on the corners of the field (caring). Both are key parts of the religion. The Laws at Mount Sinai directly require helping the poor and powerless.

Ironically, the religion has evolved in a way that puts social welfare ahead of ritual, particularly for Reform Jews. Moreover, the idea of helping others has become more than just a commandment to follow. It is viewed as an integral part of the relationship between people and God. Some say one finds God when helping others. These ideas are post-Biblical innovations.

How General Are the Prophets' Ideas

While most view the prophets' exhortation for compassion and not just ritual as generally correct religious practice, other pronouncements are probably situation specific. For example, Isaiah tells the Judeans not to flee to Egypt to avoid the Assyrian assault. In contrast, Jeremiah argues for them to do so in the face of Babylonian aggression. Both are correct predictions. The conflicting good advice suggests the prophets' recommendations should not necessarily be extrapolated to future crises. They do not provide a clear-cut answer on whether to stay and fight or flee to fight another day. And, since there are no longer prophets, responsibility for making decisions in theses cases must rest with people.

Chapter 40 - *Did Ezra And Nehemiah Have The Answer?*

Years after the Prophets, lay leaders Ezra and Nehemiah faced the same problem — how to get the Israelites to adhere to Adonai, His laws and commandments. Instead of using longer-term projections to persuade, they instituted their own laws and restrictions. Some went beyond the requirements found in the Torah. Separation from surrounding peoples and a ban on intermarriage figured prominently. Their approach did not have lasting success, however.

T he Books of Ezra and Nehemiah describe the return of the Israelites to Jerusalem from Babylonian exile, after Persia had taken over. Ezra and Nehemiah hold high positions in the Persian king's court. Each persuades the king to let him take a group of Israelite exiles back to Jerusalem, which had fallen into disrepair. Ezra's task is to rebuild the Temple. Afterwards, Nehemiah's objective is to fix the walls of the city. Both aim to restore the religion of the Torah in Jerusalem.

A Stricter Code

Two controversial decisions are made by Ezra and Nehemiah. The non-Israelite residents who had been living in Jerusalem and its surrounding areas are not permitted to participate in the construction activities. And, the Israelites are not allowed to intermarry with them. If someone already had a non-Israelite wife, he was ordered to divorce her.

The two decisions go beyond the scope specified in the Torah. The latter permits acceptance of help from non-Israelite people. And, it does not have a blanket condemnation of intermarriage. The concise history of the Israelites found in Chapter 9 shows the leaders were well aware of the contents of the Torah.

Accepting Help From Others

The Torah contains a number of instances when the Israelites rely on help from others, or attempt to do so. Moses receives advice from his father-in-law, a Medianite priest. The Israelites ask Edom (unsuccessfully) for permission to cross through its territory during their journey to the Promised Land. Abraham and Jacob go to Egypt to escape a famine. And, Lebanese masons help shape stones for the construction of Solomon's Temple.

Mosaic Law does not appear to be the reason for excluding outsiders from participating in the reconstruction of the Temple. The returning exile leadership does not use theological reasons to deny their participation. Instead, they cite a political rationale. They say, "It is not for you and us to build a House of God, but we alone will build it to the Lord God of Israel, in accord with the charge that the king, King Cyrus of Persia, laid upon us."

The outsiders' theological argument for participating is not necessarily wrong. The outsiders include non-Jews who had been transferred there by the Assyrians. Their leaders say, "Let us build with you; for we seek your God, as you do; and we sacrifice to Him since the days of Esar-haddon king of Assyria, who brought us up here." They had viewed Adonai as the god associated with that land, as mentioned in Kings 2 (Chapter 17).

Perhaps, their exclusion was a power grab by the returning Israelite leaders to control the city's decision-making and the "taxes" collected by the Temple and at the city gates. The Books suggest that Ezra and Nehemiah were astute, practical leaders, able to deal with Persian bureaucracy and hostile neighbors. They should have easily understood the implications of power sharing.

Intermarriage

The Torah is precise with regard to intermarriage. It does not condemn marriage to a non-Israelite *per se*, but only if it results in the Israelite partner turning away from Adonai to another god. Moses marries non-Israelites. And, Israelite soldiers are allowed to marry captive Midianite women who had not attempted to convert them to their own religion. Unlike the Torah, the Ezra/Nehemiah prohibition does not allow for the possibility that spouses from peoples of the land would not interfere with the Israelites' religious practice or would convert to Judaism, themselves.

There may have been practical reasons for imposing such tight restrictions. Ezra and Nehemiah may have believed that a specific injunction against intermarriage was needed to ensure the cohesiveness and unity of the Israelite group that returned to Jerusalem. Or, they may have felt it would increase the likelihood the Israelites pay for the Temple's upkeep; the prohibition precludes the possibility that a non-Israelite spouse would argue for a less costly channel to a god. This rationale gets support from the prohibition being grouped with the four pledges in Chapter 10 that involve maintenance of the Temple and sacrificial system. In either case, the intermarriage prohibition is specific to the situation in which the two leaders find themselves and should not necessarily be generalized. The Torah's less restrictive take on the issue still may be valid in other circumstances.

The Pledges

Towards the end of the Book, Nehemiah insists the Israelites agree to seven pledges in addition to following "God's law, which was given by Moses the servant of God, and to observe and do all the commandments of the   Lord, and His ordinances and His statutes." The first pledge is "not to give our daughters to the peoples of the land, nor take their daughters for our sons." The second foreswears dealing with "peoples of the land" who sell in the market on the Sabbath —perhaps the first attempt at a "blue law" and presumably aimed to prevent non-Israelite merchants from having a competitive advantage. And, the third agrees to "forgo" output and debts in the Jubilee year — meant to prevent a maldistribution of wealth between debtors and creditors. The problem was highlighted earlier in the Book. The remaining four pledges pertain to bringing food-stuffs, wood and monetary contributions for the Temple and its sacrificial system.

They Don't Work

If the Book of Nehemiah stopped there, it would teach that an overly restrictive application of the Torah is effective in getting Jews to adhere to the religion. This is not the end of the Book, however. Nehemiah returns to Persia, staying there a period of time before going back to Jerusalem. On his return, he finds the Israelites had intermarried, worked on the sabbath, and neglected maintaining the Temple and supporting the Levites. The decisions, efforts and rule-giving by Ezra and Nehemiah were for naught. The cost and difficulty of discerning Adonai's role appear to have reasserted themselves in the Israelites' religious practice.

The Real Lesson

The real lesson from the Books turns out to be that imposition of laws by society's leaders, particularly those that go beyond the Torah, is not the answer to achieving a sustained adherence to Adonai and the religion.

Chapter 41 - *A Theory Of Ethics From Amos*

Amos was the first prophet to emphasize compassion over ritual. Examining his arguments shows a basis for them in the Torah and answers some important questions about social responsibility.

There are two themes in Amos. First, social responsibility, ethics and justice are more important than ritual for God. Second, God will destroy a society that fails to act appropriately.

These themes did not make much impression in the Northern Kingdom of Israel under Jeroboam II when Amos lived, but they appear to have had a major impact on subsequent religious thinking. Not only are they echoed in the messages of future prophets, but they also influenced the writers of Deuteronomy, which was likely written after Amos. The Song of Moses that ends Deuteronomy warns the Israelites of disastrous consequences by not fulfilling the spirit as well as the letter of the Law in the same uncompromising tone of Amos.

The Book of Amos raises several questions. Why are ethics and social justice so important in the religion? Why isn't the relationship between people and God more important? Why is ritual practice meaningless if not accompanied by social justice? Why should a society be punished because of the bad behavior of only some of its members? Is the Book just the rantings of a prophet who was not listened to, or is it a well-based application of ideas found in the Torah to a bad situation?

Why Are Ethics and Social Justice Important?

Amos' idea that social responsibility, ethics, and justice are at least as important as ritual practice can be supported in Genesis and Exodus. In Genesis, Isaac and Jacob are not negligent about building altars and sacrificing to God. However, they fail to prevent members of their families from acting improperly. These failures condemned the Hebrew people to 400 years of slavery in Egypt. In Exodus, ritual and ethics appear to be equally balanced, as a good amount of space is devoted to both social laws and to the tabernacle and priesthood.

The importance of social justice in the Torah may reflect an implicit understanding that it derives from the concept of monotheism and the idea that God is the creator of all things If everyone is a creation of the same God, then each person is in some sense equal. A person cannot say he is more deserving than another because his God is better. However, the truth is that some people are more successful than others. Their success may stem from hard work, luck, or from having special abilities or talents. Does that mean people deserve all the rewards of their success?

The Torah argues not. Under the belief that God creates everything, abilities and talents are God-given. As a result, people do not deserve all the "returns" from their abilities. Some should accrue to God. This accrual can occur by people using their abilities and talents toward God's goals. Genesis and, perhaps more explicitly, Exodus indicate a goal of God is for people to be ethical, including helping the widow, orphan and poor. So, God may give people abilities in part for them to help the less advantaged. In this light, the Torah's answer to Cain's question whether he is his brother's keeper is "yes, to some extent."

Who Gets Credit?

The God-given nature of all things perhaps explains why Amos is so troubled by the Israelites' attribution of their political and military success to their own abilities and not to God. By forgetting that God grants success, the Israelites could decide they do not have to follow the commandments or to view each other as God's creation. The upper classes of the Israelite society could claim all the rewards from their successes and not share their good fortune with the poor.

The text hints at this problematical thought process. Amos cites both favorable and unfavorable events in Israel as having been determined by God, but says the Israelites do not recognize them as stemming from Him. They did not "return" to God when there was "cleanness of teeth in your cities" nor "lack of food in all your settlements, drought, blight, mildew, locusts and pestilence and military defeats." They apparently view their successes as self-won and misfortunes random.

The idea that someone's or society's success results at least in part from God is an important theme in the Torah. It arguably motivates God's testing of Abraham in the Akedah (*Why the Akedah*, Chatper 9). Also, the Israelites are warned by Moses not to forget it is God and not they who will be responsible for their good fortune in Canaan.

Problems With Rituals?

Why did Amos concentrate on ethical behavior, even though there were problems with ritual practice in Israel under Jeroboam II? A golden calf had been placed in the new temples in Bethel and Dan by Jeroboam I. Cult places were established and non-Levites appointed as priests. Nazarites were made to drink wine, and prophets prevented from making prophecies. Amos is disdainful of the Israelite temples, saying God will punish Israel for its transgressions, "cutting off" the horns of the altar at Bethel. The Israelites' only hope is to return to God (Jerusalem) and to forego the temples at Bethel, Gilgal and Beersheba.

Nonetheless, Amos perhaps understands the Northern Kingdon's temples and rituals are essentially monotheistic in nature. They are not meant to serve other gods. Jeroboam says of his new temples, "see your God, Israel, which brought you up out of the land of Egypt." While the rituals may have differed from those of the Temple in Jerusalem, the Israelite temples remained committed to a monotheistic religion. With this basic requirement met, Amos focused on the Israelite society's ethical shortcomings.

Punishing Society?

Amos' threats of social destruction because of unethical behavior has a basis in the Torah. In the Book of Genesis, there are two episodes when God destroys society – the Flood and Sodom and Gomorrah. In both cases, society is destroyed for the evil ways of the people and not for their failure to sacrifice to God.

But, God is not capricious nor uncompromising. In the Flood, the righteous Noah and his family are saved. In Sodom and Gomorrah, God is willing to spare the cities if Abraham could find ten innocent people. Moreover, God needs to see proof that these societies are corrupt. God says, "Because the cry of Sodom and Gomorrah is great, and because their sin is very grievous, I will go down now and see whether they have done altogether according to the cry of it." In the Flood, God decides to destroy humanity only when He "saw the earth, and saw that it was corrupt."

Amos appears to be aware of the considered nature of God's actions. He emphasizes that God acts only when it is clear that people do not change their ways. In Chapters 1 and 2, he hammers home the point that God overlooked three transgressions of different societies before acting on the fourth. In Chapter 4, Amos says God already sent warnings to Israel, including famine, uneven and insufficient rainfall, blight and mildew, pestilence, and military defeats. But, the people of Israel did not turn back to Him. In Chapter 7, God shows Amos three scenarios. In the first two, God creates a plague of locusts and fire, but relents from their destroying Israel after hearing pleas from Amos. In the third episode, God uses a plumb line to judge Israel and finds it lacking. He "will not again pass by them any more." God gives the Israelites plenty of opportunity to change their ways before He acts, just as Amos depicts.

As a result of unethical ways, the Israelites would see their success short-lived. God would drive them into exile and withdraw from their society – "They will wander from sea to sea and from the north even to the east; They will run back and forth to seek the word of the Lord and will not find it." God's withdrawal ensures the Northern Kingdom would never recover.

A threat of God's withdrawal has precedence in Exodus. There, a partial withdrawal of God was frightening to the Israelites after the Golden Calf episode at Mount Sinai. God tells them, "I will send an angel before you…But I will not go in your midst, as you are a stiff-necked people, lest I destroy you on the way." Despite being promised some divine help in the form of an angel, the Israelites react to this "harsh word" by mourning and removing their "jewelry."

Should Victims of Social Injustice Be Punished?

Why should victims of social injustice be punished along with the well-to-do? There is evidence in the Torah that innocent people can be impacted by God's wrath. Not everyone in Jacob's family sinned, but all found themselves exiled in Egypt. In the Golden Calf episode, there is a distinction between people who sinned and those who did not. God says, "Whoever has sinned against Me will I blot out of My book." Nevertheless, all the people are put through hardship because of the transgression: "In the day when I punish, I will punish them for their sin. The Lord struck the people, because they made the calf, which Aaron made." In Numbers, God destroys the rebels led by Korah along with their households, even though the latter did not play an active role in the confrontation with Moses. People are responsible for the moral fiber of the group in which they belong.

The idea that society is an entity responsible for maintaining morality within itself is the rod stick at the time of the Flood, Sodom and Gomorrah, Golden Calf, and Canaan, as well as to the later Jewish kingdoms. Society has a destiny that transcends individual members. Its destiny depends on its overall morality and fidelity to God.

Conclusion

Amos' fiery language may be the rantings of an ignored prophet. However, his ideas and prophesies are well founded in the Torah, albeit narrowly based with their emphasis on God's anger. Other visions of God are seen in the Torah, and the role of randomness is missing in his analysis. Nevertheless, Amos' vision may have dominated subsequent religious thinking after his prophecy of the Northern Kingdom's destruction proved correct.

Amos' argument that social morality is connected to a society's destiny is very much a part of our own modern worldview. For example, the US often justifies its actions in terms of morality or helping others. And, both Nazi Germany and the Soviet Union were castigated as evil, immoral empires that would not long survive. That Amos was able to elicit these themes from the Torah so clearly and with such single-mindedness may help explain why they have had so long-lasting influence.

Chapter 42 - *David Unhinged*

The Story of King David can be interpreted as a criticism of those people who think they communicate with God.

Everyone knows about King David – how he is chosen by God to replace Saul as king, becoming the greatest king of Israel; how he expands Israel's borders; and how his son, the wise Solomon, follows him on the throne. A more cynical tradition, ascribed to the priesthood, has Saul and David demonstrating the faults of kingship predicted by the prophet Samuel.

Both have problems. The common view does not fit the story, which shows David and Solomon having significant flaws. The cynical view doesn't demonstrate any better outcome with a dominant priesthood. More interesting from a theological perspective, the story can be interpreted as a criticism of thinking one has been picked by God. It shows how such a person turns away from the religion or becomes unhinged from reality when things go wrong. People without any putative contact with God are the ones most reliable in making a difference in the course of events.

Saul's sense of chosen-ness is undermined by failure on the battlefield. But, he doesn't look to himself for an explanation. Instead, he asks the witch of Endor if God is still with him. This reliance on a pagan ritual/conduit is expressly prohibited in the Torah, equivalent to converting to another religion.

In David's case, the consequence of losing a sense of chosen-ness is to retreat from acting responsibly. David justifies almost all his actions, good and bad, by claiming God is with him. But, when Nathan says God will punish him for the sin he committed in sending Uriah to the front, David appears to lose self-confidence. He spends his days in the castle, letting others maintain his kingdom and doing little, if anything, to stop his children from behaving badly.

David's attitude toward God changes after his efforts to reverse the promised punishment fails. When his young son dies as prophesied, he ends his fasting, saying there is nothing he could do to bring him back. He perhaps recognizes that his supposed special relationship with God has ended. The decision to stop fasting surprises his servants, suggesting it represents a pulling back from his earlier connection with God.

David seems to lose interest in ruling the country, as well. He stays within his castle, perhaps hoping to regain God's favor (by writing psalms?). He lets Joab and others keep his kingdom under control, except when Joab pushes him to join the army while it is involved in a siege. Afterwards, David reverts to reclusion.

Within the castle, David pulls back from familial responsibility. He ignores the sinful and rebellious actions of his son, Absalom, until it is almost too late. He does not stand up to his sons, giving in to Absalom's request for his half-brother Amnon to attend a festival (only to be assassinated there). David appears to be unhinged from outside events and the machinations of his sons.

David's perception of chosen-ness may have affected his sons, who behave without restraint. Absalom kills his half-brother Amnon who (himself sinning) had raped his half-sister (Absalom's sister). Then Absalom incites the Israelites outside of Judah to rebel against David, contrary to the commandment not to "curse a ruler of your people." Solomon, who God "favored" at birth, has his half-brother Adonijah killed, citing God's special relationship in making the decision. He allows his wives' pagan religions to be practiced in Jerusalem.

This way of explaining the Saul/David story stands as an allegory for the Jewish people if viewed (simplistically) as the Chosen People. When the going got tough, some Jews converted to other religions. Others retreated into their enclaves, waiting for God to save them (sometimes with disastrous consequences). Jewish history mirrors the Saul/David story at times.

Unhinging the David story from myth shows the Tanakh approaching the belief of chosen-ness cautiously. People who claim a special relationship with God do bad as well as good deeds. When their belief is undermined, as is most likely the case, fundamental ideas of the Torah can be violated. Looking to other gods undermines the unitary nature of the religion. Abdicating responsibility in the world runs counter to the idea that Jews are meant to act like God, including achieving their own destiny.

The true heroes of the Saul/David story are people, like Joab, who work to maintain the kingdom – or, from the allegorical perspective of the story, the Jews who maintain the religion as well as participate in the world. This may be the correct way to interpret the episode toward the end of the story. There, David praises God in song, which is then followed by a recitation of what his key soldiers accomplished on the battlefield. The song is unworldly, unhinged from real events. The bravery of David's soldiers as they deal with difficult situations is the final word.

Chapter 43 - *A Job On Job*

The story of Job raises doubts about applying facile theology to explain events.

The Book of Job is typically seen as a criticism of Deuteronomy's reward-punishment theology. God punishes Job, although he did nothing wrong. The Book can be viewed another way, however. It criticizes the application of seemingly plausible theology to explain events.

Job's friends offer standard, conventional ideas about sin, God, reward and punishment to explain his troubles. But, none is correct. Perhaps in irony, the author of the Book even has God distorting the truth, when He describes His creation of a non-existent Leviathan.

Job is the only one telling the truth. He protests his innocence, correctly so since the prologue indicates his being an upright person whom God punishes only to test. Job's calamities have nothing to do with any sinful action on his part.

From this perspective, the Book teaches to be cautious in applying the Torah to explain what is observed in the world. Interpretations that are ostensibly in line with the Torah, such as those of Job's friends, may not be right.

Chapter 44 - *Is The Book Of Jonah Kosher?*

The Jonah story shows that a person cannot run away from God's commands. It sheds light on Abraham's argument with God regarding the destruction of Sodom.

I s the Book of Jonah consistent with the Torah? There are three parts to consider – Jonah's failed attempt to avoid God's command, the threat to and reaction by the Ninevites, and God's conversation with Jonah at the end of the Book. All three parts can be justified by reference to the Torah.

Jonah's Attempt at Avoidance

Jonah does not want to deliver God's message to the Ninevites because he thinks He will offer them an undeserving pardon for their bad deeds. From the start, he is resigned to God's sparing the Ninevites. And, he tries to run away from the task.

Both the Book of Jonah and the Torah show, however, that people cannot escape God's command. The first example is in the Garden of Eden, when Adam and Eve try to hide from God after eating from the Tree of Knowledge. They cannot. Similarly, Jonah is caught up in a storm and swallowed by a fish when he tries to escape, as God hauls him in.

The impossibility of escaping from God's command puts the Abraham saga in a new light. When God tells Abraham to sacrifice Isaac, Abraham's trance-like acquiescence reflects this impossibility. He realizes he cannot run away from God's command. Why, in contrast, does Abraham bargain with God to save Sodom? Isn't this the same as trying to change a command? In this case, however, God just informs Abraham what he intends to do. He does not command Abraham to do anything. As a result, Abraham feels free to argue with Him.

Ninevah and Sodom

Why did God give Nineveh a chance to avoid punishment? Did God give Sodom a chance? Was this a new approach to sinful societies by God? In fact, there is little difference between God's approach to Sodom and Ninevah. Instead, the difference is in the reactions of the Sodomites and Ninevites to the threat.

In both cases, God gives the cities a chance to repent. God sends an emissary to each city – Jonah to Nineveh and two angels to Sodom. The Torah doesn't say whether the angels would tell the Sodomites to repent or face destruction. The Sodomites do not give them a chance. Immediately on hearing of their arrival, a mob tries to molest them. In Nineveh, people, up to the king, immediately repent when warned by Jonah of God's displeasure. Viewed this way, the two episodes are not much different in terms of God's approach. An emissary is sent to warn the people to change. But, people respond differently.

God's Conversation with Jonah

The key to the conversation is what it shows about Jonah's knowledge of God's ways. Jonah believes he knows how God thinks. This belief is atypical of most, if not all, the main characters in the Torah. The Patriarchs do what God commands, but do not anticipate any of them. They do not know what to expect from Him. For example, when God tells Abraham that Sarai will give birth, he laughs. Abraham asks that "Oh that Ishmael might live before you," believing God's promise of offspring would be achieved through Hagar's son. Abraham does not know God's ultimate plans.

Jonah knows more about God than did the Patriarchs because he had read the Torah! As proof, Jonah's prediction is based on attributes of God told to Moses. Jonah says, "For I knew that you are a gracious God, and merciful, slow to anger, and abundant in lovingkindness, and you repent of the evil." Even so, he does not get them entirely right, failing to mention that God does not forgive all sins and can visit punishment on future generations. He leaves out the attributes that should have assuaged his concern.

Jonah is ignorant of God's motives. Jonah cannot even figure them out from the experience of the flower. He is deeply upset about the flower's death, but doesn't see the parallel with Nineveh. Nevertheless, it is one of the few instances in the Bible where God explains his motives. He says Nineveh is a great city in which there are more than 120,000 persons who do not yet know their right hand from their left, and many cattle. The reference to right and left-handed people could be read that God believes the Ninevites did not know right from wrong and therefore should be given a chance to repent and change their ways. The traditional view of the reference to the size of the population is that it is a sign of God's compassion toward so many of His creations.

This appears to be quite different from God's actions towards sinful Jews in Exodus and later Books. Why isn't God compassionate to them? Instead, God quickly brings wrath and vengeance down against them. But, there is a difference between the Ninevites and the people in the Torah. The Ninevites do not have the Torah to guide them. In contrast, the post-Exodus Jews know right from wrong because God gave them commandments and law. For example, Aaron's sons should have known not to bring alien fire into the Tent. God did not hesitate to kill them.

Another way to look at God's reason is somewhat fanciful, but in line with ideas in the Torah. By citing the many people and cattle in Nineveh, God invokes the "Too Big to Fail" doctrine. Nineveh is apparently a wealthy city and cannot be summarily destroyed. It is not clear whether Sodom was as well endowed, although, as mentioned above, God may have wanted to give it a chance also. The doctrine is consistent with God's covenant with Noah and may help explain why God let the Israelites' enemies (except the Amalekites) co-exist with them. They were too big and wealthy to destroy.

Conclusion

The Book of Jonah clearly embodies the principles found in the Torah. Its main point is that a person cannot run away from God's commands. But, in comparing and contrasting it with the Torah shows that a lot more can be discerned. These include

CARL J. PALASH

God's approach to sinful societies, why Abraham was able to bargain with God to spare Sodom, and why God doesn't just destroy the Israelites' enemies. Not bad for a small book.

Chapter 45 - *A History Lesson In The Book Of Daniel*

The Daniel story presents too restrictive a view of history by not allowing for random developments. All is attributed to God's pre-determined plans.

T he Book of Daniel seems to be an alien way of looking at history, bordering on "make believe." Nevertheless, it allows for some general conclusions to be made about God's role in history as suggested by the Torah.

Daniel clearly is a history book. It completes the history of the Middle East where the Book of Kings ends, *i.e.*, it takes us from Babylon to the Greeks. However, the history is done in a peculiar way. The future unfolds ahead of fact through dream interpretations. While this approach strikes a modern reader as "fantastic," there are two important assumptions behind it — God controls history and history is just an unfolding of events predetermined by God. These assumptions may have dominated Jewish views of world history since the Babylonian exile. They very well may be behind many orthodox views today.

It is easily understandable why Jews liked this approach to history. Jews were a small, weak nation, and world events were generally out of their control. Believing divine control of history gave them a feeling of power, since God was on their side (assuming they followed the commandments). Looking ahead to a day of judgment ensured that enemies would get their just reward at some point.

So, is this approach just a function of the political-economic conditions of the Jews? What does the Torah say about the role of God in history? The answer is mixed – He knows what will happen at times but not others.

God's foreknowledge of the future is found throughout the Torah. He tells Abraham and his offspring their family will develop into a great nation. He also foretells his descendants spending 400 years in Egypt. At the end of Deuteronomy, God tells Moses that after his death the Hebrew people will go astray and break the covenant. As a result, evils and troubles will befall them because He will "keep his countenance hidden on that day."

There are just as many times, however, when the future seems to surprise Him. In the story of Noah, man's wickedness is so great that God "regretted that He had made man on earth, and His heart was saddened." These are not appropriate feelings for God if He knew in advance what would happen to His creations.

Similarly, the possibility of a surprising twist of history can be found in the story of the Tower of Babel. People in the story try to be like gods by reaching for the heavens. They do not know their place in the world order. God apparently understands that if He does not intercede, people could take the wrong track. He recognizes a chaotic portion of the world that can evolve independently of His desires.

Chaos can be seen elsewhere in the Torah. In Exodus, the Amalek represent chaos. They practice evil and are without constraint. God's admonition to remember or destroy the Amalek shows there is and always will be an element in the world beyond His control.

From the Torah's perspective, history evolves partly according to God's direction and partly independently of Him. So, the Book of Daniel is not necessarily a wrong approach to history. But, it is a narrow approach with no guarantee of being right. History can evolve independently of God. So, the approach taken by Daniel may very well reflect the weak political-economic conditions of the Jews at the time.

This also means the traditional view, as expressed in Daniel and Micah, that people should sit back in difficult situations and wait for God to solve their problem is too restrictive. The Torah justifies actively working to change conditions in the world without waiting for a signal from God, since the resolution of a situation is not necessarily pre-determined. People can take pride in their accomplishments. But, they should do so with a humble question in the back of their minds as to whether they are truly responsible.

Chapter 46 - *Here Comes The Judge*

The Book of Judges can be read as satire. But, it contains the theological message that people will "sin" if they are allowed to do as they please.

The perplexing issue about Judges is trying to figure out what theological purpose it has in the Tanakh. Scholarly works cite incidents from it with the utmost seriousness. But, many can be viewed as satire, with episodes bordering on the ridiculous.

The satire contrasts the behavior of the Israelites with the "true" theological elements of the Torah. Some Israelites communicate directly with God, although such communication is the privilege of only Abraham and Moses in the Torah. The Israelites act in absurd ways and often attribute their decisions to God. But, their actions tend to be contrary to the commandments found in the Torah – and over the course of the Book increasingly so.

What is this Book doing in the Tanakh? Is the answer found in the last sentence? "In those days there was no king in Israel: every man did that which was right in his own eyes." The first part of the sentence would seem to support the standard answer that the Book of Judges serves as a bridge between Joshua and Kings, and, with the many faults committed by people in Judges, provides a justification for the establishment of a kingship. This explanation, however, is not satisfying when one considers that theological/ethical problems persist under Saul, David and Solomon.

The bottom line may be tied to the second part of the last sentence. The Book shows what happens when everyone does as he pleases and the commandments are not enforced. People behave in increasingly sinful ways. Seen this way, the Book has a message for all generations of Jews: They need to find ways to enforce the commandments. People cannot be allowed to do as they please.

How to enforce the commandments has changed over time. Universal knowledge of the quid pro quo covenant along with a fear of God are the answer to the enforcement issue in most of the Torah. Deuteronomy adds love of God to persuade Jews to follow the commandments. Prophets threaten Godly retribution for people's sinful actions. A theocracy run by the priesthood is not the answer, according to the Book of Numbers. In later years, however, the rabbinic leadership in the shtetls of Europe (and in some Jewish communities today) played the role of enforcer. There is no enforcer for most Jews now, and, true to the Book of Judges, everyone pretty much does as he pleases. Reading the Book of Judges should make us more aware of the potential consequences of this fact. And, that may be why it is in the Tanakh.

Chapter 47 - **Why Is Esther In The Bible?**

Although the Story of Esther is known for not involving God, it contains two important theological points — the needs for adherence to God and for individuals to solve problems themselves. The latter point makes Purim a good balance to Passover.

T he Story of Esther has always raised questions because God is not mentioned. The Persian Jews are saved not by "heavenly" intervention, but by two individuals, Esther and Mordecai. Their actions are in stark contrast to the direct role played by Adonai in the first five Books of the Torah and in the Promised Land. The story, however, is consistent with two major theological tenets of the Torah — the need for adherence to Adonai and the need for individuals to attempt to solve problems themselves before Adonai helps.

An Approach to Following the Religion

The Esther story can be viewed as one approach to practicing the religion laid out in the Five Books of Moses. It requires adherence to Adonai. But, people's own actions matter.

The latter stands in contrast to the religious practices explored in the Tanakh's writings regarding the Israelites in the Promised Land. They emphasize reliance on Adonai. The Book of Joshua through Kings 2 show people asking Adonai for direction or help. People communicate with Him primarily through prophets, while ritual is performed by priests. A more direct, individualist approach to Adonai is displayed in the Psalms, in which praise and personal requests of Adonai are made.

These Adonai-focused approaches are embodied in the traditional Haggadah. The latter attributes the Exodus fully to Adonai's power, not even mentioning Moses' role (*Understanding the Haggadah*, Chapter 14). It aims to convince Jews to follow the commandments by establishing an obligation to Adonai for having freed them from the Egyptians. In doing so, however, it inadvertently undermines the idea that people should solve problems themselves. The conflicting approaches of the Haggadah and the Book of Esther are brought home by the proximity of Passover to Purim. Jews are to be aware of both approaches when they celebrate these holidays.

Another Interpretation of Esther

The location of the Book of Esther offers another clue on evaluating its role in the Tanakh. Esther follows Lamentations and Ecclesiastes. The former bemoans the destruction of Judah and Israel, finalizing the dire consequences predicted by the prophets. Ecclesiastes and Esther raise doubts about the significance of the covenant. Ecclesiastes questions whether material or worldly success is meaningful, since death awaits all. To be sure, a person not as wealthy as King Koheleth (who raises this question) would probably not dismiss such success so readily. Esther raises doubts about the need for God to solve problems. These questions and doubts are addressed in the Book of Daniel, which comes after Esther. Daniel describes not only how God helps in the world, but also how He ministers justice (reward and punishment) in the after-life. In this interpretation, Ecclesiastes and Esther are there to acknowledge important issues, but not to change the God-centric message of the prophets.

Adherence to Adonai

Mordecai and Esther clearly do not stray from Adonai. Mordechai instructs Esther not to let the king know she is Jewish until doing so is needed to save her people. And, he attributes his decision not to bow to Haman to being Jewish. By asserting their Jewishness, they, in effect, affirm their adherence to Adonai. Indeed, Persians viewed Jews as a distinct national group, with their own god — Adonai.

Adherence to Adonai is arguably the most important commandment in the Torah. It is the first of the Ten Commandments. Adonai's wrath and severe punishments are seen almost only in cases when the Israelites turn to other gods or attempt to undermine His appointed leaders. Although the Torah also requires commitment to the other commandments to obtain

Adonai's favor, Mordecai's and Esther's assertion of their Jewishness was an important step. They satisfied the basic demand made by the prophets — that Jews not turn to other gods.

Equating Jewish identification to obeying the First Commandment may be an implicit message of the Esther story. It emphasizes that Jews of all stripes — today, Conservative, Reform or Orthodox — are all in harmony with this fundamental principle of the religion.

Solving Problems

Neither Esther nor Mordecai asks for Adonai's help, either through ritual or prayer. By leaving out Adonai, the story goes to the extreme in illustrating Genesis' point that one has to attempt to solve a problem before expecting Him to help.

To be sure, the Balaam/Balak episode in Numbers suggests Adonai may be helping in the background. And, Esther and Mordecai possibly had this subtle understanding, though it is not mentioned in the text. Appreciating the possibility of Adonai in the background is a more sophisticated approach to understanding God's role in the world than a demonstration of magic and accurate predictions by prophets.

The Esther story argues against focusing solely on Adonai to the exclusion of everything else. It reaffirms that Jews are to be involved with the overall society in which they live and to take responsibility for ensuring their proper place in it. They are not to recuse themselves from the real world and devote themselves fully to Adonai through prayer or poetry, contrary to what David did in his later years. It implicitly critiques the unconditional requests for Adonai's assistance made in the Psalms.

Conclusion

As an approach to practicing the religion, the Esther story may be more important in the Tanakh than generally recognized. It demonstrates how to do so without depending on unworldly evidence provided by people who claim to communicate with Adonai and without divorcing oneself from the real world through psalms and prayer. The story implicitly shows the need to profess adherence to Adonai. At the same time, it underscores the need to solve one's own problems, although the possibility of Adonai helping in the background cannot be ruled out. The story carries a large responsibility as it balances against the message found predominantly in other writings of the Tanakh and the Haggadah, that is to rely on Adonai.

Chapter 48 - Making Sense Of
The "Song Of Songs"

The Song of Songs is difficult to make sense of. But, it turns out to be a critique of King Solomon and the centralization of the religion in Jerusalem.

T he imagery contained in Song of Songs makes it difficult to draw out the book's meaning and purpose. But, it can be done. It does not require imposing outside characters, such as "other nations" or changing the words, found in traditional interpretations. Instead, it requires "tilting" the words so they read somewhat differently from how they appear at first glance. It is like a book whose pictures change when it is moved back and forth.

Song has three messages. First, the book may echo the complaint of the people in northern Israel against the centralization of the religion in Jerusalem. Solomon was taking God away from them. There is a sense that God is tied to a location, which was clearly the view at the time. Second, the Song hints of the disagreement between Samuel and the Israelites whether to anoint a king. Samuel's argument that Israel needs only God for a king is used to deprecate Solomon. Third, the book criticizes outside influences on the Israelites. Keeping them away is what God wants. These messages are seen by going through each chapter.

Chapter 1

The need to tilt the words occurs in the opening four verses. With its emphasis on kissing, virgins, etc., the sexuality of the text hits the reader up front. Moreover, as the Song of Songs is said to be Solomon's, and the woman says the "king has brought me into his chambers," the natural conclusion is the woman is in love with Solomon and her love is about to be consummated.

This conclusion, however, is farthest from the truth. Instead, all the fervent, passionate language should be seen as a final affirmation of the woman's love for God (her true lover) before she is brought into the presence of Solomon to defend her position (among which is that God belongs to her and not just to Jerusalem). The comment that the "king has brought me to his chambers" is more an aside from her other statements, and meant to set the scene. It should be read in hush, fearful tones. In this sense, the woman's effusion of passion should be seen in the same light as the fervent prayers of the early Christians before being thrown to the lions. Both show a fierce dedication to their god before being sacrificed because of it. In Song, the woman's dedication is expressed in terms of a personal, sensual and intimate relationship. So, what we have in the first four verses sets the scene. A woman is appearing in front of King Solomon to make her case. The rest of the book is a linear progression of her appeal.

In verses 5-8, the woman begins her appeal by identifying herself. She describes herself as different from the "Daughters of Jerusalem" because she was scorched black by the sun. She is from a rural area, in contrast to the women of the city. Throughout the book, the use of bucolic words to describe the woman and her lover reflects her rural background. Here, the woman's comments are defensive, saying she is comely despite being black. This protestation hints at a sense of inferiority often associated with country folk in the presence of "sophisticated" city dwellers. But, the difference between the woman and the Daughters becomes more significant as the book progresses. In particular, while she knows God (her lover), the Daughters of Jerusalem do not.

She hints at why God left her. She is the keeper of vineyards, although not her own. In a Cinderella-like comment, she says her siblings were angry with her and forced her to care for their vineyards. This comment may reflect an actual event, possibly when the other tribes discriminated in some way against the tribe in the north. In any case, it is clear by the end of the book that God prefers the woman to stay in her own garden. Throughout the book, the term, "garden," should be understood as community, own area, or particular group of people.

In verse 9-16, the woman makes the point that she and God are well acquainted. She describes a dialogue of mutual admiration. She says their house is made of cypress and cedars, trees from the North that could be meant to underscore the location where they knew each other. This passage is important because it establishes a basis for her complaint that Solomon is taking God away from her -- she had been with God before Solomon.

Chapter 2

Here, the woman reminisces about events when she and God were together. This too establishes a basis for complaint. As an aside, she warns the Daughters of Jerusalem "not stir up nor awaken love until it pleases." Its meaning becomes clearer later.

Chapter 3

The woman now proceeds with her story. She had gone to Jerusalem to find God. Neither the watchman nor Daughters of Jerusalem had seen Him. This shows that whatever the Jerusalamites were doing, it was not good enough to have God make Himself known to them. The woman then finds God, at least in her imagination. And, she mockingly tells the Daughters of Jerusalem to go see Solomon, who is coming to the city with his soldiers -- a poor substitute for God. This hints at the argument of Samuel that a king cannot take the place of God. She also says to go "see king Solomon with the crown with which his mother crowned him on his wedding day." Today, this sentence is used in some siddurs to glorify a wedding. But, in terms of this analysis, the comment is not a compliment. Instead, it is a put-down. The woman makes the point that Solomon was anointed by his mother, unlike Saul and David who were anointed by God through the prophet Samuel.

Chapter 4

This could be the woman's dream, in which she and God are talking together. There are some key elements. First, God's description of the woman is of a dual nature. God starts out by praising her fair looks. But, then God describes her neck to be like "David's tower." This latter description is not as sensual as the other phrases used to describe her. But, it is critical to understanding the kind of person she is. She is strong and defiant, more a Statue of Liberty than a Venus de Milo. Her virtue is being steadfast against outside influences. This is praised by God when he says, "A locked up garden is my sister, my bride; A locked up spring, A sealed fountain fountain locked, a sealed-up spring." The imagery of an enclosed garden comes up elsewhere, most importantly at the end. It should be viewed in contrast to the connections Solomon made with the outside world -- marriages, concubines and temples to other gods.

The rest of the chapter describes the woman's wish that she and God be together again. She says, "Awake, north wind; and come you south; Blow on my garden, that its spices may flow out. Let my beloved come into his garden, And taste his precious fruits."

Chapter 5

The climax of the story is in this chapter. It begins with the woman waking from a dream as God "knocks." But, she gives excuses why she does not get out of bed to open the door. Her coat is off, her feet washed, how could she now dirty her feet? When she finally brings herself to open the door, God is gone. This passage is important. It shows God did not forsake her, but instead came to her. It was her fault they did not get together. This fits with the view that it is the Israelites' own fault when God is not there to help them.

When she realizes what she did, the woman panics. She runs wildly through the streets of Jerusalem. There, she is struck and wounded by the people. This is more punishment for not making an effort to bring in God. And, it could be read as a description of what will happen to the Israelites when they are exiled in the future -- also seen as a result of their drawing away from God. The Daughters of Jerusalem are scornful of her fixation with God when they say, "How is your beloved better than another beloved?" In other words, why is your God better than the other gods? The woman then describes God in a fit of powerful imagery.

Chapter 6

This chapter seems to be the denouement after the climax in the prior chapter. The woman still cannot find God, but asserts that God is back in His garden. Importantly, this is not her garden, so she still is without Him. In the rest of the chapter, the woman imagines God praising her and saying she is better than the sixty queens and eighty concubines and young women without number, presumably Solomon's. This is another place where a pure Israel is asserted to be preferable to the "strangers" at Solomon's court in Jerusalem.

Chapter 7

The denouement continues, with beautiful imagery describing the woman. It is like a cathartic outpouring of praise.

Chapter 8

In this chapter, the woman sobers up. She begins by acknowledging reality, wishing things were different, *i.e.*, that God were her brother. She repeats her charge to the Daughters of Jerusalem, telling them not to wake God "until it so desires." This now can be understood. The Daughters should not practice the religion, *e.g.*, sacrifice to God, until they eliminate the foreign elements in Jerusalem. Only this will please God, and then will they have the right to "stir up" God with their sacrifices or prayers. The sober mood continues, with some general comments about love. Then, the woman turns to the future, talking of her little sister. And, here, the true meaning of the book comes through. She wants her little sister to remain separate from the influences of the outside world "when she is to be spoken for." She says that if her sister were a wall, a battlement of silver would be built upon her; if a door, she would be enclosed with boards of cedar. The woman emphasizes that she herself was a wall with breasts like towers. This made her lover find "peace." Finally, she scorns Solomon and his riches. She emphasizes that her vineyard is "her own," not shared with strangers. She remains in her garden and implores God to "come away! Be like a gazelle or a young stag on the mountains of spices."

Conclusion

"Song of Songs" can be read as an assertion that staying true to God is what He wants. The book is critical of turning to foreign influences. Along with the beautiful language and imagery, this underlying message may help explain why Song of Songs is included in the Tanakh.

Judaism Found

A fter more than twenty years studying the Torah, I feel
comfortable with an understanding of the theological
foundations of Judaism. My approach kept the analysis close
to the text, asking why the Torah says what it does from a
theological perspective. In so doing, I believe to have derived
logical and satisfying rationales for the main Jewish concepts
and answers to much-asked questions. Some match common
explanations. Others may not. Overall, the insights have made
me appreciate the religion to be a challenging and meaningful
enterprise.

Chapter 49 - *A Jewish Theology*

B ased on my analysis, the purpose of the Torah simply is to indicate what is needed to make society compatible for God. Why should Jews want to do so? The answer is straightforward. God's presence helps society achieve its goals, which, from the Torah's perspective, mean essentially materialistic or worldly success. This exchange — making society compatible for God in exchange for His help — is essentially the covenant between God and the Israelites.

While these conclusions may not sound grand or noble, their social implications are profoundly positive. The Torah's prescriptions for a God-compatible society include interpersonal relationships marked by respect, compassion and justice.

Some popular ideas about Judaism turn the Torah's bottom line on its head. Tikkun Olam, for example, reverses the covenant saying people are meant to help God, particularly to fix the world. It reflects the compassion and sense of justice implicit in the Torah. But, it can serve to deemphasize the importance of commandments not directly related to these ideals. The Torah's goal of making society compatible for God can be undermined.

The Torah's instructions can be divided into three groups of commandments. The first relates to approaching God. It establishes the basis of the relationship between God and the Jews, as well as a set of rituals to be practiced. The second set deals with ways to incorporate these "religious" ideas into everyday life. A sense of spirituality is superimposed onto everyday activities such as eating. And, the third puts restrictions on interpersonal relations.

The three groups are not independent. The Torah's specification of the Kosher Laws, part of the second group, proxy for the sacrificial rituals of the first and bolster the ethical requirements of the third. Similarly, the need to show respect for others can be derived from how one is to approach God. The religion is not so neatly divided into different spheres as may appear.

Covenant Between God and Jews: Motivating Jews

The Torah examines a number of ways to motivate adherence to the covenant. They are the reward/punishment, quid pro quo, guideline and code approaches. Viewing people as God's property and love of God also are brought into play. Emphasis on each changes throughout the Torah.

Genesis examines and rejects the reward approach, in which God grants economic success to the Patriarchs. Success fails to induce proper behavior, as each generation of the Patriarchs after Abraham makes mistakes. All subsequent covenants contain threats of punishment as well as promises of success, depending on whether the Israelites follow the commandments. The Book of Genesis can be interpreted to justify the commandments and threat of punishment found in the following four Books of the Torah.

Exodus starts with the quid pro quo approach. The Israelites are to obey the commandments because God freed them from Egypt. They owe Him. This approach has problems, however. The Israelites have difficulty discerning whether Moses or God is responsible for their situation. And, the Israelites understandably question a god who, though powerful, permits bad things to happen.

Both problems impact the religion throughout the Torah as well as in the post-Torah part of the Tanakh. Gideon, in Judges, asks God directly, "If the Lord is with us, why then is all this befallen us? Where are all His wondrous works which our fathers told us of, saying, 'Did not the Lord bring us up from Egypt?" God's answer -- Gideon should lead the battle against the Midianites but He will be with him in this endeavor -- reflects the implications of the guideline approach developed subsequently to quid pro quo. Jews should take responsibility and act to resolve issues, but with the understanding that God may be helping.

Exodus shifts from quid pro quo to the guideline approach

at Mount Sinai, giving the Israelites more responsibility. God gives a set of commandments to keep the Israelites on a broad but straight path. It involves a separation between God and the Israelites and permits them leeway in determining their destiny. The specifics of the commandments can be modified as long as the changes do not violate the overall intent laid out by God.

The Israelites reject this approach in the Golden Calf episode, preferring direct guidance by God. So, the guideline approach is replaced by the code approach, which requires the Israelites to follow a set of laws and commandments without question.

The guideline and code approaches can be viewed as alternative ways of practicing the religion. The guideline approach encourages a rational practice, seen by the Torah's providing explanations for many of the commandments. Along with the implication to act like God, the rational element of the guideline approach means the religion can be followed in a somewhat flexible way as laws are adjusted to fit circumstances. The code approach is more rigid, requiring adherence to the commandments without question. From a psychological perspective, the two approaches allow people to find different degrees of structure in the religion. In some ways, the difference between the guideline and code approaches is similar to the distinction between Reform and Orthodox Judaism today. They differ on the extent to which the commandments are malleable.

At the end of Numbers, there is a suggestion the commandments do not cover all situations. The religion needs to evolve to meet new circumstances. This evolution is implemented in Deuteronomy. The Torah concludes that the flexibility of the guideline approach is needed for the religion to work.

The Torah identifies each approach by the rationale given for the Fourth Commandment to honor the Sabbath. For the guideline approach, the rationale contained in the first set of Ten Commandments in Exodus is that God rested on the seventh day of Creation. Thus, one should rest on the Sabbath because

God did so, with the inference being a Jew should act in general like God. The code approach is identified by the absence of a rationale in the second set of the Ten Commandments in Exodus, consistent with the acceptance without question of the laws in this approach. And, the quid pro quo approach is highlighted in Deuteronomy by the rationale that God freed the Israelites from Egyptian slavery and thus they owe Him.

The Torah offers other ways to motivate the Israelites to adhere to the covenant. In Leviticus, the land and the Israelites are said to be God's property. As such, they should be treated with respect. This idea can serve as a basis for ethics and sustaining the land. In Deuteronomy, the Israelites are commanded to love God, while Moses states that God loves the Israelites. Psychology is brought into play with this approach. The prophets offer longer-run reasons for the Israelites to obey the commandments. They argue the rewards and punishments will be meted out in the future, depending on how the Israelites behave. And, if the Israelites adhere to the covenant, God will resurrect them from the most dire consequences of worldly events. In the end, the Torah retains a sense of ambiguity on how one is to view and practice the religion. There is more than one way.

Relationship Between God and Jews: Responsibility

The ambiguity is even deeper. The Torah does not have a consistent position on the distribution of responsibility between people and God. Who is to be responsible for achieving success – God or people? The Torah struggles with this issue throughout, just as Americans continually debate how much government intervention in the economy or society is desirable or necessary.

Orthodox Jews, who believe God is omnipotent and consequently responsible for everything, may not accept the legitimacy of this issue. However, there is nothing in the Torah to preclude the possibility that a level of chaos or uncertainty was left over from Creation, enabling people to have free choice. People can play a role in determining the outcomes of events.

Also, the Torah can be read to argue that God, while powerful, is not omniscient. He displays a lack of foreknowledge at times. Moreover, theological reasons can be made why God likes chaos for people — it prompts a demand for Him and also allows people to create.

A tug of war winds through the Torah centered on who should take responsibility for the destiny of the Israelites. The issue appears in all five Books. From Genesis to the guideline approach at Mount Sinai, the Torah aims to have people take responsibility, albeit with God's help if needed. Then, from the code approach in Exodus to the love relationship in Deuteronomy, the Torah emphasizes reliance on God to achieve desired results. In grand irony, though, the Torah cannot escape the realization that people need to make decisions themselves. A division of labor between God and the Israelites is established in Numbers. And, Deuteronomy acknowledges the need for new laws to meet changing circumstances. In the final analysis, God and the Jews partner in taking responsibility for their destiny, consistent with the typical message heard today.

The Book of Esther takes exception to the idea that Jews need God to solve problems, since it leaves out any mention of Him. God's absence in the story has sparked many discussions on why it is in the Tanakh, given the prevalent emphasis on God elsewhere. Perhaps the Book offers an alternative way to understand the religion, just as the Torah examines a number of approaches. The proximity of Purim with Passover, for which the traditional Haggadah excludes any mention of Moses, allows Jews to keep both ideas — self reliance and reliance on God — in mind during this holiday period.

Judaism: A Practical Religion

Considering the Torah's multiple approaches to adhering to and implementing the covenant, Judaism should be seen as a practical religion. Judaism is open to a variety of ways to achieve a society that is compatible for God. Even God modifies his plans to make them successful. For example, the first

Ten Commandments can be interpreted to replace the failed attempt to get humans to act like God by cohabitating with the Nephilim. And, the Balaam/Balak story serves to soften the guideline approach by indicating that God is there to help in the background.

In this light, as long as an approach, even one not explicitly stated in the Torah, does not violate the commandments, it presumably can be used to promote the religion or to address a problem. So, the currently popular practice of drawing psychology-type lessons from the Torah would seem to be legitimate. People like to hear how the religion can help them resolve personal problems.

In choosing an approach to "sell" the religion or to analyze a problem, however, it is important to consider its implications for human action. Pushing the idea of heavy reliance on God, for instance, might persuade people not to try to solve problems themselves – sometimes with disastrous consequences.

While approaches, such as psychology or Kabbalah, may attract people to Judaism, it is not clear they, by themselves, will attract God. Jews presumably still need to follow the commandments for God to feel comfortable enough to reside among them.

Relationship Between God and Jews: Belief in God

The need to follow the commandments to bring in God may be moot for many non-orthodox Jews who doubt His existence. Although the Torah, naturally, does not allow for such doubt, it approaches the issue cleverly. It shows God's actions may or may not be observed. God's presence is seen at Mount Sinai. But, in the story of Balaam and Balak, God acts behind the scene, helping the Israelites without their knowledge.

A "behind-the-scenes" God is a difficult idea on which to base belief, however. Moses and the subsequent prophets resort to symbols, magic and supernatural phenomena to convince people of God's power. People need proof. The prophets' predictions make explicit God's role in worldly events, presumably to provide examples of the "behind-the-scenes" actions of God. Although, at least to a modern reader, these examples may appear fanciful and unconvincing, they become more meaningful if understood as highlighting the idea that God acts in the world and therefore should be held in awe and respect.

In Exodus, the Ten Plagues demonstrate the difficulty of discerning God's actions from natural events. A   fear of God – conceiving Him in terms of awe and respect -- is needed to appreciate His role in the world.

The Torah leaves open the question whether God is responsible or not for an event. From a Jewish perspective, either case is possible. And, without direct knowledge, it behooves a Jew to allow for either possibility. Judaism requires a sense of wonder about the world – a Jew should always ask, "Is an event random or God determined?" As there is no definitive answer, both possibilities need to be accorded some measure of credibility.

Relationship Between God and Jews: Why Do Bad Things Happen?

A problem faced by many Jews, including the orthodox, is disbelief or discomfort in accepting God's responsibility for evil, such as the Holocaust. And, even if such an event is random, they ask why He did not act to stop it quickly? The Torah's answer to the existence of evil is that God's responsibility cannot be ruled out. He may be testing someone or inflicting punishment. But, it is also possible an evil event is random.

Although I have not found an answer to the second question regarding God's procrastination in solving a problem, there is clear precedence for God not acting quickly. In Genesis, God waits to the last minute to prevent Abraham from sacrificing Isaac. He also waits for Sarah to be old before enabling her to have a child to carry on the covenant. In Exodus, He takes time to go through Ten Plagues before freeing the Israelites from Egyptian slavery.

There also is evidence that people need to act to solve a problem before God provides assistance. Nonetheless, acting by oneself is a necessary, not sufficient condition to obtain God's help. Otherwise, God would not be independent, but a servant of people if He were to respond to every request for help. God decides when to help, just as when to express anger. Perhaps a degree of uncertainty regarding the timing of God's help is needed to dissuade people from waiting for Him rather than acting to solve problems themselves.

God's wrathful actions in the Torah leave open the possibility that some post-biblical disasters are His doing. In episodes such as the Flood, Sodom and Gomorrah, the Golden Calf, and Korah's rebellion, God kills or wants to kill many people unless a leader, such as Abraham or Moses, persuades Him not to do so. There appears to be a lot of collateral damage in God's wrathful actions, as people die who are not necessarily guilty, such as Korah's family. The multitude of deaths resulting from God's anger is not dissimilar to the many deaths that occur in post-biblical disasters. So, God's responsibility for them, typically viewed as natural events, cannot be readily dismissed. Although no one such as Abraham or Moses is here these days to intervene, congregational prayer services in response to a disaster might substitute. Prayers to praise God and to acknowledge sin should be part of the service to match the message from the Torah.

While modern Jews may have difficulty coming to terms with the wrathful side of God, it is part of the religion. The Second Commandment says He visits "the guilt of the parents upon the children, upon the third and upon the fourth generations of those who reject Me." But, God's anger is not so persistent nor indiscriminate in the Torah. It is seen when the Israelites turn toward other gods or when they try to overturn their leadership. The intensity of the anger shows the importance God attaches to fidelity. He does not countenance a switch to another god nor an undermining of His chosen leaders. Nonetheless, the Torah tries to soften the implications of God's wrath by introducing more lenient commandments after He shows his anger.

A saving grace may be that God's wrath, for the most part,

manifests itself against groups of people, rather than against an individual. Individual transgressions are meant to be adjudicated by society. Indeed, God's punishment of individual transgressions would run counter to the Torah's aim to minimize His involvement in mundane problems. Judaism should not be considered a religion that promotes a personal fear of Godly retribution for failure to follow a commandment.

Relationship Between God and Jews: Compassion

Jews and others emphasize the compassionate side of God, which is one of the attributes that God ascribes to Himself. The Seconod Commandment states that He shows "loving kindness to thousands of those who love Me and keep my commandments." His forbearance for the faults of the Israelites certainly supports belief in this side. This forbearance apparently goes beyond the Israelites. As Amos says, God overlooked three transgressions of different societies before acting on the fourth.

There are specific cases when His compassion comes through. But, these examples have Him partly to blame for the problem. He shows concern for Hagar after she and Ishmael are expelled by Sarah. In part, this may be because He advises Abraham to permit their expulsion, telling him "in all that Sarah says to you, listen to her voice."

Another may be His instruction to Isaac not to go to Egypt to avoid a famine. While it might not seem compassionate to tell someone not to act to avoid hunger, God may not want Isaac to have to deal with Elohim – defined as other gods — who were responsible for the Akedah. God understands Isaac was put through an exceptional test because of them and would feel uncomfortable having to deal with them in Egypt.

God shows compassion for people performing special tasks for Him. He agrees to take some of the burden of leading the Israelites off Moses' shoulders. He does so because, as He says, "for you have found favor in My sight, and I know you by name." His compassion does not reappear, however, when Moses fails to give Him credit for obtaining water from rocks. He could have attributed Moses' mistake to a succumbing to pressure. Instead, He bans him from entering the Promised Land, possibly because He viewed the ommission as too significant to ignore. As in Amos, God's compassion is seen going only so far.

Relationship Between God and Jews: Getting Close to God

Most Jews, fortunately, prefer to have a positive view of God. Many aim to get "close" to Him through prayer and other ways. The Torah, however, raises questions regarding this goal. Genesis argues against it in the Tower of Babel episode, as God thwarts people's attempts to reach the heavens through constructing a tower. In Exodus, the relationship between God and the Israelites first established at Mount Sinai features a separation between them. All five Books recognize that people would die in His presence.

Although the Torah raises doubts about the possibility of getting close to God, following the commandments -- including prayer, studying Torah, keeping Kosher, and treating others ethically – inherently is meant for Jews to feel God's presence or at least as if He is present. For the most part, the Torah posits that this feeling should reflect a fear of God – meaning that He is to be thought of with awe and respect. Deuteronomy expands this feeling to include love. In these ways, the religion provides for Jews to be emotionally attached to God and to believe they can reach the eternal. To be sure, they represent another irony or ambiguity in the Torah -- while the actions make Jews feel they are moving up toward God, in truth they aim to bring God down to help them in the world.

In other words, having Jews feel they are approaching God is not the ultimate purpose of Judaism. The goal is to obtain God's help for Jews to attain success. This purpose is driven home at the end of the Book of Exodus, where the outcome of the Israelites' renewed commitment to the covenant and building of the Tabernacle is a practical set of signals, by way of a cloud, through which God informs the Israelites whether to travel or rest.

Were the goal different, the Torah presumably would not be centered on the Israelites' journey to the Promised Land, but on how they achieved spiritual heights. Such focus would serve to divorce the Israelites from the real world. Instead, the idea of striving to be close to God is made a limited endeavor in Numbers, which specifies a term limit and costs for being a "Nazirite" -- one who sets "himself apart for the Lord."

A potential problem could arise when people think they can get close to God. They could place greater reliance on Him than on themselves to solve problems. Such inclination is apparent in the popular petition prayer, which asks unconditionally for God's help. Praying for God to help someone recover from illness, to help obtain a new job, and to do well in an endeavor are examples. Requests for God's help are almost always made conditionally in the Torah, especially in the sacrificial system on which prayers are based. A petitioner must vow to do something in return for God's assistance. Consistent with the Torah's overall view of how God relates to the Israelite society, the conditionality underscores a desire for people to take on responsibility. And, costs are associated with involving God in worldly events. Thus, the effectiveness of the typical prayer heard during services is doubtful.

Relationship Between God and Jews: Love

Perhaps the most touted aspect of the relationship between God and Jews is mutual love. Introduced in Deuteronomy, this personalization of the relationship is meant to inspire Jews. It adds a psychological motivation to the array of approaches promoting adherence to the religion -- follow the commandments because God loves you.

The love relationship can lead to incorrect conclusions about the religion, however. It could be interpreted to mean God's favor will be forthcoming just because of love. This is not Judaism, which emphasizes the need to follow His commandments. Deuteronomy links each mention of love with this requirement.

Love between Jews and God risks fostering overdependence on Him to solve problems. Why would God forsake someone He loves? When faced with difficulty, Jews might feel praying for God's help is all that is required. Or, to paraphrase Micah, they should wait patiently for God to come as a savior. This way of solving a problem can have disastrous consequences. The introduction of love of God demonstrates how fixing a deficiency may create other problems.

Incorporating Religion Into Everyday Life

In addition to sacrifices or prayer, the Torah commands Jews to observe several practices that in effect bring an awareness of God into their everyday lives – the second group of commandments. This group includes the Kosher laws and the need to bathe in the Mikvah. Both map into rituals and events known from the Torah to be holy. Also, prohibitions against certain sexual activities map into fundamental ideas regarding life and fear of God. So, despite all the chapters devoted to the building of the Mishcan, to the sacrificial system and to the priesthood, the Torah shows how Jews can live with a sense of God without the existence of these religious structures.

This set of commandments is probably the most controversial for modern Jews. Since there are no apparent practical reasons for them, and because some serve to separate Jews from Christians, many non-orthodox Jews feel they can ignore them either partially or in their entirety. Most Jews do not keep Kosher nor go to the Mikvah. There is controversy among both Jews and Christians about the legitimacy of homosexuality.

More Jews might see these commandments differently if they had a better understanding of their motivation. Jews could sense a connection with God through keeping Kosher if they realize how it is meant to mimic the restrictions on what can be sacrificed to Him. By keeping Kosher and following the other commandments, Jews would not have to resort to programs that have little basis in the Torah to achieve feelings of spirituality. Also, opinion about homosexuality might become more accepting once people understand the Torah's underlying problem with it – lack of procreation -- can be resolved.

Interpersonal Laws

The third leg on which Judaism rests is the need to apply ethics in interpersonal relationships. The Torah requires ethical relationships in the sense that people are to treat others with respect.

The Torah derives the need for ethics in at least five ways. Ethical behavior is specified directly in Exodus with the laws that follow the Ten Commandments. It also can be derived from the Ten Commandments through the guideline approach -- the Commandments imply that Jews should treat others with the respect they would assume in approaching God. Leviticus then underscores the importance of ethics by introducing the concept of love of neighbor and of treating a stranger as oneself. The Book also suggests that Jews should treat others with the respect they would show God's property. Finally, ethics can be derived from the idea that God creates everything, so Jews "owe" Him for any success they might have – the motivation subscribed to by Amos.

The most widely recognized of these bases for ethical behavior is the concept of love of neighbor as oneself. This idea, however, may be flawed in several respects. Relations with others are not fixed, but dependent on how one feels about himself. In the limit, the idea argues for equality in income and wealth distribution that is not required in the rest of the Torah. And, it represents a degradation of the guideline approach, which bases interpersonal relationships on the respect one shows God.

As if ethics are not enough, the commandments that bring religion into everyday life – those of the second group – reinforce good behavior. These commandments remind Jews to act as if in God's presence. They add another level of constraint on interpersonal relationships. One presumably would not treat others unethically in the presence of God. Once more, the three main groups of commandments interconnect.

Among interpersonal relationships, the Torah emphasizes a need to help the poor, begging the question why God does not eliminate it, Himself. The Torah views the elimination of poverty as impossible, stipulating in Deuteronomy that there always will be poor people despite the richness of the Promised Land. Arguably, the guideline's implication that people should create means that poverty is a problem they should address.

Strikingly, the laws concerning donations to the poor mirror those pertaining to sacrificial offerings to God. Leaving the fallen grain in the fields for the poor and offering the first fruits of the harvest frame this agricultural endeavor. They are two ends of the same activity. The symmetrical relationship between them support the prophets' contention that ritual without caring for the poor is unacceptable to God.

The Torah can be read to show what is needed for a society's members to act appropriately to each other. God is there to be the primary source of law. Ritual ensures that people will acknowledge Him as such. And, the commandments specify proper behavior. This interpretation of the Torah, however, turns around its true purpose, which is to show what it takes to have God help a society achieve its destiny. Correct social behavior is a means to an end, rather than an end in itself.

Inter-Society Relationships

Besides relationships with other people, the Torah addresses the question of how Jews should interact with other groups. The most widely known aspect of this issue is probably the prohibition to intermarry. God is incensed at Israelites who co-habited with Moabite women. The problem, however, is not the co-habitation, itself, but its consequence -- the foreign women persuaded the Israelites to sacrifice to another god. Intermarriage *per se* is not necessarily a problem. Moses, for example, married non-Israelite women, but God does not view his marriages negatively when Aaron and Miriam criticize Moses for doing so. The Torah opposes intermarriage when it turns Jews away from the religion.

The Torah does not oppose all interactions with other groups. Moses learns a better way to conduct a judicial system from his father-in-law, Jethro, a Median priest. Moses indeed offers Jethro part of the Promised Land for help in directing the Israelites' travels through the wilderness, a precedent that should be highlighted perhaps in current discussions about Israel and the Palestinians. And, Abraham and Jacob permit their families to reside in Egypt to avoid starvation. The Torah posits that Jews are not to isolate themselves. Even while having a relationship with God, Jews need to work with others to solve problems.

The Books of Ezra and Nehemiah impose more severe restrictions on the interactions between the Israelites and their neighbors than are found in the Torah. In particular, they prohibit intermarriage. Practical reasons seem to be behind the tighter requirements, so the latter should not necessarily supercede the less stringent rules found in the Five Books, generally speaking. Their restrictions do not have a lasting effect on the Israelites to boot.

Can The Commandments Be Amended?

With the Torah seen to be supple and flexible in specifying how a Jew is to relate to God and people, it is not surprising that it also may permit flexibility in applying the commandments. What is surprising is that this flexibility is found largely in Deuteronomy, the Book with the reputation for containing the strictest statement of the religion. Deuteronomy seems to hint that commandments can be dropped or de-emphasized depending on circumstances. This view is similar to the guideline approach, which permits Jews to change some of the commandments to better achieve the religion's goals.

Does the Torah permit an individual to decide which commandments to follow? The answer is not clear. When some Israelites differ from Moses in interpreting God's wishes, in Numbers, Moses has the final say for the most part but there can be compromise. The Torah's establishment of a social hierarchy, including priesthood, presumably is there to make such decisions after Moses. Today, there is no authority, outside of some Orthodox communities, to make the superseding decision on how to follow a commandment. In the absence of authority, it would seem important that an individual have a sense and knowledge of the commandments in deciding whether or how to adhere to any specific one.

Insight into the commandments does not necessarily mean acceptance. For example, one of the post-biblical Kosher laws – separation of meat and dairy – is based on an incorrect interpretation of the commandment not to boil a kid in its mother's milk. This commandment is a prohibition of a Canaanite ritual rather than part of the Kosher laws in the Torah. The commandment does not map into any sacrificial or holy part of the Torah. And, it is not tied to the Kosher laws in Exodus or Leviticus. Deuteronomy inverts the commandment with the one it is truly tied to – to sacrifice the first fruits of the harvest to God -- and juxtaposes it with the Kosher laws.

Promised Land, Chosen People, Messiah, and Resurrection

In addition to commandments, Jews throughout the ages have been motivated by the notions of the Promised Land, the coming of a messiah, resurrection of the dead, and Chosen People.

The Promised Land is the ultimate favor God bestows to the Israelites. The reward for adhering to the covenant is grounded in the real world. The Promised Land can be viewed as a sanctuary for the Israelites, just as the Mishkan serves as a sanctuary for God. An historical perspective today demonstrates the importance for Jews of having a sanctuary in the form of their own country, a remarkable foresight in the Torah.

The Torah does not treat the Promised Land as sacrosanct, however. Two of the tribes can reside outside of it, although they must promise to assist the other tribes in capturing the land. (This episode justifies decisions by modern Jews to live outside Israel, although they must provide help and support to it.) Moses is willing to offer part of the Land to a non-Israelite, Jethro, for short-term help. And, the Israelites could lose the Land if they do not follow the commandments. The Israelites do not own the Land unconditionally or because they are the Chosen People.

There is no mention of a messiah or individual resurrection in the first Five Books of the Torah. They were developed by the prophets afterwards, promising future rewards for adhering to the covenant when the immediate outlook looked bleak. The Torah incorporates the idea of resurrection of the Israelite people. In Genesis, God promises to make his descendants a great nation, although they will be slaves in Egypt for 400 years. In Deuteronomy, Moses promises the Israelites that God will take them back if, after having gone astray, they revert to following the commandments. The Book does not incorporate the idea of individual resurrection, perhaps because the latter has a theological problem. Claiming people will have eternal life runs counter to the concern of God that Adam and Eve would eat from the Tree of Life and become divine-like.

The Israelites are the Chosen People because God decided to reside in their midst. It has nothing to do with their being inherently special. While God says in Exodus that the Israelites are to be a "kingdom of priests and a holy nation," the phrase is probably best interpreted to mean they are to serve Him by following the commandments and that the Israelites' holiness is conferred by His presence among them.

Reform versus Orthodox

With this general framework to understand the Torah, how can the controversy between the Orthodox and Reform be evaluated? The issue is not one-sided.

Reform Jews conform to the first and third parts of the commandments. They acknowledge the supremacy of God and focus on practicing ethical behavior. Many, however, do not follow the commandments of the second group, embodying ritual practices in everyday life. Most Reform Jews feel they can approach God through prayer services or spiritual moments. The fundamental problem from the Torah's perspective is that all three sets of commandments need to be followed to have God in a society's midst. By not performing all, Reform Jews may be fooling themselves in thinking they can reach God.

Reform Judaism asserts that, as rational beings, Jews can choose which commandments, if any, to follow. The earlier Books of the Torah, of course, prohibit such individual choice, as seen in the punishment of those Israelites who gathered manna on Shabbat in Exodus. Deuteronomy, in contrast, opens the door to selective emphasis of the commandments. Based on the latter, the Reform allowance for individuals to choose which commandments to follow cannot be dismissed out of hand.

Some Reform Jews feel they can meet the commandments half way. They may keep Kosher at home but not outside. Does the Torah permit partial observance of the commandments? There is no case for such in the Torah. Perhaps the strongest support is the possibility that Deuteronomy drops some commandments that are no longer relevant once the Israelites reach the Promised Land or if special circumstances intervene. If the dropping of commandments in response to changed circumstances is permitted, then partial adherence to them might be considered acceptable, as well, if the situation requires.

Orthodox Jews conform to all three parts of the religion. Their application of the religion, though, appears too rigid relative to the flexibility of the Torah. By not treating women equally, for example, some Orthodox Jews fail to evolve in a way that would better realize the principle of respect for others that is inherent in the Torah. The Ultra-Orthodox, who attempt to isolate themselves from overall society by what they dress or by studying all the time, contradict the Torah's emphasis on taking responsibility in the world. From the episode of Jethro to the penultimate goal of reaching the Promised Land, the Torah's message is that Jews are to be involved with their own destiny and to engage with other groups as long as they are not converted to their religions.

Can the Orthodox and Reform Jews be reconciled? The Torah requires all Jews to adhere to the commandments. The adherence by each group is a matter of degree. Numbers, however, also permits diversity within the community. And, without a leader like Moses to judge the merits of each side, the Orthodox need to recognize that other Jews can differ in their application of the Torah. All groups satisfy the basic requirement of adhering to Adonai.

The Torah is particularly mindful of the potential for infighting among Jews. After God makes a mistake favoring Abel over Cain, He rewards economically the Patriarchs' offspring who are not chosen to carry the covenant. He does not want jealously to persist between the chosen and the bypassed brothers. A concern for the potential of fratricide colors laws and commandments throughout the Torah. Joseph eventually forgives his brothers. In Leviticus and Numbers, the Torah is careful to prevent the Levites from acquiring too much power that could result in resentment by the other tribes. The other tribes are admonished to treat the Levites properly. The conflict between the Orthodox and Reform runs counter to the desires of the Torah.

In Sum

The theology of Judaism, as described above, covers a lot of ground. While there may be truth in Rabbi Hillel's statement on the essence of Judaism -- to the effect that one should not do to others what one would not do to oneself -- there is a lot more to the religion than that.

Chapter 50 - *Concluding Thoughts*

These, then, are the basic principles behind Judaism that I have deduced from my multi-year study of the Torah. They boil down to a view on how Jews relate to God and what Jews have to do to gain God's favor. While there are some fixed ideas, such as the primacy of God and the need to stay within the broad sense of the commandments, the Torah encompasses a variety of approaches to the religion. The Torah shows Judaism to be a flexible and practical religion in many regards.

There is no question a number of the ideas presented here are controversial. Some people disagree with the conclusion that God is not omniscient or that He makes mistakes. Others do not like the desired separation between God and the Israelites seen in Exodus through Numbers. Their criticisms likely reflect the ideas of God's dominance and love found in Deuteronomy.

Many people could be disturbed by the idea that the Torah's purpose is to show how to bring God down into society. Instead, many believe Jews are meant to ascend toward God, particularly by helping Him repair the world. Helping God is not the main thrust of the Torah, however. Perhaps the Torah recognizes that people can distort the meaning of doing God's work. The Book of Job points out that no one can understand God's intentions. And, the story of Saul and David can be read as a critique of those who believe they hear the voice of God.

In another vein, some readers feel the Torah is not a coherent statement of theological ideas, but just a recitation of sequential historical events written by different sources. I reject this conclusion, arguing the apparent diversity of sources is at least partly a reflection of the many ways the Torah tries to "sell" the religion. Some of the distinctive elements of the Torah pointed to as indicative of different sources, such as various names of God, actually have theological significance. Even the most "historical" portion, in Exodus, is didactic in intent.

Based on the cohesion I found in the text, my guess is the editors of the Torah did a careful job making the various sources compatible with each other. A critique of the Torah on the basis of its many roots may be just a way to justify picking and choosing which commandments to follow.

The Torah is often said to be amenable to many interpretations. The text, however, does not support all interpretations. For example, interpreting it as written by and for the priests does not sit well with the text. Parts of the Torah (even the parts supposedly written by priests) should not be as they are if the purpose were to bolster the priesthood's position. Also, I have heard some say that Abraham is testing God in the Akedah rather than the other way around. This modern reading, though, directly contradicts the text and is not supported by analysis either.

On balance, my analysis presents a way of reading the Torah that helps make Judaism a logical, meaningful religion today. I hope its broad conclusions, as well as specific insights and points, help readers better appreciate the purpose and practices of the religion. I also hope the analysis contributes to an understanding of the text for the many people who engage in Torah or Bible Study each week.

I, myself, have become impressed by the importance of the Torah's implicit insistence on respect for others. Having sat in front of a newswire everyday at work and reading so often about atrocities around the world, I am convinced that bad things happen in places where such respect is not the overriding principle.

The Torah's position that ethical rules are not enough to ensure good behavior represents a powerful message, as well. Incorporating practices, such as keeping Kosher, into daily lives to remind one to act as if God is present serves to reinforce the requirement to act ethically.

The other broad idea that has impressed me is the point from Numbers and Exodus that God's role in world events is not necessarily discoverable but cannot be ruled out. Given the existence of randomness, implicit in the Torah, God is not necessarily involved. However, with a fear of God, one's interpretation f an event has to take this possibility into account. In sum, there has to be a degree of uncertainty about the true nature of an event. Is it random or God-determined? There cannot be a definitive answer. However, by appreciating the possibility of God's role, a Jew could find prayer and ritual and thus the religion meaningful even if he has doubts about God's existence.

In total, this twenty-year effort has made me much more knowledgeable about Judaism. The theology behind synagogue services, sermons, and Jewish practices has become transparent. As a result, I have reached a point where I can appreciate the depth and truth of the religion. I hope those who have read these papers feel the same.

About The Author

Carl J. Palash is an accomplished financial markets economist for over 40 years. He received a Ph.D. in economics with honors from the University of Pennsylvania.

Made in United States
North Haven, CT
15 April 2022

18304376R00168